Bernard Boedder

Natural Theology

Bernard Boedder

Natural Theology

ISBN/EAN: 9783744653459

Printed in Europe, USA, Canada, Australia, Japan

Cover: Foto ©Lupo / pixelio.de

More available books at **www.hansebooks.com**

MANUALS OF CATHOLIC PHILOSOPHY.

(STONYHURST SERIES.)

NATURAL THEOLOGY.

BY

BERNARD BOEDDER, S.J.

NEW YORK, CINCINNATI, AND CHICAGO:

BENZIGER BROTHERS,

Printers to the Holy Apostolic See.

1891.

PREFACE.

THE manual of Natural Theology which now makes its appearance before the English-speaking public, existed in manuscript substantially ready for print in the year 1889. Through a combination of untoward circumstances its publication has been delayed till now. The delay in its appearance has not been without advantage for the book itself. Its subject makes it most suitable to be the last in order of publication among those volumes of the Stonyhurst Series which are concerned about Speculative Philosophy; for though the utmost care has been taken to make it intelligible even to those who have studied no other branch of Philosophy, yet minds prepared for the reading of this manual by a careful perusal of its companions in the department of Speculative Philosophy, will arrive at a far deeper and fuller understanding of its contents. The better readers are versed in the laws of right reasoning by the study of *Logic*, the more thoroughly convinced they are of the absolute

necessity for the human mind to admit the existence, sources, and criteria of Certitude, as laid
down in the *First Principles* of our Series, the
greater diligence they have bestowed upon acquiring a firm grasp of the fundamental notions and
principles treated of in *General Metaphysics*,
and the more solid the knowledge is they have
gained of the moral freedom, spirituality, and
immortality of the human soul expounded in
Psychology, the greater will be their ability to
appreciate and to turn to practical account the
doctrine about God which is explained and defended
in the present volume.

This manual embraces not only those questions
which in our Latin compendia usually are treated
of under the heading *Theologia Naturalis*, but also
those which commonly are discussed as a part of
Cosmologia. This was done in order to give the
necessary completeness to the treatment of my
subject. Our English volumes are in the first
place intended to help those who do not intend
to study in detail Catholic Theology to a sound
understanding of the most important questions of
Philosophy, and particularly to show them the way
to judge intelligently and to solve clearly modern
difficulties against those natural truths which form
the basis of Christianity.

In the celebrated Catholic controversy about the manner of Divine foreknowledge of and concurrence in human actions, it has been my endeavour to give a good account of the opposite opinions and of my own position. I have purposely avoided quotations, as often as I could conveniently without doing harm to the cause of truth, in order to eliminate any element of prejudice or party strife.

B. BOEDDER.

St. Mary's Hall, Stonyhurst,
April 4, 1891.

CONTENTS.

———

BOOK III.—THE ACTION OF GOD UPON THIS WORLD.

NATURAL THEOLOGY.

INTRODUCTORY.

1. NATURAL THEOLOGY is the science of God, so far as God can be known by the light of our reason alone. In order to make the meaning of this definition clear, we have first to explain what we understand by *Theology;* then what signification we attach to the compound term *Natural Theology;* and finally, what right we have to call Natural Theology a *science.*

First, then, as regards the word *Theology.* It is derived from two Greek nouns, θεὸς and λόγος, and means literally *speaking or reasoning about God.* In this sense the word occurs in both Plato and Aristotle.[1] By *Natural* Theology is meant that kind

[1] Plato (*Republ.* 379 A) speaks of οἱ τύποι περὶ θεολογίας, meaning the forms in which tales about gods should be shaped. Aristotle (*Meteorolog.* Lib. II. c. i.) gives us the opinion of οἱ διατρίβοντες περὶ τὰς θεολογίας on the sources of the ocean. He refers to the old poets, Orpheus, Hesiod, Homer, and their fables about the gods. St. Thomas, in his commentaries on Aristotle, calls them the *poetæ theologi;* by Aristotle himself they are styled οἱ θεολόγοι. (*Metaph.* Lib. XI. al. XII. c. vi.) According to Max Müller, Θεός, Deus, is connected with the Sanscrit Deva, signifying "the Brilliant," a very suggestive denomination of the Supreme Being who, according to St. Paul, dwells in light inaccessible (1 Tim. vi. 16), and according to St. John, is "Light" (St. John i. 5). (Cf. M. Müller, *Science of Language,* Second Series, pp. 405, 449, and *Science of Religion,* p. 269.)

B

of reasoning about God, which starts from principles, the truth of which can be known to us by the
light of our *natural* reason left to itself, that is, to its
innate capacity of perceiving and judging the facts
as well of common as of scientific experience, and of
drawing conclusions from these facts according to
principles that either are self-evident or have previously been proved. If this reasoning is carried on
systematically, it results, as we shall discover, in *a
system of truths about God, the First Cause of all things,*
and may therefore be rightly called *the Science of
Natural Theology.*

It is the object of this science to vindicate the
existence and honour of the one true God against
the denial of Atheists, the doubts of Agnostics, the
misrepresentations of Pantheists, and the absurdities
of Polytheists.

2. There is another system of truths regarding
Almighty God which is called *Supernatural*, or more
commonly, *Dogmatic Theology.* Between this and
Natural Theology there is a wide difference.

(1) In the first place they differ in their foundation. For whereas Natural Theology is based upon
principles known by reason with human certainty,
Supernatural Theology has for its foundation principles accepted by faith which rests on the authority of God Himself, who has declared them to us
by Divine revelation.

(2) From this difference there results another
regarding the method of demonstration used in the
two sciences. *Natural* Theology draws its arguments
from the intuitions of reason and from facts of ex-

perience; *Supernatural* Theology finds the premisses of its conclusions in the sources of Christian Revelation, which are the Canonical Scriptures and the documents of Divine Tradition.

(3) Finally there is a vast difference between the achievements of the one and the other. Natural Theology inquires into the existence, the attributes, and works of the one infinite God, without being able to treat of the inscrutable mysteries of the Blessed Trinity and of the Word Incarnate; whereas Supernatural Theology, although it does not pretend to make these mysteries comprehensible to reason, yet, guided by Divine revelation, which has established their reality, analyzes their meaning, shows their consequences, illustrates their harmony with known truths, and thus throws light upon the Divine beauty of Christian Revelation.

Hence we see that the chief subject-matter of which Natural and Supernatural Theology treat, is the same; but the aspect, under which they view it, is altogether different, or to express this in the language of the schoolmen, Natural and Supernatural Theology agree to a large extent in their *material* object, but they differ in their *formal* object.

3. The very nature of Supernatural or Dogmatic Theology implies and demands that Natural Theology should precede it and prepare its way. For it is the duty of reason to prepare the minds of men for the acceptance of Divine revelation, upon which Dogmatic Theology is built. Before an infidel can reasonably feel obliged to acknowledge a creed as

Divine, he must be convinced that there is a God, who can communicate truths to men, and that men can accept these truths without danger of deception. It is Natural Theology that opens the way to this conviction by strict logical reasoning. Christian Doctors therefore rightly call the truths developed in Natural Theology the *præambula fidei;* and the office assigned to Philosophy in general, when it is called the *handmaid of (Dogmatic) Theology,* belongs especially to the particular branch of Philosophy now under consideration.

We may add that Dogmatic Theology taught under the supervision of the Infallible Church, is for the Catholic philosopher a guiding-star even to his philosophical reasonings about God. This is a most sound and intelligible proposition, but it is one peculiarly liable to misrepresentation. We are far from claiming the right to draw the course of philosophical reasoning away from its natural paths in order to bring the results into fictitious conformity with those of revelation. Such a procedure would be as foolish as it would be dishonest. Our claim is to imitate the mariner to whom the star is a guiding-star, not because it dispenses him from the due use of the compass, but because it enables him to check the errors into which he may have fallen in his estimate of the records of the needle. The Catholic philosopher is conscious that human reason, particularly when it embarks on the difficult sea of philosophical speculations, is liable to go astray through defective observance of its own laws. On the other hand he has sure grounds for his conviction that the Church's teaching is absolutely reliable. What more reasonable than that on finding a discrepancy between the results of his philosophical reasoning and his Dogmatic Creed, he should conclude the former to be in some point defective and should retrace his steps to discover where the defect may lie?

4. In what we have said about the stand-point of a Catholic writer on Natural Theology, we cannot reasonably expect to be fully understood by those outside the Church. All that we ask for from non-Catholic readers is to judge our conclusions in Natural Theology by the light of principles which must be admitted by every reasonable man. Let them consider whether we ever make an undue use of authority to establish a truth which should be proved by reason alone; let them judge for themselves whether we meet our adversaries with solid arguments or with empty phrases, and whether we enunciate any opinion which is out of harmony with well-established scientific facts.

5. Approaching our subject in this spirit, we have a reasonable claim to the sympathy and interest of our readers. For what subject of inquiry can be compared with the first source of all things, the Infinite Majesty of God? Moreover, if as reasonable beings we are irresistibly drawn to inquire into the causes of things, must not all our researches suffer from want of solidity and completeness, if we lack a true knowledge of God, the First Cause of all things, and of His relation to this world? Such knowledge throws light upon the origin of

the universe, upon the nature and destiny of man, upon the true meaning of life, upon our duties here on earth, upon our prospects for the future, upon the wonders as well as the woes of human history. Nay, there is no department of knowledge which is not ennobled when viewed in the light of these truths : because from God, and through Him, and in Him, are all subjects that can possibly have a claim on man's attention.

What makes this study still more important is that without it we cannot hope truly to estimate and solidly to refute the charges brought forward against the reasonableness of Christian faith by atheists, agnostics, and pantheists, who know well how to support their statements with an array of specious arguments. If we wish to diminish the harm inevitably caused by the spreading of such false opinions, we must be able to produce a good store of arguments by which the existence of God, His attributes, and His relation to this world are proved, in such a way, that their force may come home to the mind of every one who does not obstinately prefer darkness to light.

For some of our readers it may be useful to call attention to the danger of resting content with a partial knowledge of our subject, or thinking that a thorough grasp of it can be obtained without patient study. Beginners who have not perseverance enough to reason step by step, but who pick out one question or another at random, must not wonder if they very soon find themselves hopelessly confused, and utterly unable either duly to appreciate or clearly to solve the difficulties of adversaries.

6. The order of our discussion is suggested by the three following questions:

I. Can we know for certain that there exists One first intelligent and infinitely perfect Cause of all things, that is to say, One personal God of infinite perfection, Creator of the world?

II. Granted that there exists One personal God of infinite perfection, what are the special attributes of this One infinite Being?

III. If there be such a personal God, what can we know about His action upon this world?

Following the line of thought suggested by these three questions, we shall divide our treatise into three books: the first treating of the existence of God, the second of the attributes of God, the third of the influence which God exercises upon this world.

NATURAL THEOLOGY.

BOOK I.

OF THE EXISTENCE OF GOD.

CHAPTER I.

VIEWS OF MONOTHEISTIC PHILOSOPHERS ON THE
NATURAL FOUNDATION OF A REASONABLE BELIEF
IN GOD.   REFUTATION OF ONTOLOGISM AND OF
THE SO-CALLED ONTOLOGICAL ARGUMENT.

SECTION I.—*Explanation of the different opinions about God's
existence and the proofs for it.*

7. THE chief object which we aim at in the first
part of Natural Theology, is to discover the true
reasons why the existence of an intelligent First
Cause of the universe must be admitted as certain.
To clear the ground, we first give a short review
and estimate of the different opinions held by philosophers who believe in a personal God, concerning
the natural relation of the human mind to that
belief.

8. The more noteworthy opinions on the subject
in question may be reduced to these four headings:

(1) The opinion that we have naturally an immediate consciousness of God's existence. This opinion is known under the name of *Ontologism.*

(2) The opinion that we can prove the existence of God *a priori* from the, mere concept which we form to ourselves of God. This kind of proof for the existence of God is commonly called the *Ontological Argument.* The name is unfortunate, as it suggests a connection of the argument so styled with the system of Ontologism. In reality there is none.

(3) The opinion, that the existence of God, although it cannot be perceived by us immediately, nor be proved *a priori*, can yet be proved evidently *a posteriori* by reasoning from the contingent and finite things of this world to God, the necessary, self-existing, infinite Being.

(4) The opinion, that it is reasonable and man's duty to believe in the existence of God, but that it is impossible to prove by evident arguments that the denial of that existence is an untruth.

9. Of these four opinions, the first has its most eminent representatives in Nicholas Malebranche (1715),[1] Vincenzo Gioberti (1852), Antonio Serbati Rosmini (1855), and Casimir Ubaghs (works published 1854—1856). The second can boast of such great names as St. Anselm of Canterbury (1109), and in later times, René Descartes (1650), and Leibnitz (1716). The third was generally held by metaphysicians of all ages, from the bright

---

[1] The figures added to the names of philosophers in this section refer to the year of their death, with the exception of Ubaghs.

dawn of metaphysical inquiry in Plato's *Dialogues*
up to the bold revolution attempted in the realms
of philosophical thought by Kant in his *Critique of
Pure Reason.* That the human mind is able to rise
from the knowledge of the finite things which surround us to a certain, though inadequate, knowledge of God, the first and the intelligent Cause of
the universe, was unanimously asserted by Plato
(348 B.C.) and Aristotle (322 B.C.), by St. Augustine
(430 A.D.), by St. Thomas Aquinas (1274), and the
long series of the schoolmen, by Bacon (1626), and
Locke (1704).

Moreover, although St. Anselm, Descartes, and
Leibnitz thought the ontological argument to be
a very easy proof of God's existence, they were
by no means of opinion that it is the only one
possible. On the contrary, in the writings of all
three we find also arguments for God's existence
drawn from the contemplation of finite things.[2] In
recommendation of this third line of argument, we
may further say that it is supported by scientific
men of the first rank, such as Kepler, Newton, Faye,
Sir John Herschell, Sir William Thomson, &c.[3]

But, notwithstanding the great authority of the
third opinion, its hold over the best minds of
educated Europe was shaken considerably by Kant's
Critique of Pure Reason. In this work, the first
edition of which was published in the year 1781,
the fourth opinion mentioned above was advo-

---

[2] St. Anselm's *Monolog.* cc. i.—iv. inclusive; Descartes' *Principia
Phil.* Part I. pp. 17, 18; Leibnitz, Opera (Edit. Erdm.), p. 506.
[3] See below, § 40.

cated as the only reasonable defence of the belief in God. According to the author of the *Critique*, convincing proofs for the existence of a Supreme Being are not attainable by the Speculative Reason. In order to confute atheism, he therefore appeals to what he calls the Practical Reason. Man, he says, feels himself under the sway of an internal voice which categorically commands him to do good and to avoid evil. He cannot despise this voice without violating his human dignity, nor can he follow it consistently, unless he acknowledges a supreme Lawgiver and Judge, to whom he is responsible for his moral conduct. Consequently it is man's duty to believe in God's existence, although he is not able to show convincingly that the denial of that existence contains an objective untruth.

10. The opinion of Kant has been adopted under various forms by many philosophers of our century, who nevertheless have been far from committing themselves to the whole of his theory of human knowledge. Thus Jacobi (1819) maintained that God's existence can be known neither by reasoning nor by immediate intuition, but is manifested to us by a kind of irresistible spiritual feeling. On the Continent, De la Bonald (1840) found what he thought a sufficient proof for God's existence in the necessity of a primitive Divine revelation, without which, according to his views, the origin of intellectual human knowledge cannot be explained. Lamennais (1854), in order to show how unreasonable the denial of God's existence is, fled for refuge to

the universal consent of mankind, which he took to be the general criterion of truth and certainty. In England, Hamilton and Mansel, urging that we necessarily entangle ourselves in glaring contradictions as soon as we compare the attributes of the Infinite with one another, deduced the obligation of faith in God, as He is put before mankind by Christ and His Apostles, chiefly from the perfect harmony between that faith and our moral instincts.

This last way of defending God's existence against atheism proved injurious to the good cause on behalf of which it was undertaken. For the most striking of the arguments, by which Mr. Herbert Spencer in his *First Principles*, tries to prove that nothing definite can be known about the underlying cause of the universe, are borrowed from Mansel's *Limits of Religious Thought*.

11. We shall now proceed to give our reasons for adhering to the third of the opinions we have just mentioned, which maintains that man can come to a certain knowledge of God by means of his natural understanding, not however by way of immediate intuition, nor by reasoning *a priori*, but by arguments *a posteriori* based on the essence and properties of the things comprised under the term "world."

Section 2.—*Refutation of Ontologism.*

12. As we said above (§ 8), Ontologists are those philosophers who believe that the mind of man, by its very nature, has a certain direct consciousness of God's existence. They do not affirm that man

by his natural faculties is able to see God face to
face, to perceive Him as He is in Himself, or to
have a direct intuition of His Essence.   Indeed,
they could not say so without exposing themselves
to ridicule, and to the charge of contradicting the
Christian Creed which they profess.   What they
mean is that man's knowledge begins by some dim
perception of God, considered not in His Essence,
but in His relation to creatures.

13. A germ of Ontologism thus explained is
found in Descartes' *Principia Philosophiæ*.[4]   He says
that the idea which we possess of an infinitely
perfect Being, could not be produced in us but by
this Being Himself.   Malebranche developed this
germ into a philosophical system.   In his celebrated
work, *Recherche de la Vérité*, he tells us that the
human mind knows all things save its own existence,
through the ideas it forms of them.   These ideas
are occasioned by sense-impressions ; but they are
not the mere result of sensations, nor are they the
product of our mental activity.   They are perceived
in God, who is immediately present to us.   He is,
so to say, the Sun in the midst of the world of
thinking created spirits, and only inasmuch as He
pours out the light of His eternal ideas upon our
minds do we see truth in Him, who is the First
Truth, the Prototype of all things and of all
thoughts that are true.

Since Malebranche, no one has defended Ontologism more vigorously than Gioberti in his *Intro-
duzione allo studio della Filosofia*.   He represents the

---

[4] Part I. pp. 17, 18.

immediate intuition of God, which he believes to be natural to man's mind, as a direct perception of God's influence upon this world. Consequently the starting-point of all human learning is this judgment : " Being creates existences." (*L'Ente crea le esistenze.*) By *Being* he understands the self-existing Divinity; by *existences*, creatures, which he does not call beings, because they have no independent being of their own, but are dependent upon the creative act of their first cause. His opinion consequently is, that our first intellectual act is a direct intuition of God creating the world.

Another and milder form of Ontologism is to be found in Rosmini's *Theosophia,* and in Ubaghs' *Theodicea.* Rosmini holds that the idea of being, which according to his theory respecting the origin of ideas is innate in us, must be nothing else but the idea of God, the Creative Cause of finite beings. Ubaghs thinks that we are born with the idea of the Infinite God, and that this idea is in the beginning unformed, but becomes formed by reflection, to which we are led by our education in human society.

Similar views on our natural knowledge of God are defended by Maret in his *Essai sur le Panthéisme,* by Gratry in his work *De la Connaissance de Dieu,* by Fabre in his *Défense de l'Ontologisme,* and by others in France, Belgium, and Italy.

Notwithstanding the wonderful ingenuity which these authors exhibit in support of their hypothesis, we must, in the interest of truth, lay down the following thesis.

Thesis I.—*Immediate intuition of God, as held by ontologists, is beyond the reach of man's natural understanding.*

14. In stating this proposition we admit with the ontologists as a fact of Christian revelation, that all men who die in the grace of God, shall in Heaven see Him as He is. And they on their part admit that this Beatific Vision, reserved for the servants of God, is not the natural endowment of our human understanding, but the supernatural reward of living faith. Consequently, to explain the possibility and truth of this Vision does not belong to the domain of Philosophy. So far we are at one with our adversaries. What we have to prove against them is, that God *in His relation to creatures* cannot be the object of our *direct* intuition here on earth. The first reason for which we assert this, is drawn from our internal experience.

15. If the direct intuition of God in His relation to creatures is a natural endowment of the human soul, we certainly must be able to become with the greatest facility perfectly convinced by *mere reflection* of the fact that we are in God's presence, and no thought should be easier to us than the thought of God. However, this is not so. *Effort* is required to raise our mind from things visible to their invisible First Cause. Even those who are perfectly convinced of God's existence, may live hours and days without thinking of Him. Nay, at times doubts may arise in their minds against their faith

in God, and how can they put off these doubts?
Not by mere reflection, but either by dwelling upon
the strong reasons from which God's existence is
mediately evident, or by calling to their minds certain
practical maxims, the reasonableness of which has
been once understood, and with which the doubt
about God's existence is incompatible. Every well-
instructed Christian knows that the existence of an
all-wise, all-powerful, and infinitely good God is a
fundamental dogma of Christianity. Moreover, he
has satisfied himself about the reasonableness of
adhering to the truths of Christianity. After this
it is a practical maxim with him, that a wilful doubt
about God and His attributes is a serious sin.
Appealing to this maxim, he rejects the doubts
against God's existence as unreasonable sophistries.
This is a reasonable process, and corresponds to
a palpable need of the believing mind. But on
the ontologistic hypothesis, such a need would not
arise.

16. If we examine a little more deeply into our
subject, we find that the conflict between experience
and Ontologism has its root in the very nature of the
human soul. This soul is neither an outgrowth of
matter, as materialists would have us believe, nor
is it a pure spirit, that is to say, a thinking and free
being altogether independent of matter in the exercise of its natural functions. Man's soul is a spirit,
organizing and quickening matter. The fact that
our soul cannot exercise its vegetative and sensitive
energies except in a material body and by the help
of material organs, necessarily reacts upon its

spiritual faculties of understanding and free-will, albeit the acts of these faculties considered in themselves are not organic acts. The conclusion drawn from this state of things, the fuller discussion of which belongs to Psychology, is this. Man's mind has for its immediate and direct object only such things as can be perceived by the senses. It can arrive at the knowledge of immaterial beings only by reasoning, and by faith in reliable authority. Convinced of this, Aristotle uses language which implies that it is as impossible for man's mind, left to its natural resources, to have a direct perception of spiritual things, as it is for an owl's eye to find delight in the rays of the mid-day sun.[5] Experience fully verifies this conclusion, for in order to explain things not accessible to sense perception, we constantly have resort to illustrations drawn from the objects of sense. If, then, no spiritual thing is directly accessible to our mind, how can we have an immediate vision of God the Infinite Spirit? If there were any truth in the Ontologist hypothesis, such a direct intuition of God would be natural to us. For the ontologists say that we

[5] Aristotle, *Metaph.* Lib. I. brev. c. i. Aristotle's words are: ὥσπερ γὰρ καὶ τὰ τῶν νυκτερίδων ὄμματα πρὸς τὸ φέγγος ἔχει τὸ μεθ' ἡμέραν, οὕτω καὶ τῆς ἡμετέρας ψυχῆς ὁ νοῦς πρὸς τὰ τῇ φύσει φανερώτατα πάντων. According to this passage, our understanding is like the eyes of nightbirds for daylight, as regards the beings most intelligible in themselves. Now spiritual beings are more intelligible in themselves than material beings, inasmuch as the pre-eminence of internal intelligibility follows the pre-eminence of natural being. Cf. the beautiful remarks of St. Thomas on this passage of Aristotle. *Comment. in Metaph. Aristot.* Lib. II. Lect. i. § "Ostendit causam præmissæ difficultatis," etc.

C

directly perceive God's relation to creatures. Now it is evident that a relation between two terms cannot be *directly* perceived unless each is the object of direct perception.

17. No wonder that a theory so inconsistent with experience and with human nature is also inconsistent with itself. Ontologists say that we perceive immediately something of God, yet do not immediately perceive His essence. In this there is a contradiction. For in God, as the ontologists willingly grant, there are no accidents. His essence is absolutely simple. It is therefore impossible to see anything of Him immediately without seeing His essence. From this conclusion ontologists recoil, and rightly, for it is opposed to Revealed Truth; but it logically follows from their hypothesis, and therefore that hypothesis must be rejected as false.

18. Nor can the reasons which ontologists bring forward to support their theory move us to give a more favourable verdict on it. The more important of their arguments are the following, to each of which we shall add its respective answer.

A. We have an idea of the Infinite. This idea cannot be got by abstraction from finite beings nor by reasoning about them. Therefore it must be admitted that it was given to us together with our existence; in other words, that the direct intuition of the Infinite is natural to the human mind. (Thus Malebranche, Gioberti, Ubaghs.)

Answer. It is true that every Christian, nay, every monotheist who understands his position, has a genuine idea of the Infinite. His idea of the Infinite is not a merely negative one, as Sir William Hamilton would have it. He does not only know that the Infinite is altogether different from the Finite; he knows something positive about the attributes by which it is characterized. But from this it in no way follows that the representation of the Infinite by the human mind has its origin in direct intuition. On the contrary, from the fact that our idea of the Infinite expresses its object not in a *purely* positive way, but *by the help* of negation, it is evident that not the thought of the Infinite but the thought of the Finite is most natural to our mind. Why is it that when we speak of God, who is pure reality, or, so to say, *pure affirmation without negation of perfection*, we speak of Him in such a way as to predicate of Him perfection, and at the same time remove the limits of these perfections, calling Him infinitely wise, infinitely powerful, and so forth? No other sufficient reason can be given save this, that the power, the wisdom, and the other positive perfections of creatures which we predicate of God, are directly known to us only within certain limits. We first think of finite things according to their own being, not paying attention to their limitation; then comparing less perfect finite beings with more perfect, we become aware of their limitations; finally, thinking of all possible finite perfections united in one Being, and denying all limitations which are necessarily proper to them in finite beings, we form a *negativo-positive* concept, as it is called, of the Infinite. In this manner we do really think of the infinitely perfect Being, although we think of it in a very inadequate way.

Now it is true that such an idea of the Infinite cannot be got from finite things by mere abstraction, nor can it be arrived at by *one* step of reasoning, but it can be reached by a *chain* of lawful reasonings from absolutely certain premisses. And this is what we have to make clear in the course of our treatise. For the present it may suffice to indicate the principal links in this chain. Things produced suppose a first unproduced cause; an unproduced cause exists by virtue of its own essence, or is self-existing; there can be but one self-existing being; the one self-existing being must be the source of every possible being—in other words, it must be infinitely perfect; otherwise the total first cause of all contingent being would be less perfect than the effects which it can produce.

B. There must be harmony between the order in which things follow one another in their real existence, and the order in which they are ideally expressed in our minds; otherwise our mental representations would not be true. Now of all existing beings God is the first. Consequently the first judgment of the human mind must refer to God. (Thus Gioberti.)

Answer. For human cognition to be true, it is not requisite for antecedent to be known before consequent, cause before effect. I may first come to know a book, and thence proceed to learn by inference the existence and character of the author. Or I may first come to know the author, and thence infer the nature of his book.   In either case my knowledge of the book and the author can be true. It would only be false if it were to represent to me the book as the cause of the author, instead of the author as the cause of the book.   The requisite of truth, alleged by Gioberti, is not the requisite of *truth in general*, but that of *perfect* truth, which comprehends all possible truths.   And this exists nowhere but in the Divine intellect.   To have *truth in general*, it is enough that everything mentally affirmed to be real, really is what it is affirmed to be ; it is not necessary that the order of mental affirmation follow the order of real existence.

C. The human mind is naturally directed to God as to its last end.   Consequently, as God is the first object of the human will, so must He be the first object of the human understanding.   (Thus Malebranche.)

Answer.   From the fact that God is man's last end, it follows that the human soul at some time or other (at least after death, in the case of one who dies before attaining the use of reason), must come to some knowledge of God carrying with it a natural tendency of the will towards God.   But it does not at all follow that man from the beginning of his existence must have the actual use of his intellect ; much less that the first acts of his intellect must have God for their object.

D. As God alone exists by Himself, so He alone can be intelligible by Himself.   Therefore created things cannot be known except so far as God is known.   (Thus Gioberti.)

Answer. In a certain sense it is true, that God alone is intelligible by Himself. His is the only existence which is essential, which cannot not be; or, in other words, He alone has the reason of His existence in His own essence. In all creatures actual existence is not essential, but only possible existence; or, in other words, the essences of creatures considered in themselves are merely possible things, only existing on the condition of God's creative act, which is not necessary, but free. However, this truth is of no force to prove that really existing creatures cannot be known but in God. A creature which really exists is really distinct from a merely possible creature. It is not a pure essence, but a created essence, and therefore has an existence of its own distinct from God's existence, although it owes its existence to God's free creation. Now as intelligibility results necessarily from existence, so from an existence distinct from God's existence there must result an intelligibility distinct from God's intelligibility, although God is the efficient cause of the creature's existence, and consequently of the creature's intelligibility.

E. The universal attributes which we give to creatures, when we predicate, for instance, that "John is a man," or that "Bucephalus is a horse," express something necessary, eternal, unchangeable. But created things are contingent, temporal, changeable. Therefore we cannot have drawn our universal ideas by abstraction from created things; but they must be due to a direct intuition of their uncreated cause.   (Thus Vercellone, Milone, Fabre, Sans-Fiel, and other modern ontologists.)

Answer. Properly speaking there is, as St.Thomas rightly affirms, only *one* being which is necessary, eternal, unchangeable, namely, God.[6] If we say that the universal attributes of created things are necessary, eternal, unchangeable, we mean simply that God is the necessary, eternal, unchangeable source of all kinds of possible things which we express by universal ideas, and that consequently these things are understood by God necessarily, eternally, unchangeably, as imperfect imitations of His own essence, and producible out of nothing by His infinite power.   Hence we may say that universal attributes, or, in other words, the objects of universal ideas, are *negatively eternal;* but we may not say that they are *positively eternal.* A thing is *positively eternal,* if it exists by its own essence, unchangeable, without beginning and without end.   It is *negatively eternal,* if, as a thinkable, conditionally-existing object, it is not limited to a certain time. Thus the object of the universal idea " man " is negatively eternal, because no possible time can be given at which by the power of God that idea might not be verified in one or many individual men. The human mind is obviously capable of forming such a negatively eternal idea.   Perceiving with our senses an individual thing, we at once grasp with our intellect that which *is*, or at least *may be*,

---

[6] Cf. *Sum. Theol.* i. q. 9. a. 2. and q. 10. a. 3. especially ad 3m. A more full explanation of the eternity of all truth is given by St. Thomas, *Qq. Disp. de Veritate*, q. i. a. 5.

common to many such individual things. This we
do without penetrating into their individual constitution. It is therefore a baseless assertion that
the formation of universal ideas is conditioned by
a direct intuition of God.[7]

SECTION 3.—*Criticism of the Ontological Argument.*

19. Having proved that the Ontologistic hypothesis, according to which all our knowledge is based
on a direct intuition of the Infinite, cannot be admitted, we have now to explain our objection to the
opinion of those who think they can prove the *existence*
of the Infinite from the *idea* of the Infinite. Their
argument is known among scholastic philosophers
by the name of the " Ontological Argument," a
term which we must distinguish from the "Ontologistic Hypothesis." It has three celebrated forms,
of which the first was proposed by St. Anselm, the
second by Descartes, and the third, virtually at
least, by Leibnitz.[8] We give the substance of all
three.

20. St. Anselm reasons thus : By God is understood the greatest Being which can be thought of.
But a Being which not only exists in the mind as

[7] For further discussion of Ontologism, we may recommend
Stöckl, *Geschichte der neuern Philosophie,* Vol. I. pp. 123, seq., Vol. II.
pp. 570, seq., 579, seq., 621, seq.; Lepidi, O.P., *De Ontologismo;*
Zigliara, O.P., *Della luce intellettuale e dell' Ontologismo;* Kleutgen,
Phil. Scholastique, nn. 377—490; Liberatore, *Psychol.* Edit. I.
novæ formæ nn. 200—206; *Theol. Nat.* n. 3 and n. 6; *On Universals*
(Translated by E. H. Dering), pp. 64—95, and pp. 180—196.

[8] Cf. Opp. S. Anselmi, *Proslogium,* c. 2; Descartes, *Principia
Philosophiæ,* Pars I. 14; Leibnitz' Opp. (Edit. Erdm.), pp. 374, seq.

an object of thought, but has also actual existence outside the mind, is greater than a Being which exists in the mind only. Therefore God exists actually outside the mind.

In Descartes the argument takes this form: Whatever is contained in a clear and distinct idea of any object must be affirmed of that object. But a clear and distinct idea of an absolutely perfect Being contains the notion of existence. Consequently, we must say that there really exists an absolutely perfect Being.

Leibnitz remarks on the two forms of the Ontological argument just proposed that the scholastics were wrong in rejecting them. He says they are not fallacious, but need to be completed. They do not offer any reason for their assumption that the idea of the greatest and absolutely perfect being is possible and not self-contradictory. He thinks, however, we may safely assure this possibility as long as no one proves the contrary. Thus in his mind the Ontological argument should be cast into this shape: God is at least possible, for in the concept of Him no repugnance is discovered. But if He is possible, He must exist, because the concept of Him implies existence.

21. It has been said in answer to St. Anselm and those who took up his argument, that it only proves the existence of the infinite being in the world of ideas, not in the world of realities; that it proves the ideal possibility of such a being, but not its real existence. Even in St. Anselm's time this objection was raised by a certain ingenious thinker named

Gaunilo. After having first objected to the validity
of the premisses, this man argued thus against the
conclusion :

"There are people who say that somewhere in
the ocean there exists an island, which certain men,
because of the difficulty or rather impossibility of
finding what really does not exist, have surnamed
the *lost island*. This island is by fiction represented
as possessing in incredible abundance all sorts of
precious and delightful things, far more than the
celebrated Isles of the Blessed; nay, as surpassing
in riches all the countries inhabited by men, although
no proprietor or settler is living on it. If somebody
were describing all this to me, I should of course
easily understand his explanation : there could be
no difficulty in that. But if he went on thus to
argue : You cannot any longer doubt but that the
island I spoke of, the idea of which you admit
without hesitation to be in your mind, exists also
in reality somewhere. Indeed, you cannot deny it,
if you only attend to what I now say : It is more
excellent to exist not in the mind only, but in
reality, than to exist in the mind only. Therefore
the aforesaid island must really exist ; for if it did
not, any other real country would surpass it in
excellence, and consequently the island which you
have thought to be superior to all, really would not
be superior to all. If the speaker attempted thus to
make me admit the real and undoubted existence
of that island, I should either believe him to be only
joking, or I should not know which of us to think
the more stupid, myself, if I granted such a con-

clusion, or him, if he really thought that he had proved the actual existence of that island with anything like certainty.   Assuredly, I should not yield to him, unless he convinced me that its excellence was thought of by me as something really and undoubtedly existing, ånd not only in the same way in which we can think of what is false or un-certain."⁹ Nevertheless, this mode of putting the objection is not so strong as it may seem at first sight.   St. Anselm answered it thus: "If any one can find anything whatsoever, either really existing or only represented by the mind, *with the one exception of the greatest being conceivable*, such that he can reasonably apply to it the form of this my argument, I promise to find him the 'lost island' with such success that it shall never be lost again."¹⁰

So far the Saint is perfectly right.   Whoever grants as certain that we have a true idea of an infinite being, cannot deny that existence is implied in that idea without contradicting himself: for an infinite being cannot be otherwise than self-existing. A being which is not self-existing is necessarily limited: for it cannot possess anything but what it has received from its cause; and its cause cannot give it the perfections of self-existence.   Therefore, when there is question of *finite* being, it may be granted that I can think of a finite being better than any that really exists; and yet quite con-sistently with this concession it may be denied that such a being as I think of does really exist.   For

---

⁹ *Opusculum pro Insipiente*, inter Opp. S. Anselmi, c. **6.**
¹⁰ *Liber Apologeticus*, inter Opp. S. Anselmi, c. 3.

a finite being is contingent, and without internal
contradiction can be conceived as not existing. But
if it be admitted as certain, that I really think of
an *infinite* being, the actual existence of such a being
must be allowed; for an infinite being cannot without internal contradiction be conceived unless it be
conceived as self-existing.

Thus far, then, we do not find any serious fault
with the advocates of the Ontological proof. Our
reason for not admitting the demonstration as a
valid refutation of agnosticism is its failure to
provide us with a warrant for the absolute certainty
of the assertion, that *we have an idea of an infinite
being*. We therefore state our objection thus :

Thesis II.—*In the so-called Ontological Argument
the supposition underlying the premisses that the idea
of an infinite being is not self-contradictory, is assumed
without sufficient warrant. Consequently, that argument
is not a perfect demonstration of God's existence.*

22. Of course we readily allow that the idea of
an infinite being is in fact not self-contradictory. We
only deny that this can be ascertained with certainty
otherwise than by the *a posteriori* argument.   It
must be established by consideration of contingent
things, and by inference from their existence of the
necessary existence of *One* First Cause. As long as
this has not been shown, the agnostic may justly
reply to the Ontological proof: " Possibly there
may be many self-existent beings. In that case the
idea of an infinite being is self-contradictory. For
none of the many self-existent beings would be the

source of the perfections of all other beings; and consequently none of them could be really infinite; because a being which does not unite in itself all thinkable perfections, must be finite. Of the many self-existent beings, then, ,which I suppose there may be, none can be infinite. And as you yourself allow, no contingent being can be infinite. But all being is either self-existent or contingent. The conclusion is that an infinite being is absolutely impossible, and consequently we can have no real idea of such a being."

To this objection the advocate of the Ontological argument has no satisfactory answer. He can say nothing but what Leibnitz said: " We may safely suppose the possibility of an infinite being, till it be disproved." Perhaps we may. But a supposition made on these terms is no basis of certainty. In short, the Ontological argument is a very strong argument *ad hominem* against one who does not challenge the supposition of the premisses ; but in no way an objectively evident proof.[11]

[11] St. Thomas Aquinas criticizes and rejects the argument of St. Anselm in I. dist. 3. q. 1. a. 2. ad 4m.; *Sum. Theol.* i. 2. 1. ad 2dum, and *Contra Gent.* i. c xi. § "Nec oportet ut statim cognita." An estimate of it is also given by Kleutgen, *Phil. Schol.* nn. 937—942. The history of this argument, which may be seen in the *Life of St. Anselm,* by Martin Rule, M.A., Vol. i. pp. 195, seq. is very interesting.

CHAPTER II.

PROOFS FOR THE EXISTENCE OF AN INTELLIGENT FIRST CAUSE OR PERSONAL GOD.

SECTION 1.—*Method of Proof.*

23. THE object of the three following chapters is to prove not only that there is a First Cause of all things else that exist, but also that this First Cause has the attributes which are associated with the conception of a First Cause in the minds of monotheists, especially of Christians. This is most necessary if we are to make our ground sure. In a certain sense materialists and pantheists maintain the existence of a First Cause. What else are the eternal atoms out of whose combinations and movements the materialist believes the cosmos to be composed? What else is the Absolute of the pantheists, alleged to be eternally evolving itself under manifold aspects and conditions, and thereby creating the world out of its own substance? In truth, what is denied, particularly in these days, is not so much self-existence, as personal self-existence. We have to prove the existence of a Personal First Cause, that is to say, of an intelligent self-existing Being who is distinct from the cosmos of which He is the ultimate cause.

24. The proof of this position is three-fold. We have the argument of the First Cause, the argument from Design, and the so-called Moral argument. The argument of the First Cause draws from the simple fact that some things exist the conclusion that there must be a First Cause, and then from the fact that intelligent beings, namely, men, exist, the further conclusion that this First Cause must be intelligent. It can thence proceed to the ultimate conclusion that such a First Cause must be One and Infinite in all respects.

The argument from Design starts with the order observable in the world, and infers the existence of a supra-mundane intelligent Designer. It then continues, in accordance with the method of argument already pursued by the argument of the First Cause, to argue for the self-existence, unity, and infinity of this Designer.

The Moral argument is that drawn from the general recognition of the existence of an invisible Lawgiver, a superhuman Lord and Ruler. It contends that a recognition of this character must be taken as the genuine voice of nature, and not as the outcome of any of the deceptive influences to which nature is subject. However, this argument, like that from Design, only proves the existence of an intelligent, superhuman ruler of the world. It does not tell us whether this ruler is self-existent or himself dependent on some previous Maker or Ruler. For this we must again go back to the argument of the First Cause.

Thus it is seen that the argument of the First

Cause is the only one which is sufficient in itself.
Absolutely, therefore, the others might be dispensed
with. Nevertheless, they have their useful purpose.
The argument of Design brings out more impressively the need of recognizing Intelligence in the
First Cause, and the Moral argument fortifies our
minds in their grasp of the previous arguments,
for it shows them to be no mere outcome of an
individual speculation, the conclusion to which
the minds of men are impelled in such numbers
and under such conditions that we are constrained
to recognize in the impelling force the voice of our
intellectual nature.

SECTION 2.—*The Argument of the First Cause.*

Thesis III.—*Not all things are effects of causes, but
there exists an unproduced First Cause, endowed with
intelligence and free-will, in other words a personal God.*

25. Kant, in his *Critique of Pure Reason,*[1] acknowledges that the human mind cannot divest itself
of the idea that everything that has a beginning
has a cause. However, he demurs to the objective
certainty of this principle when applied to particular cases without limitation. According to him it
is one of those judgments which he was pleased to
call *synthetic a priori judgments,* judgments, that is to
say, which we are constrained by a natural necessity
to accept as universally true, although they are
neither self-evident nor verifiable by experience.

[1] Kant's *Critique of Pure Reason* (Translated by M. Müller), p. 8.

26. Yet if we would not fall into the abyss of universal scepticism,[2] we must admit the objective validity and universal range of the principle of causality rightly understood. Our reason demands absolutely that we should say that *whatever does not exist of absolute necessity, cannot exist without a proportionate cause.* That this principle must be admitted as universally valid, will become clear by showing its connection with the principle of contradiction. We lose all hold on truth the moment we cease to acknowledge the principle of contradiction, that is to say, as soon as we allow that the same thing under the same aspect may be and not be at the same instant. But the principle of contradiction stands or falls with that of causality. That which does not exist of absolute necessity is of itself only contingent, depending for its existence on a condition outside itself: otherwise, existing unconditionally, it would be an absolutely necessary being. If we suppose that there was in any particular case a beginning of existence without cause, in other words, that a violation of the principle of causality took place: this could not happen without there being an instant in which a mere possible thing—a thing, that is to say, which depends for existence on a condition external to itself—really depended upon itself as the condition of its existence; and this would be a manifest violation of the principle of contradiction.

[2] To understand fully the intrinsic absurdity of universal scepticism, the reader may consult *The First Principles of Knowledge*, by the Rev. John Rickaby, especially c. viii. pp. 134—147.

D

Moreover, this principle is not only violated if we admit a beginning of existence without cause, but also if we admit such a beginning without a *proportionate* cause; namely, without a cause which *considered in its totality* contains a perfection at least equal to that of the effect. For if it did not, the *excess* of the effect over its cause would really be without *any* cause, in violation of the principle of contradiction.

27. By means of the same principle of causality we now go on to prove that there must be something self-existing. For the present we do not inquire whether the thing self-existing be matter or mind, whether it belong to this world as a part of it, or whether it be above this world. The only truth to be established is this. Not all beings can be effects; there must be something which is a cause without being the effect of another cause, and this something must be self-existent.

Our argument is as follows: Everything in so far as it is an effect is indebted for its actual existence to some other thing. But supposing there be no . self-existent being, then the totality of being must be an effect, no matter whether it be a finite or an infinite series of various kinds of being. Consequently in that supposition whatever falls under the concept of existing being past or present, must be indebted to another being for its existence. But this is evidently absurd; for it cannot be true without the existence of *something beyond the bounds of what falls under the notion of existing being.* Therefore the supposition that there is no self-existent being is unreasonable, and the assertion of a self-existent being is demanded by reason.

28. A strong confirmation of this truth is to be found in the fact already mentioned, that neither materialists, nor evolutionists, nor pantheists are bold enough to give an explanation of the origin of the present world, without supposing an eternal *something*, either " Matter," or the " Unknown," or the so-called " Absolute," or the pure " Ego," or the " Idea " of Being, or the " Will," or the " Unconscious." What they all refuse to admit is the existence of an *intelligent and free* self-existent being, a personal God, distinct from and superior to this material world and to mankind. The task now remains to show that the same principle of causality, which led us to acknowledge a self-existent being, leads us further to the conclusion that this self-existent Being is personal.

29. The human soul is an immaterial (spiritual) and free being. But the First Cause of an immaterial and free being cannot be a material being, and one constrained by an irresistible natural impulse to the production of its effects. Consequently the First Cause of the human soul must be an immaterial free being, which implies that we must consider a self-existent spiritual and free being to be the first cause of man. But such a being is manifestly distinct from, and superior to the material world and to man. Therefore the existence of a self-existent being, immaterial and free, superior to the material world and to man, cannot reasonably be

denied ; or what amounts to the same, the existence of a personal God is evident.

30. Is there any flaw in this reasoning? Surely no one who admits the first premiss upon which the argument is based, can reasonably object to the rest. What it means is this. The human soul, that is to say, the inmost principle of thought and will in man, differs altogether from everything material. We call it therefore a spiritual being, by which we understand a being not composed of parts, as matter is, but complete in its simple essence, and able to act and to exist by itself without being united to matter. Freedom also we attribute to the soul, by which we mean a power of self-determination existing in the will. The human soul is free inasmuch as its will is able to choose or not to choose any object presented to it by the understanding, as long as that object does not appear desirable under every possible aspect.

But are we sufficiently warranted in making these assertions? Are they more than an attempted answer to some of the deepest psychological problems, supported, it is true, by the authority of mediæval schoolmen, but directly opposed to the tendency of modern thought? Can it then be reasonable to take for the basis of the solution of the most important philosophical questions such a debatable fact as that of the existence of a spiritual human soul endowed with free-will?

These are questions which no doubt suggest themselves to some of our readers, and we are bound not to pass them by unanswered, although the complete answer belongs to Psychology.[3]

31. The answer to the question, whether our soul be an outgrowth of matter or an immaterial being, must not be given *a priori*, but must be based on facts. As the tree is known by its leaves, its flowers, and its fruit, so does the human soul manifest its nature by its ideas, its judgments, and its desires. It is to these that we must give our attention in order to become convinced of the spirituality of the soul.

There are two sorts of ideas in us, sense ideas (or phantasms, imaginations) and intellectual ideas. A *sense* idea is an internal representation of a *phenomenon*, or of a combination of phenomena, that have impressed themselves upon one or more of the organs of sensation with which the human body is endowed. An *intellectual* idea is the expression of *being* under a more or less general aspect. The difference between the two will be best seen in concrete instances. I have a sense idea of a circle, if I represent to myself a perfectly round plane figure; I have an intellectual idea of a circle, if I know what constitutes the being, the essence of a circle, its "whatness," or what is commonly

---

[3] These questions, all-important as they are, do not belong to a treatise on Natural Theology. For anything like a satisfactory discussion of them we must refer back to the Manual of *Psychology* (Stonyhurst Series), by the Rev. M. Maher, pp. 361—393, also pp. 443—467; and to the Manual of *Logic* (*ibid.*), by the Rev. R. F. Clarke, pp. 105—120, also pp. 140—157. We shall, however, be consulting the convenience of our readers by indicating at least the outline of the argument of which the fuller development is to be found in the books referred to.

called its definition. My sense idea of a circle is as variable as the magnitudes of circles are, but in each representation it corresponds only to *one* magnitude; my intellectual idea of a circle on the contrary is as invariable as the definition of a circle considered not in its *verbal expression*, but in its *meaning*; and at the same time it is applicable not to a limited number of circles, but to all possible circles. In the same way the sensile idea or phantasm of a man corresponds either to one particular man or to several men perfectly resembling one another in external appearance, but the intellectual idea of man or the mental expression of what is meant by the word "man" is applicable to all possible men.

32. This premised, we admit readily that our sense ideas or imaginations are caused directly by organic impressions, and require the immediate co-operation of a material organ, the sensitive nerves and the grey matter of the brain. Moreover, because of the substantial union between soul and body, the formation of intellectual ideas and the rise of indeliberate desires connected with them, is also largely dependent upon the imagination, and consequently upon the state of the brain and the whole nervous system as acted upon by the external corporeal world. We allow therefore that the human brain may be called the organ of understanding inasmuch as it is the organ of imagination, the operation of which in this our mortal state is a prerequisite to the working of the understanding. To this must be added that we cannot by direct

intuition get intellectual ideas except of things represented by our imagination. The consequence is that to a certain extent a change in the operation of the imagination naturally carries with it a change in the operation of the understanding. There is thus some foundation for the expression borrowed from mathematics, that the understanding is a "function of the brain;" since by "function" mathematicians mean a quantity so connected with another quantity that any change in the one is accompanied by a corresponding change in the other. But the expressions referred to must not be taken to mean that our intellectual knowledge consists of sense impressions. Mr. Herbert Spencer is therefore wrong in saying: "Feelings are in all cases the materials out of which in the superior tracts of consciousness, *Intellect is evolved by structural combination.*"[4] And again, he is wrong in speaking of our senses thus, "The impressions received by these senses form the materials of intelligence which arises by combination of them, and must therefore conform to their development."[5]

33. Against theories such as these we maintain that our intellectual ideas, our rational judgments, and our deliberate resolutions cannot possibly be the effects of organic impressions either hereditary or acquired.

A man who knows what mathematicians mean by the word "circle," and what philosophers understand by the term "rational being," has an intellectual idea of the words "circle," and "rational

---

[4] *Principles of Psychology,* Vol. I. p. 192.   [5] *Ibid.* p. 388.

being." No doubt he has also in his brain the phantasms of circular figures seen before, and the phantasms of many rational beings with whom he has conversed. Again, there are in his brain the organic impressions of the words in which the explanation of "circle" and "rational being" are given to him. But there is a vast difference between these phantasms in whatever combination they may be taken, and the *meaning* of the words, "circle" and "rational being." Organic impressions can only lead to the representation of what has really affected our organs. But the meaning of a word cannot really affect an organ; for it is not an existing particular thing which can move and change, it is the term of an act of our mind, it is that which our thinking mind manifests to us as something really belonging to those particular things which, on account of their similar natural properties, are denoted by the words in question. Consequently, the meaning of a word as known by our minds is something which has no proportion to organic movements, and therefore cannot in any way be considered as the result of organic action. This holds good about the meaning of any word, but especially of such terms as, "Being in the abstract," "Impossibility," "Causality," "Spirit," "Infinite perfection," "Consciousness," "Intellectual idea," "Infinitesimal," "Differential calculus," finally, "the Unknown," as explained by Mr. Spencer himself.

34. Moreover, as intellectual ideas expressing things in general, by their very applicability to an unlimited number of things, infinitely surpass the

effects which can reasonably be attributed to organic impressions, so neither can the concomitant consciousness which we have of the existence of these ideas in us be explained on the hypothesis of mere organic causation. I think for instance of the signification of the word "spirit," and whilst I entertain this thought I also know that I am entertaining it. Thus the thinking principle denoted by the pronoun "I," is at once the thinking subject and the object of its own thought. Assuredly this could not be, unless this principle is an immaterial being; for in matter no particle acts upon itself, but one particle acts upon another. Therefore the thinking principle in man which is called the soul, must be an immaterial spiritual being.

35. If intellectual ideas and the reflection of the mind upon them are due to quite another principle than matter, much more must this be said of intellectual judgments and the concomitant reflection on them. Let us take the principle of contradiction : "Nothing can be and not be at the same instant and under the same respect." As often as we enunciate this principle, we affirm that there is absolute opposition between any perfection and the negation of the same. We feel certain about this opposition, not only with regard to the past and present, but also with regard to all future time, and with regard to all possible perfections to which the concept of being may be applied. How could the knowledge of the unlimited value of that principle be attributed to an organic impression, without

admitting an effect infinitely superior to its total cause?

36. The spirituality of the human soul, following as it does from the preceding considerations, is the foundation of that freedom of will by which man is enabled to become master to a large extent, not only of the rest of the visible creation, but of his own actions, so far as they are dependent upon his deliberate resolutions. It is because we have a spiritual soul, that we are able to consider one object under many aspects, and to weigh the motives which recommend its choice or dissuade it. As our reasonable will is a property of the same spiritual soul, which is the spring of our intellectual ideas and judgments, we cannot be necessitated to the choice of any object, so long as reasons against that choice present themselves to our mind. We often have to decide whether we will follow the reasonable counsel of a friend, or stubbornly and selfishly take our own way; whether for the sake of charity we will undergo an inconvenience, or for the love of pleasure procure ourselves a superfluous comfort; whether we will act upon an approved moral maxim, or yield to the mere impulse of anger, pride, or other passion. In all these cases we are responsible for our choice, unless the use of reason be so disturbed in us as to make reflection impossible. Our own consciousness bears witness to the fact that whatever we choose deliberately, we choose without being necessitated to the choice. It is for this reason we experience remorse and self-reproach, when we have chosen ill. And as we naturally

hold ourselves responsible for our deliberate volitions, so our very nature inclines us easily to forgive indeliberate offences committed by others, however grave they may be; whereas nothing provokes us more than deliberate malice. All these internal facts can be explainèd only on the admission of the truth, firmly recognized by mankind taken as a whole, that our deliberate resolutions depend upon the free choice of our reasonable will. Whoever, with the pantheist Spinoza [6] and other monists or determinists, denies this freedom of will, not only puts himself in glaring opposition to the common good sense of mankind, but also implicitly denies the essential distinction between praiseworthy virtue and blameable vice;[7] nay, he teaches a doctrine which leads to absolute scepticism; for he cannot hold his opinion without confessing a natural and indelible tendency of the human understanding to accept what in his view is a mere delusion, the notion that man in some of his actions is a deliberate, free, and responsible agent.

37. If man's soul were nothing more than a principle of growth, of individual and specific bodily development, of sense-perception, and of animal appetite, then, of course, he could strive after nothing but what is in harmony with animal craving, or tends to individual organic comfort, or to the good of kith and kin; and he would do even

---

[6] Cf. Spinoza, *Ethics*, Part II. prop. 48, and Part I. Appendix.

[7] Spinoza denies this distinction explicitly: "No action considered in itself is either good or bad." (*Ethics*, Part IV. prop. 59, towards the end of the demonstration.)

these actions with a certain specific uniformity, as
dumb animals do them, always in the same way.
But man by his free-will rises infinitely higher. He
alone in the whole animal creation, sits down deliberately to meditate how he may do things better
than his ancestors have done for centuries before
him; he alone has invented and continually makes
progress in the arts; he alone cares for the study of
nature; he alone utilizes it for intellectual purposes.
He alone is free either to yield to the immoderate
cravings of animal appetites, or to subject them to
the demands of reason and conscience; nay, he
is able deliberately to struggle against sensible
pleasure, deliberately to mortify his passions, deliberately to aim at the "higher things." The evidence
of these facts has induced Mr. A. R. Wallace, who
is called by Mr. Mivart "the surviving chief of
the encompassed and besieged citadel of Darwinism," to throw in his lot with those who maintain
the spirituality of the soul.   In his *Exposition of the
Theory of Natural Selection*,[8] after having shown that
man's mathematical, musical, and artistic faculties
cannot be accounted for by the hypothesis of evolution,[9] Mr. Wallace thus continues: "The special
faculties we have been discussing clearly point to
the existence in man of something which he has not
derived from his animal progenitors —something
which we may best refer to as being of a spiritual
essence or nature, capable of progressive development under favourable conditions.   On the hypothesis of this spiritual nature, superadded to the

    [8] London: Macmillan and Co., 1889.   [9] Pp. 466, seq.

animal nature of man, we are able to understand much that is otherwise mysterious or unintelligible in regard to him, especially the enormous influence of ideas, principles, and beliefs over his whole life and actions. Thus alone we can understand the constancy of the martyr, the unselfishness of the philanthropist, the devotion of the patriot, the enthusiasm of the artist, and the resolute and persevering search of the scientific worker after nature's secrets. Thus we may perceive that the love of truth, the delight in beauty, the passion for justice, and the thrill of exultation with which we hear of any act of courageous self-sacrifice, are the workings within us of a higher nature which has not been developed by means of the struggle for material existence."[10]

38. We have therefore a right to say that the fact affirmed in the major premiss of our argument for the existence of a personal God, viz., the spirituality of the soul (§ 29), cannot be reasonably doubted. But if we must admit this fact, we cannot but allow its legitimate consequences. It is evident that there must be a cause of the human race. Astronomers and geologists, palæontologists and historians agree, that man did not always exist. How then did the first man come into existence? We pass over the question as to the origin of his body; but whence came his spiritual freely-electing soul? A spiritual and free being cannot be the outcome of a mere organic development. Therefore the cause of

---

[10] *Ibid.* p. 474; cf. *ib.* as far as p. 476; cf. *Dublin Review*, Jan. 1890, "Darwinianism," by M. Mivart.

the human soul must be an agent itself spiritual and free. And if you suppose this agent to be not a self-existing but a created spirit—which hypothesis we shall discuss later on—that created spirit must have a self-existing spirit for its First Cause. This follows evidently from the impossibility of any series of produced causes which is not dependent upon an unproduced First Cause; an impossibility we have proved in § 27. The conclusion is that the First Cause of the human race is a spirit, self-existent and freely-choosing, in other words, a personal God.

SECTION 3.—*The Argument from Design.*

Thesis IV.—*The manifold and beautiful order of nature is the work of a designing mind of vast intelligence; and must be ultimately explained by the existence of a personal God.*

39. The argument from Design is built upon the fact that material things do constantly and in a most complex way group themselves together into well-ordered wholes and systems. This fact cannot be explained sufficiently otherwise than by admitting an Intelligence presiding over nature's works, designing and adapting means to ends with foreknowledge of eventual results. That the Intelligence we speak of is self-existent, we cannot directly prove by this argument. We shall have to supplement the deficiency in this regard by the argument of a First Cause. Yet considered apart from it, the argument from Design is in itself a striking refutation of materialism, whether in the shape of a fortuitous

mechanical concurrence of atoms, or in the monist's mystic vision of the undifferentiated developing into the differentiated and individualized.

40. The order which prevails throughout the visible world has excited the attention of thinkers from the very dawn of Philosophy. According to Cicero,[11] Thales, the leader of the Ionian school, held God to be that Intelligence which out of water forms all beings. Anaxagoras[12] believed likewise in a Superior Reason pervading the whole of nature. Plato[13] attributed the harmonious order of celestial and terrestrial bodies to a designing mind; and Aristotle, at the end of the twelfth book of his *Metaphysics*, concludes from the unity of the order in the physical world to the unity of its Ruler. The same argument was treated more fully by the Stoics, a fine specimen of whose reasoning is preserved by Cicero in the second book of the *De natura Deorum*.[14]

To say nothing of scholastic philosophers,[15] Bacon[16] held it for absolutely certain, that the attributes of God, and particularly His wisdom and His ruling providence, are traceable in creation. Leibnitz[17] expressed it as his persuasion, that the material

---

[11] *De Natura Deorum*, i. 10. Cf. Aristot. *De Anima*, i. 5.

[12] Cf. Stöckl, *Geschichte der Philosophie*, p. 51 ; Ueberweg, *History of Philosophy*, i. p. 63.

[13] *Philebus*, pp. 30b, seq.

[14] Cf. especially the beautiful illustrations in c. xxxiv. and c. xxxvii.

[15] Cf. St. Thomas, *Sum. Theol.* i. q. 2. a. 3. c. " Quinta via."

[16] Bacon de Verulam, *De dignitate et augmentis Scientiarum*, Lib. III. c. ii. pp. 207, seq. Cf. Stöckl, *Geschichte der neuern Phil.* I. p. 21.

[17] Leibnitz, Opera (Edit. Erdm.) p. 506.

elements of the world, considered in themselves, are
capable of quite another order than that by which
they actually are connected; whence he concludes
that the realization of this one order out of many
possible orders must be attributed to the determining mind of God.   Kepler's reverence for the
Author of Nature is well known.   Newton concludes
his *Scholia* with a *scholion generale* in praise of the
Creator, whose infinite wisdom in arranging the
solar system had struck him with admiration.
"This most elegant contrivance, consisting of the
sun, planets, and comets," he says, "could not
originate but by the design and power of an intelligent Being."   What this great astronomer saw so
clearly, the great biologist of modern time, Charles
Darwin,[18] felt instinctively and "with overpowering
force," although he did not care to draw the conclusion suggested to common-sense by his own
observations.   Let us add here that although John
Stuart Mill doubted whether the Darwinian principle
of the "survival of the fittest" be not able "to
account for such truly admirable combinations as
some of those in nature," he was nevertheless of
opinion, "that it must be allowed that in the
present state of our knowledge, the adaptations in
nature afford a large balance of probability in
favour of creation by intelligence."[19]

Of far more weight, however, than Mill's timid
admission of a large balance of probability, is the

---

[18] *Life and Letters of Charles Darwin*, by F. Darwin, Vol. I. p. 316,
note.
[19] *Three Essays on Religion*, pp. 172, 174.

firm conviction of many of the best scientific men of our own century, that it is absolutely impossible to explain the adaptations we meet with in all departments of nature, otherwise but by intelligence and design. St. George Miyart tells us that the cause of the phenomenal universe "must be orderly and intelligent, as the first and absolute cause of an orderly series of phenomena which reveals to us an objective intelligence in the bee and the ant, which is not that of the animals themselves, and which harmonizes with and is recognized by our own intellects."[20] Dr. W. B. Carpenter, after having given us in his *Vegetable Physiology* a highly interesting chapter on the Secretions of Plants,[21] pauses to contemplate with his readers "the important inferences which may be drawn from the foregoing details, in regard to the Power, Wisdom, and Goodness of the Almighty Designer."[22]

With the two great biologists just mentioned, A. R. Wallace, in the work already quoted above, agrees at least to a certain extent. According to him, the "three distinct stages of progress from the inorganic world of matter and motion up to man, point clearly to an unseen universe—to a world of spirit, to which the world of matter is altogether subordinate."[23]

No less pronounced statements in favour of the existence of an intelligent arranger of the universe,

---

[20] *Lessons from Nature*, p. 358.   [21] *Vegetable Physiology*, c. x.
[22] Op. cit. n. 404, pp. 258, 259 in First Edition.
[23] Cf. *Exposition of the Theory of Natural Selection*, pp. 475, 476.

E

came from other quarters of modern science. "Overpowering proofs of intelligence and benevolent design," said Sir William Thomson some years ago,[24] "lie around us, showing to us through nature the influence of a free-will, and teaching us that all living beings depend upon one ever-acting Creator and Ruler." Two years later, Sir William Siemens repeated the same judgment in these words: "We find that all knowledge must lead up to one great result, that of an intelligent recognition of the Creator through His works."[25]

At the same conclusion which English scientists drew from the order of nature, the French astronomer, Faye, in his work *Sur l'origine du monde* (Paris, 1884), arrived from the consideration of the human mind. After having stated that human intelligence must owe its origin to an intelligence higher than human, he thus continues: "*Plus l'idée qu'on se fera de cette intelligence suprême sera grande, plus elle approchera de la vérité.*"[26]

But what seems to us the best extrinsic evidence of the great strength of the argument from design, is the fact that such a judge of the value of arguments as Kant thinks it a blameable imprudence not to conclude from the order of nature to an intelligent designer. "This proof," he says,[27] "will

---

[24] Presidential Address, 1882.

[25] See also statements made by Professor Stokes, Professors Stuart and Tait, and Sir John Herschell, in *The Month* of January, 1889, pp. 39, seq., in "The New Genesis," a criticism of E. Clodd's *Story of Creation*, by Rev. John Gerard.

[26] Op. cit. p. 114.

[27] *Critique of Pure Reason* (Translated by M. Müller), ii. p. 535.

always deserve to be treated with respect. It is the oldest, the clearest, and most in conformity with human reason. It gives life to the study of nature, deriving its own existence from it, and thus constantly acquiring new vigour. It reveals aims and intentions, where our own observation would not by itself have discovered them, and enlarges our knowledge of nature by leading us towards that peculiar unity, the principle of which exists outside nature. This knowledge reacts again on its cause, namely, the transcendental idea, and thus increases the belief in a Supreme Author to an irresistible conviction. It would therefore be not only extremely sad, but utterly vain, to attempt to diminish the authority of this proof. Reason, constantly strengthened by the powerful arguments that come to hand of themselves, though they are no doubt empirical only, cannot be discouraged by any doubts of subtle and abstract speculation. Roused from all curious speculation and mental suspense, as from a dream, by one glance at the wonders of nature and the majesty of the cosmos, reason soars from height to height till it reaches the highest, from the conditioned to conditions, till it reaches the supreme and unconditioned Author of all." Later on,[28] Kant refers to the objection that we must not argue from the need of foresight in human workmanship to a similar need in nature. His answer is: "We cannot do better than follow the analogy of these products of human design, which are the only ones of which we know completely both cause and effect. There

would be no excuse, if reason were to surrender a
causality which it knows, and have recourse to
obscure and indemonstrable principles of explanation, which it does not know." [29]

It is true that Kant, while granting thus much,
has nevertheless some speculative difficulties against
the argument from Design. We shall treat of these
later. For the present we are satisfied with knowing
that one of the most acute leaders of modern
thought, forced by the voice of reason, bears testimony to the great truth that "the heavens show
forth the glory of the Lord," [30] that " by the greatness of the beauty and of the creature, the Creator
of them may be seen so as to be known thereby," [31]
and that "the unknown God " [32] "left not Himself
without testimony, doing good from Heaven, giving
rains and fruitful seasons, filling our hearts with
food and gladness." [33]

We now proceed from authority to argument.

41. Order is the adaptation of diverse things to
one definite result. Order of simple coexistences is
called *statical;* order of motions and activities is
called *dynamical.* Thus for instance, in a well-
arranged library we have statical order, in machinery
not only statical, but also dynamical. These definitions supposed, it cannot be doubted that the visible
universe in all its parts bears marks of a most
varied and beautiful order. Darwin was so struck
by this complex final order, that he did not hesitate
to pronounce " nature's productions far truer in

---

[29] P 538   [30] Psalm xviii. 1.   [31] Wisdom xiii. 5.
[32] Acts xvii. 23.   [33] Acts xiv. 16.

character than man's productions;" and to maintain that they are "infinitely better adapted to the most complex conditions of life, and plainly bear the stamp of far higher workmanship."[34]

Any good popular treatise on astronomy and physiology will serve as a rich source of illustrations bearing on the truth of these statements, nor is there any one who will be foolish enough to dispute them. It must, however, be carefully noted, that we do not as yet affirm that *everything* in this world is well-ordered, nor do we say that there is a *universal combination of things for the fulfilment of one common purpose.* Were we to claim all this, we should indeed be claiming only what, if rightly understood, is most true. But so far-reaching a proposition is not necessary for the argument from Design, nor would it be sufficiently warranted until we have carried our inquiry further.

42. Confining, therefore, our attention to those manifestations of order which are obvious to every one who cares for the study of the workings of nature, we ask : How did these orderly arrange- ments, their harmony, beauty, and usefulness, come to be ? May we suppose, with Epicurus, that they are the effect of chance ? in other words, that they are owing to an accidental concurrence of atoms, moving in infinite space, and meeting one another in such a way as to form, after many failures, various kinds of inanimate and animate bodies ? Such an hypothesis would be not only inadequate to account for the laws and results of chemical combinations,

[34] *Origin of Species,* c. iv. p. 65.

and for the origin of life ; it would be intrinsically
absurd, conflicting with the universality of the Principle of Causation, inasmuch as this fortuitous concurrence would be an uncaused concurrence.[35] There
must then have been a cause of the formation of
the heavenly orbs and their arrangement in systems:
a cause again which, on our earth, grouped together
the elements into organized structures, moving,
growing, repairing themselves, and reproducing
their kind according to definite laws.   Where shall
we find this cause ?   It must either be inherent in
the elements of matter, or it must be something outside these.   If it is outside matter, it can only be a
mind, understanding and designing the order of
matter.   But will not the inherent forces of matter
suffice to explain this complex order ?   Let us see.

[35] On this point not only all sound metaphysicians, but also all
true scientists, are at one.   "The one act of faith in the convert to
science," says Professor Huxley, "is the universality of order, and
of the absolute validity, in all times and under all circumstances, of
the law of causation.   This confession is an act of faith, because,
by the nature of the case, the truth of such propositions is not
susceptible of proof.   But such faith is not blind, but reasonable,
because it is invariably confirmed by experience, and constitutes the
sole trustworthy foundation for all action."   Then picturing, for
illustration's sake, the raging sea, he thus continues : "The man of
science knows that here, as everywhere, perfect order is manifested;
that there is not a curve of the waves, not a note in the howling
chorus, not a rainbow glint on a bubble, which is other than a
necessary consequence of the ascertained laws of nature, and that
with a sufficient knowledge of the conditions, competent physico-
mathematical skill could account for and indeed predict every one
of these 'chance' events." (*Life and Letters of Charles Darwin*, by
F. Darwin, Vol. II. c. 5, written by Professor Huxley, p. 200.)   We
agree fully with all of this, *inasmuch as it implies that nothing happens
without a proportionate cause*, and that consequently an accidental
concurrence of causes is nonsense.

43. In the first place, the inherent forces of matter cannot be appealed to as the cause of the order prevailing in the inorganic world. We know that material elements produce different effects according to their different collocations in regard to one another.[36] Consequently, each effect is the natural outcome of a previous disposition of the parts of matter. This being so, every orderly effect is due to a pre-arrangement of particles suitable to the production of such an effect. That is, the order which is worked out by the elements of matter, presupposes order in the combination of the working elements. Thus the question of order in the world of inanimate matter is thrown back to the origin of that combination of elements which generated order.

Nor do we escape the necessity of seeking a cause external to the combinations themselves, by pleading the possibility of an eternal series of combinations. In the first place, eternal succession is a self-contradictory conception. Succession implies links of a series, it is constituted by the continuous addition of link to link. Now links added to one another are always numerable. Links of a series must always be in some number, however immense the number may be. But to be in some number, is to be finite : for every number is made up of finite unities. Thus eternal succession would be essentially finite, because it was succession, and yet infinite because eternal.

[36] " The last great generalization of science, the Conservation of Force, teaches us that the variety in the effects depends partly upon the *amount* of force, and partly upon the diversity of the collocations." (Mill, *Three Essays on Religion*, p. 145. Third Edit.)

In the second place, even if eternal succession were possible, it would furnish no explanation of the phenomenon of orderly combination which the world exhibits: any more than infinite extension of a chain hung in air would supply the want of supports for it. Consequently, although we have nothing to say against the assumption made by astronomers, that our cosmic system resulted from the condensation and division of a primitive rotating *nebula;* yet we cannot admit this *nebula,* without observing that there must have been a *first* arrangement of the material elements which constituted it, one which already contained in germ the present system, or else the said system could never have resulted from it. Now this first arrangement was neither the effect of the forces of matter, nor was it essential to matter. Had it been the effect of material forces, it could not possibly have been the first disposition of matter, but was rather the effect of a preceding disposition of the elements. Again, had it belonged essentially to matter, it could not have yielded to another disposition so long as matter existed, and thus the present cosmic system could never have been formed. Therefore, if we would explain the origin of that system without violation of reason, we are forced to say that its first beginning, nebular or otherwise, is due to an intelligent cause.[37]

[37] Professor Huxley supports our conclusion, when in defence of Darwin's *Origin of Species* he writes: "The teleological and the mechanical views of nature are not, necessarily, mutually exclusive. On the contrary, the more purely a mechanist the speculator is, the more firmly does he assume a primordial molecular arrangement of

44. If the forces of matter are inadequate to explain the order of the inorganic world, much less can they account for the existence of life and the orderly relations which exist between animate and inanimate beings.

Whence comes the adaptation of inanimate nature to the support of life ? The natural tendency of brute matter cannot explain it. The relation of brute matter to life is accidental to its nature. Whence then did the relation originate ? No satisfactory answer to this question can be given except this : that an Intelligent Ruler of this world arranged the material elements of which the universe is built up in such a way that they gradually became adapted to the service of living beings whose existence he intended and foresaw. This answer must be insisted upon all the more from the fact that man, the most noble being on earth, finds it rich with an innumerable multitude of things accommodated to his bodily and mental wants. As we have proved before (§ 32, seq.), the soul of man is not the outgrowth of matter, but the work of an intelligent Creator only. No evolution of matter, of plants, and of animals, could culminate in the existence of man, composed of a human soul and a human body; and yet matter and

which all the phenomena of the universe are the consequences, and the more completely is he thereby at the mercy of the teleologist, who can always defy him to disprove that this primordial molecular arrangement was not intended to evolve the phenomena of the universe." (*Life and Letters of Charles Darwin*, by F. Darwin, Vol. II. pp. 201, 202, in Professor Huxley's chapter on "Reception of *The Origin of Species*.")

life inferior to man, conspire to furnish him what he needs for the maintenance of his body, and to help him in the cultivation of his intellect. Certainly no reasonable explanation of this great fact can be given but by recurring to an intelligent mind, superior to man and the irrational world, which arranged the latter, ere man was created, with a view to prepare him a fit dwelling-place.[38]

45. We have then seen hitherto that the adaptations to one another which connect the various groups of beings in the macrocosm of the universe must be attributed to a Designing Mind. The same conclusion we arrive at by pondering the order prevailing in the microcosm of each living organism, from the tiniest unicellular plant up to the most highly organized animal. Just as in scientific inquiry, the further that it proceeds, the more it becomes evident that brute matter by its own forces alone never developes into organized living structures; so, when we look at the subject from a metaphysical point of view, we are forced to maintain that the vast differences which separate the natural tendencies of living bodies from those of lifeless matter, are a sufficient evidence of the impossibility of a natural evolution of the latter into any species of the former. And with this conclusion coincides the verdict of scientific experience.

[38] " A successively increasing purpose," says St. George Mivart, "runs through the irrational creation up to man. All the lower creatures have ministered to him, and have, as a fact, prepared the way for his existence. Therefore, whatever ends they also serve, they exist especially for him." (*On Truth*, p. 495.)

Mr. St. George Mivart speaks on this point with authority.   He says :

" That there is an absolute break between the living world and the world devoid of life, is what scientific men are now agreed about—thanks to the persevering labours of M. Pasteur.   Those who affirm that though life does not arise from inorganic matter now, nevertheless it did so 'a long time ago,' affirm what is at the least contrary to all the evidence we possess, and they bring forward nothing more in favour of it than the undoubted fact that it is a supposition which is necessary for the validity of their own speculative views.   There is, then, one plain evidence that there has been an interruption of continuity, if not within the range of organic life, yet at its commencement and origin.   But we go further than this, and affirm, without a moment's hesitation, that there has, and must necessarily have been, discontinuity within the range of organic life also.   We refer to the discontinuity between organisms which are capable of sensation and those which do not possess the power of feeling.   That all the higher animals 'feel' will not be disputed.   They give all the external signs of sensitivity, and they possess that special organic structure—a nervous system—which we know supplies all our organs of sensation.   In the absence of any bodily mutilation, then, we have no reason to suspect that their nervous system and organs of sense do not act in a manner analogous to our own.   On the other hand, to affirm that the familiar vegetables of our kitchen-gardens are all endowed with sensitivity, is not only to make a gratuitous affirmation, but one opposed to evidence, since no vegetable organisms possess a nervous system, and it is a universally admitted biological law, that structure and functions go together. If, then, there are any organisms whatever, which *do not* feel, while certain other organisms *do* feel (as a door must be shut or open), there is, and must be, a break and distinction between one set and the other."[39]

What then was it which gave birth to organic life ? To say, it had no beginning, but that from eternity there existed one or several series of living organisms, would involve the postulate of succession without beginning, which we have proved to be self-contradictory. (§ 43.) But, if organic life can neither be considered as an effect of the forces of dead matter, nor have the source of its own existence within itself, we cannot reasonably explain its origin except by admitting that an intelligent Being, ruling over the matter of our earth, first put into it the germ of life, although we are not able to point out *when*, and *in what way*, this influence was exercised. Hence, the countless living organisms that people our globe are the realizations of ideas conceived by an immaterial superhuman Intelligence. This Intelligence drew the plans on which they are built, foresaw the stages of evolution, through which they run with so astonishing a regularity, furnished them with a multitude of skilfully-contrived organs, and adapted their whole structure to the environment in which they are placed.

[39] *Origin of Human Reason,* pp. 10, 11.

46. That the Ruler in whose mind the order of the world originated is a self-existing intelligence, and consequently a personal God, does not follow immediately from the fact that the order of the world must be the work of a superhuman Intelligence. What does, however, follow immediately is, that the Intelligence which rules the physical world is so vast, that no human understanding and wisdom can be compared with it. For many ages the cleverest of men have been occupied in studying the relations that exist between the different parts of living beings, and between these parts and their functions, and yet there is no man who understands completely the mysteries hidden even in one living cell. Far indeed then above human comprehension must be the excellence of that Mind whose ideas were the models after which the universe was fashioned, with its wealth of marvels and complexity of order.

If, however, we would show that the order of the world is due, not only to an Intelligence far exceeding all intelligence of man, but ultimately to a self-existent Intelligence—in other words, to a personal God, we must go back to the argument of the First Cause. Either the intelligent mind who designed the order of our world is dependent upon a series of other minds without beginning, or it depends upon a first mind, or it is itself the first mind. The first alternative is absurd, because it implies a series of causes produced without a self-existent cause to produce them (§ 38); therefore either the second or the third must be admitted. But this is equivalent to an admission that the order of the world depends upon an intelligent, self-existent cause; for the cause of the cause of order must also, at least mediately, be the cause of order itself.[40]

SECTION 4.—*The Moral Proof.*

Thesis V.—*Mankind has at all times believed in the existence of an intelligent nature superior to the material world and to man. This universal belief can only be explained as the result of the real existence of such a nature. But to grant this much is to grant implicitly the existence of a personal God.*

47. When we have convinced ourselves by a train of reasoning that some proposition is true, we are always anxious to know if our conclusion is identical with that of other minds. Our own minds may have been the victims of some lurking fallacy, but it is less likely that other minds should have been simultaneously deceived in the same manner. Thus we gain confidence when we find them to be in agreement with us, and our confidence becomes very great indeed when these other minds are in immense number and belong to various classes of persons acting independently of one another. It is natural therefore that now that we have completed our proofs of the existence of God drawn from intrinsic evidence, we should go on to inquire how far the Divine existence is universally

[40] On the argument from Design, cf. Janet, *Final Causes.* Translated into English by William Affleck, B.D. Second Edition. Edinburgh: T. and T. Clark, 1883.

recognized, and that we should claim the result of the inquiry as a signal corroboration of our position.

We claim more, however, than this in the present argument. We claim to find in this universal recognition which we assert, not only a corroboration of what has preceded, but an argument of absolute value in itself. We claim that a fact like this of the consent of nations in the recognition of God must be deemed the voice of universal reason yielding to the compelling evidence of truth. The cause must be adequate to the effect. A universal effect must imply an equally universal cause. But truth alone is such a cause. Error is always partial, local, temporary; truth alone is everywhere the same.

48. This is the outline of the argument we now advance. Its force will become more manifest when we have examined into its details.

First, about the fact. From the ancient writers, pagan as well as Christian, many well known passages have been collected in which this universal recognition of a Divine government of the world is attested. Thus Plutarch says: "If you go round the world, you may find cities without walls, or literature, or kings, or houses, or wealth, or money, without gymnasia, or theatres. But no one ever saw a city without temples and gods, one which does not have recourse to prayers, or oaths, or oracles, which does not offer sacrifice to obtain blessings or celebrate rites to avert evil." [41] And Cicero has declared that "there is no nation so wild and

[41] *Adv. Coloten Epicureum.*

fierce, as not to know that it must have a God, although it may not know what sort of a God it should be." [42]   From among Christian witnesses we may take Clement of Alexandria, who tells us that "all nations, whether they dwell in the East or on the remotest shores of the West, in the North or the South, have one and the same rudimentary apprehension of Him by whom this government (of the world) has been established." [43]

One is prone nowadays to suspect passages like these of resting too little on solid information, too much on the inferences and generalizations of oratory.   Still they have their value, and attest to us the results of such actual experience as came within the reach of former generations.   They have a right also to be taken together with the results of modern inquiry which, if they are found to agree with them, they can complete.   And they do agree with the discoveries of the most recent times. There are few tribes of the earth which have not been scrutinized by the active-minded explorers of the present century, and scrutinized on the whole with scientific care and skill.   Out of the entire number thus examined it is just possible that a few are altogether without religious ideas.   Sir John Lubbock has maintained that there are such.   But it is a task of no small difficulty to elicit from savages a true account of their religious beliefs.   They are shy in the presence of the white man, and they have also often a superstitious fear of mentioning the names of their gods.   Thus it becomes likely that

[42] *De Leg.* I. c. 8.   [43] *Strom.* Lib V. n. 260.

even this small residuum is not really as atheistic as it has been alleged to be. This is the judgment of one who is in the front rank of anthropologists, and is. clear from any suspicions of undue partiality in favour of the religion of theists. Mr. Tylor writes:

"The assertion that rude non-religious tribes have been known in actual existence, though in theory possible, and perhaps in fact true, does not at present rest on that sufficient proof which for an exceptional state of things we are entitled to demand. . . . So far as I can judge from the immense mass of accessible evidence, we have to admit that the belief in spiritual beings appears among all low races with whom we have attained to thoroughly intimate acquaintance." [44]

That the facts brought forward by Sir John Lubbock to prove the contrary, are not really to the point, has been clearly shown by Gustav Roskoff.[45] The conclusion at which he arrives is, that "hitherto no tribe has been found to be without any traces of religious sentiments." In this he is fully borne out both by the distinguished German ethnologist, Oskar Peschel,[46] who denies categorically that any tribe has been met with without religious ideas, and

---

[44] *Primitive Culture*, Vol. I. pp. 378 and 384.

[45] Gustav Roskoff's words are as follows: "Es ist bisher noch kein Volksstamm ohne jede Spur von Religiösität betroffen worden." (*Das Religionswesen der rohesten Naturvölker*, p. 178, Leipzig, 1880.)

[46] "Stellen wir uns die Frage, ob irgendwo auf Erden ein Volksstamm ohne religiöse Anregungen und Vorstellungen jemals angetroffen worden sei, so darf sie entschieden verneint werden." (Oskar Peschel, *Völkerkunde*, p. 260. Fifth Edit. Leipzig, 1881.)

F

also by F. v. Hellwald, in his *Natural History of Man.*[47]

49. Even if there were a few races altogether without religion it would not touch our argument. Our object is to ascertain the voice of nature, and of rational nature. It is only to be expected that we shall find its tones affected by an admixture of the tones of error in degraded races, and that the extent of the confusion should follow the degrees of degradation.

Here, however, the very natural objection will occur to the reader's mind : Do we not find an opposing voice at the other end of the scale of civilization ? Do not those who deem themselves and are perhaps deemed by the mass of men to represent the acme of intellectual culture, proclaim themselves to be conscientiously agnostic in reference to this important doctrine? That there are these apparent exceptions to the general law must of course be admitted. But we must not allow our adversaries to assume too much. Undoubtedly there is an increasingly large number of persons who profess themselves to be agnostics. Still only a small portion of these can be regarded as persons of special culture : and if there are some such, it must not be forgotten that there are many more of equal culture who are earnest theists. The fact thus alleged against us when reduced to its proper

---

[47] " Mit Fug und Recht darf man von einer Religion der Wilden sprechen ; denn bisjetzt sind noch keine vollständig religionslosen Völkerstämme gefunden worden." (F. v. Hellwald, *Naturgeschichte des Menschen*, p. 95. Stuttgart, 1883.)

proportions becomes this. In the present age there are many agnostics who declare that they do not see grounds for admitting the Divine existence, and some among them are in the front rank among the thinkers of the day. After all, this is a fact not peculiar to the present age. It can be paralleled by similar instances in the last century, and it can be paralleled also by similar instances among the philosophers of ancient Greece and Rome. Even the reasonings on which modern agnostics rely are substantially the same with those which we find in the writings of these ancient atheists.

If any one, certainly Professor Huxley must know, whether the scientific progress of our age has really created new and formidable difficulties against Natural Theology. Yet he says: " There is a great deal of talk and not a little lamentation about the so-called religious difficulties which physical science has created. In theological science, as a matter of fact, it has created none. Not a solitary problem presents itself to the philosophical Theist at the present day which has not existed from the time that philosophers began to think out the logical grounds and the logical consequences of Theism." [48]

50. Thus we are able to state as generally true the fact with which we have to deal. The acknowledgment of a superior and invisible intelligence governing the visible universe is common to all ages and all regions, to civilized and uncivilized tribes alike. We find a disposition on the part of

[48] *Life and Letters of Charles Darwin*, by F. Darwin, Vol. II. c. v. p. 203.

some few philosophers to dispute the validity of the belief, but nevertheless the belief has proved to be persistent and indestructible in the mass of mankind. It is this persistency among the mass of men, retained even in the teeth of sceptical opposition, on which our argument is based.

Now for the interpretation of this important fact. How comes it that minds are so accordant in their inference that the nature and movements of the visible world imply the existence of an invisible over-ruling spirit? There must be motives acting on the mind to induce it to draw this conclusion: and the motives must have been the same everywhere, since the effect, the inference, is the same everywhere. If the inference is of the character which we have investigated in the previous theses, and if this inference is true; if it is true that the universe bears upon its face the characteristic marks of an effect, and an effect presupposes a proportionate cause, if the universe bears upon its face the marks of design and purpose, and the only pro portionate cause of design and purpose is a cause endowed with intelligence, then the world-wide recognition of such an intelligent ruler of the world is fully justified and explained. And that this is the true explanation we may establish by way of elimination. What other explanation is there in the field? Bayle in the seventeenth century undertook to suggest other possible causes. He named the following:

(1) Ignorance of natural causes. Men observed the marvellous course of nature in the midst of

which they lived, and, unable as yet to detect the physical causes from which they actually spring, attributed them to the action of invisible beings which they anthropomorphically invested with form and qualities resembling their own.

(2) Fear excited by the stupendous forces of nature, by the flash of the lightning, the roll of the thunder, the fury of the waves, and the shock of the earthquake.

> Primus in orbe deos fecit timor ardua cœli
> Fulmina dum caderent.

(3) The fraud of the ruling classes, of priests and kings, who played upon these natural predispositions of the people by stamping them with the seal of their own superior authority: so doing because they perceived that the tendency of the beliefs was to exalt their own character as priests and kings by causing them to be regarded as the Divine representatives and as the mediators through whose instrumentality alone the Divine anger could be appeased.

Of these three reasons only the first is radical and need be considered. Given a belief in the existence of a Divine ruler, fear would naturally ensue, and where the idea of God was mingled with error, as it undoubtedly has been among barbarous nations, this fear would take an unreasonable form. But fear alone could not *create* a belief in God. In like manner, given belief in the existence of God formed on other grounds, the natural consequence would be a conviction that earthly rulers are His representatives holding authority under Him, and this conviction might lend itself to the interested motives of unworthy rulers where the people were sufficiently untutored to credit such fraudulent representatives.

What then is to be said of the first alleged cause of the belief in question? And be it noticed, that this self-same cause which is said to have originated the belief in God in past ages, is alleged to be sustaining it now among the ignorant theists, who, according to our modern men of progress, shut their eyes to the enlightenment of modern thought. You discover final causes, is the charge against us, and you then infer from them the existence of an architect of the universe, because you fail to see that the existing physical causes are quite able of themselves to evolve the complicated system which we call the world.

This charge, however, is a little out of date now. Those who used confidently to make it are beginning to realize what was seen by their adversaries all along, namely, that the appeal to physical causes and even to a long course of evolution under their action only results in pushing back the need of a designer to an earlier stage, and indeed makes the need itself the more imperative. However, this is a point that has already been sufficiently considered. All that we are at present concerned to notice is, that if failure to regard physical causes as containing within themselves an adequate explanation of the cosmos has been the motive which has engendered this universal recognition of the Divine existence, the failure is not one which can be confidently appealed to as discrediting the recognition. We are merely reduced to this, that whereas a certain argument seems to modern agnostics unsound and to modern theists sound, the general consent of mankind is on the side of the theists, not of the agnostics. And this is just what the theist appeals to as constituting an independent argument in his favour. How explain, he says, this persistent general belief without seeing in it the voice of rational nature ratifying the truth of the conclusion and the validity of the inference?

51. Of course it must not be supposed that we deny that here and there some among the thinkers of former ages have erred, just as barbarous tribes even may err now, in attributing to the immediate action of the Divinity results of which the immediate cause was the action of some physical agent. Errors in assigning wrong causes to physical facts have no doubt been committed repeatedly, and have been corrected by our superior information. Herein, in fact, we see, from the opposite side, an illustration of the value of our principle that persistent universal belief is an evidence of truth. The errors in question proved themselves to be errors by dropping out with the march of discovery. They have proved not to be universal and persistent. But these crude notions of immediate Divine action in the movement of the storm or the flash of the lightning, are ,not what we are appealing to. The question is not why some men multiplied their gods, or attributed to them this action or that; but why mankind in

general have agreed in thinking that the world as a whole presupposes the existence of an intelligent governor, and why this belief has shown itself, and continues to show itself to be as persistent in the face of all attacks made upon it by the agnostic thought of the various ages, as the other beliefs have shown themselves to be yielding and transitory. Error, we know, cannot live for ever. It is always in danger of destruction, because its foundations are insecure. Truth, on the other hand, though it may lie for a time obscured, must persist, because its foundation is on the rock of evidence.

52. It will help to render the force of our argument more distinct, if we bear in mind the difference between what were once happily called by Cardinal Newman "Implicit and Explicit Reason." To reason, that is to say, to be intellectually moved by certain premisses to the adoption of the conclusion towards which they point, is one thing. To give an accurate account of the nature of the premisses grasped by the mind, is quite another. To quote the Cardinal's words:

" Let a person only call to mind the clear impression he has about matters of every-day occurrence, that this man is bent on a certain object, or that man was displeased, or another suspicious: or that one is happy and another unhappy; and how much depends in such impressions on manner, voice, accent, words uttered, silence instead of words, and all the many subtle symptoms which are felt by the mind, but cannot be contemplated; and let him consider how very poor an account he is able to give of his impression, if he avows it and is called upon to justify it."[49]

The illustration is taken from one class of inference, but is applicable to others. To give an accurate account of one's reasoning is a faculty confined mainly to those who possess the art of reflection and analysis, born of the discipline of philosophical training. To reason correctly is a faculty much more widely found. It is noticeable that most men reason correctly concerning practical matters which come within their special sphere of interest and experience. All men who are in their right senses reason correctly concerning those matters which are of fundamental importance for the conduct of life. And thus it comes to pass that in a certain sense untrained minds are given to reason more correctly than philosophers. The latter, although enjoying the power to analyze their reasonings into its elements, do not always enjoy this power to perfection. Accordingly they set down the premisses inaccurately, and then, finding them insufficient to bear the weight of the inference, discard as unsound conclusions which are really valid. Meanwhile the untrained mind, undistracted by any such false notions, pursues its natural course, and arrives with certainty at the true conclusion. Here, then, we have the justification of the stress we have been laying on the appeal to the persistent universal consent of mankind in recognizing the existence of a superior intelligence. The appeal is from the mind caught in philosophical mazes through its

[49] *Sermons before the University of Oxford*, p. 274. Third Edit.

inability to grasp with sufficient accuracy the true
premises on which the arguments for God's existence rest; and it is to minds free from this dis-
tracting influence which by their concord in such
number, variety, and persistency, prove themselves
to be dominated by the evidence of truth.

53. In the last clause of the thesis we are proving,
we assert that to admit this universal recognition
of a superior intelligence governing the universe is
implicitly to admit the existence of a personal God.
The word "implicitly" must be carefully noticed.
The argument from universal recognition is often
misapprehended, because it is understood to aspire
to more than it really does. Cicero, long ago, said,
in words already cited: "No nation is so wild and
fierce as not to perceive that there must be a God,
although ignorant what kind of God it must be."
The two questions, whether God exists, and what
is the true nature of God, are to be distinguished.
As to the latter, the grossest and most absurd of
notions have prevailed, and it might be urged
against us that if we desire to take the beliefs of
the mass of mankind as in itself an evidence of
truth, we ought in consistency to take their gross
and absurd notions as an integral part of the belief.
What right have we to pick and choose? What
right have we to cite as valuable witnesses the
polytheists and even the fetish worshippers, and
at the same time disregard as valueless their belief
in polytheism and fetichism? However, the answer
is reasonable enough. The element of persistent
universality on which we lay stress is to be found

in the belief in the existence of a supreme intelligence. But as soon as men went beyond this, and
sought to conceive to themselves the form and
manner of this overruling intelligence, they fell into
error, and their error is revealed as such by its
want of universality and its want of persistency.
The forms which mythology has assumed among
the various tribes may resemble one another in
certain general characteristics, because even erroneous thought is an attempt to understand realities,
and must be governed to a certain extent by what
it sees; still, on the whole, the mythologies are
characterized by their dissimilitude: they are racy
of the soil where they spring up.

We are content, then, to appeal to the consent
of mankind for the rudimentary conception of a
governing intelligence (or intelligences) overruling
the world. But we contend that in this rudimentary
conception is contained implicitly the doctrine of
a personal God. To show that this is the true
inference from the premisses is not the task of the
present thesis. It has been partly demonstrated
already, and remains to be more completely
demonstrated in the theses yet to come.

Such is the Moral proof, grounded upon the
belief of the human race in the existence of God.
It is not absolutely conclusive, except when
taken in conjunction with the argument of the
First Cause. That argument shows perfectly the
existence of a personal God; yet it gains much in
practical value, when accompanied by the other two

(the argument from general consent and the argument from Design), which appeal more directly to
ordinary understandings. To confirm our conclusion
now indirectly, by evincing the untenableness of the
opposite, we will point out some of the practical
consequences that flow from agnosticism.

SECTION 5.—*Logical consequences of Agnosticism.*

Thesis VI.—*The logical consequences of Sceptical
Atheism or Agnosticism in the practical order show
clearly that the position of the agnostic is opposed to
reason.*

54. The word *atheist* suggests the idea of a man
living without regard for God. If he does so,
because he thinks that there is no sufficient reason
for believing in God's existence, he may be called
a *theoretical* atheist; if on the other hand, he admits
that existence, but disregards the law of God in
regulating his free actions, he will then be called a
practical atheist. In this place we have not to treat
of the consequences of practical atheism except
in so far as they are included in those connected
with atheism maintained as a theory. Confining
ourselves to the theoretical atheists, we have again
to distinguish *dogmatic* and *sceptical* atheism. A
dogmatic atheist is one who asserts without doubt,
"There is no God;" whereas a sceptical atheist,
commonly called an *agnostic*, maintains only that
we can know nothing definite about the First Cause
of things.

If the logical consequences of Sceptical Atheism
are disastrous, those of Dogmatic Atheism will

not be less disastrous, though they can hardly be more. We may, however, limit our attention to the consequences of the former only. Dogmatic Atheism is not very common now-a-days, at least among men of culture. Agnostics, we know, are wont to protest very strongly against the designation of atheists being applied to them, and the protest, whether reasonable or not, proves at least this much, that in their estimation the intellectual position of one who should claim to have demonstrated the non-existence of God is altogether irrational. Under these circumstances it is not necessary to consider the practical consequences of Dogmatic Atheism, but only those of Agnosticism. This we call Sceptical Atheism, since the name is one that is founded on truth and required by symmetry. The objection that may be raised to it by agnostics may become less if they will observe that the name atheist taken by itself has been defined to mean one who acts as if there were no God. Agnostics can hardly deny that they do this. "Worship of the silent sort" has indeed been pronounced fitting before the "altar of the Unknowable." But is such an evanescent homage, whether it be fitting or not, really sufficient ?

We assert then, in the present thesis, that the logical consequences of sceptical atheism in the practical order are so opposed to reason as to involve a condemnation of its tenets. There are pessimists in the world, and their number is said to be increasing with the spread of " modern thought." But although these may be cited as valuable wit-

nesses to the force of the argument about to be
advanced, the thesis is not addressed to them. It
is rather addressed to those who cannot think that
Nature is a fraud or a pest, but believe its course to
be stamped with the promise of a true hope.

In proof of our thesis, we will first invite attention to the moral paradox in which the agnostic
finds himself entangled, or rather would find himself
entangled if only he would reflect sufficiently. Few
agnostics would deny that, *if* the Christian assumption were correct and the existence of such a God
as Christians believe in were an ascertained truth,
it would follow at once that He must desire the
worship of loving reverence. Just as it is inconceivable that, if two persons hold towards each
other the physical relationship of father and son,
the father should not desire to enter into the moral
relationship of intercourse with his son and have it
reciprocated by loving and reverent affection and
obedience, so also, *if* there is a personal God from
whom man, has received his being, faculties, and all
else that he can call his, it is inconceivable that God
should not desire to enter into moral relationship
with him and receive a loving and obedient service
and worship. The conception of a God who, at
some past moment, made the world, set it spinning
like a top, and then ceased to care about it, has
always been rejected by the larger part of civilized
nations, and at the present day has fallen into
discredit. If, therefore, God desires this worship,
man ought to render it, and in the case of his
not rendering it, the requirements of natural

equity are violated and an indignity is offered to God.

So much as this will be generally conceded to us by agnostics. They do not challenge the inference as to conduct and worship which Christians draw from Christian premisses. They only challenge the premisses, that is, the certainty of the existence of God. They do not go so far as positively to deny the existence of God. They merely contend that it is uncertain. But in declaring it to be uncertain most of them go farther, and admit with Darwin that it is more probable than the opposite opinion. That is to say, it is probable that there exists a God desirous of receiving love and worship from His creatures, and therefore reciprocally probable that it is man's sacred duty to render it to Him. This the agnostic, by the very fact that he protests against being called an atheist, is bound to admit, and yet because he professes himself unable to go farther and convert the probability into a certainty, he cannot render the worship. Such is the moral paradox to which the agnostic is reduced.

And the paradox will be felt the greater if the agnostic will observe that, on his own principles, the hypothesis of the existence of an intelligent ruler of the world is not only probable, but even the most probable theory to account for the facts. When he forgets his philosophy, and as a man of science, that is, of physical science, adopts the attitude of the pure realist, he professes himself agnostic on the ground that Evolution in its extremest form may account for that order reigning through Nature which is the theist's foundation-stone. Now, Evolution thus conceived, however it may be dressed up in modern fashions, is in essence nothing but the old theory of the fortuitous concourse of atoms: the theory that, given eternal atoms and eternal motion, eventually order will result from their interaction, since order is self-sustaining and chaos is not. Although in answer to this we have given clear reasons to show that neither the theory of chance nor that of evolution can account for the orderly arrangements of the universe (§§ 42—46); nevertheless let us grant again, for the sake of argument, that either of the two is a conceivable explanation of the genesis of the cosmos. Can it possibly be claimed as relatively probable, or anything but relatively most improbable when set in competition with the rival theory of a personal Designer?

If the agnostic puts on his philosophic cloak and becomes a transfigured realist with Mr. Spencer, the existence of an " Infinite " is admitted, and all denied is the lawfulness, in face of the relativity of knowledge, of attributing to the Unknown Cause of the universe any attributes derived from the consideration of the things of this world, man not excluded. The protest made against the practice of assigning them to Him is made on the ground that they are likely to be altogether beneath Him: that is to say—if logically explained—on the likelihood that He may possess attributes which may go so far beyond even the most noble qualities of the human mind, that the latter are nothing but a dim and comparatively insignificant image of a

First Mind, and that human personality is but a dim and comparatively insignificant image of the Personality of the First Cause. In other words, that the great " Unknowable " is supereminently a person.

If the agnostic declines to be in any sense a realist, and shuts himself up in some form of pure idealism, we will not attempt to press him with the statement of the present thesis. The idealist is guilty of inconsistency in his every act of intercourse with the outer world. With such a burden of inconsistencies upon him, and all so easily borne, we cannot expect him to shrink from one more. But we may say this, that for realists the hypothesis of the existence of a personal God ought to count as the most probable of the theories in the field, and thus the moral paradox which has been described as arising out of the agnostic position becomes the more acute.

55. Such is the logical consequence of agnosticism as regards the duties more properly called religious. Its logical effects on the observance of the moral law in general are also fatal. We maintain that *in the great mass of mankind, were agnosticism ever universally accepted,* its effects, moral and social, would be most pernicious. Individuals of the average human type cannot lose the belief in an all-seeing and infinitely holy and just God without being exposed to commit many crimes, which they would not have committed if they had persevered in that belief. If God does not exist, no one is able to point out any sufficient principle of morality, which he can prove that man is absolutely bound to abide by. Of course certain

G

actions will be more becoming than others, because
more suited to rational nature. If a man is a man
of good taste he will so far forth abide by these
actions and abstain from their opposites. But
suppose he does not care to be a man of taste,
what is to oblige him to it? On that supposition,
no one has a right to blame his fellow-man for
enjoying life as he thinks fit. What is man, if you
take God away? What else but a machine made
of matter, held together by material forces? What
shall oblige me to have more respect for that
machine called man, than for another called ox or
sheep or monkey, which anatomy proves to be con-
structed on quite a similar plan and to be made
of the same organic elements? Why is it a greater
crime to destroy a man-machine than to destroy a
monkey-machine? Unless there is an immaterial
Divine Spirit, there cannot possibly be an immaterial human soul, and if there is not an immaterial human soul, our so-called freedom of will
is an illusion. But if our freedom is an illusion,
moral responsibility is an empty name, and if
that is an empty name, nobody is to be blamed,
however erroneous may be the misdeeds by which,
in the opinion of men, he sins against the dignity,
as it is called, of man. These and the like are the
practical lessons which *logically* follow from agnosticism. How can they be put into practice without
giving free rein to the most revolting vices in the
mass of men?

Again, if agnosticism with these moral consequences, which *objectively* are implied in it, were

universally prevalent, all social relations would sooner or later be in hopeless confusion. The good order of a commonwealth rests above all upon a healthy family life. Where domestic relations, domestic authority, domestic virtues are not respected, civil relations will constitute a very frail machinery: civil authority will only rest upon changeable party-passions; civil virtues will degenerate into hypocritical egotism. But if in the family God is not acknowledged, if His fear does not check the impetuosity of vicious cravings, the most sacred bonds of family life will soon be broken. A nation of agnostics soon would suffer from so many evils that, to quote the saying of the Roman historian, Sallust, "neither the evils nor their remedies would be bearable." If such a nation did continue to exist for awhile, if agnostic philosophers succeeded in stemming the deluge of universal disorder by the moral principles of utilitarians and altruists, the reason could only be this, that human nature is too good to suffer a universal application of the moral principles which strict logic would recommend as the consistent outcome of the agnostic theory. To sum up, Agnosticism is a hypothesis which in its logical consequences leads to the destruction of the most fundamental principles of reason, and to the moral and social ruin of mankind. Therefore it must be out of harmony with human reason, it must be altogether untrue and unreasonable.

No doubt it will be objected to this reasoning, that agnostics are numerous now-a-days, and are found to be as respectable as Christians in their

moral conduct. If by agnostics are meant select individuals of that body, mainly persons in comfortable
circumstances, no imputation on their moral conduct
is intended. Their probity is quite recognized, and
is consistent with our argument: although it must
be admitted that agnosticism has yet to show that
it can scale the moral heights on which Christian
heroism is so much at home. The question is as to
logical consequences: and these must be sought, not
in individuals, but in masses. Moreover, a suffi-
ciency of time must be allowed for the tendencies to
work out their natural results. If agnosticism and
Christianity are compared in their effects on the
masses of men, already the baneful tendency of the
former is disclosing itself in a growing corruption
of morals wherever it prevails.

This, we may infer, is only the beginning.
Centuries of recognition of the Christian sanctions
of the moral law have bequeathed a strong hereditary bias in favour of morality which will hold out
for awhile against the adverse forces. But this bias
must abate, if the world continues to drift away from
the only sound form of theism, which is Christianity.
Mr. Spencer, we know, anticipates a blissful age
when the feeling of moral constraint, of the "ought,"
will die of atrophy, because the path of right and the
path of pleasure will, under the influence of more
suitable education, have been made to coincide.
We can only say that the present outlook, if we go
by observation, not by questionable *a priori* inferences, offers no anticipations of any such eventual
coincidence.

CHAPTER III.

ON THE FUNDAMENTAL ATTRIBUTES OF THE PER-
SONAL GOD AND HIS FUNDAMENTAL RELATION TO
THINGS DISTINCT FROM HIM.

Introductory Remarks.

56. THERE exists a personal God, that is to say,
a self-existing, intelligent Being, upon whom the
material world and mankind depend. This statement is the outcome of the proofs given in the
preceding chapter. Against it and the evidences for
it several difficulties have been advanced, which it is
our duty to weigh and to solve. However, to do
this with greater clearness, it will be useful first to
treat of the most fundamental attributes of the
personal God, His unity, simplicity, and infinity;
and then to state the fundamental relation, in which
all things distinct from God stand to Him; in other
words, to show that there is no being besides God,
which does not owe its origin to creation out of
nothing by God's power.

SECTION I.—*The Unity of God*

Thesis VII.—*There can be but One personal God.*

57. When we say that God is One, we mean
that the Divine Nature exists undivided, and con-

sequently is not something belonging to several
Beings. From what Christian Revelation teaches
about the incomprehensible mystery of the Blessed
Trinity, the Christian student is acquainted with
the dogma that God is One and Three; that there
are three Persons, the Father, the Son, and the
Holy Ghost, each of whom is the same One God.
Therefore if we say the Father is God, the Son is
God, the Holy Ghost is God, we do not wish to be
understood as predicating the Divine Nature of the
Divine Persons in exactly the same sense in which
we predicate the human nature, when we attribute
it to three human persons, Peter and Paul and
Andrew. By the affirmation that one human nature
is common to three human persons, we do not
mean that really *one and the same* existing human
nature belongs equally to the three, for, as St.
Thomas expresses it, in three individuals of the
human nature there are three humanities;[1] that is
to say, three human persons are not rightly spoken
of as having one human nature, but as being perfectly *similar* to one another, in regard of those
attributes, which, being contained in our general
idea of human nature, are predicable of each of
them. But quite another meaning is to be given to
the statement that One Divine Nature is common
to the Father, Son, and Holy Ghost. It means
that the three Divine Persons are One real Divine
Existence, One undivided Divine Essence. In the
language of St. Thomas we may thus express the

---

[1] St. Thomas, *Sum. Theol.* i. 39. 3. " In tribus suppositis humanæ
aturæ sunt tres humanitates."

difference between the meanings of the terms "one" and "common" in the two phrases mentioned: "The unity and community of the human nature is not an objective reality but a subjective conception of objective reality, . . . but the actuality signified by the name 'God,' that is to say, the Divine Essence, is in its objective reality both one and common."[2]

58. The mystery of the Blessed Trinity and its relation to the Unity of God is in our thesis neither affirmed nor denied. Its truth transcends human reason, and is to be believed on the authority of that personal God whose unity and infinity we can prove, and whose infinite perfection guarantees His veracity. The Divine character of the doctrine of the Blessed Trinity is to be vindicated by Dogmatic Theology, whose task it is also to show that there is no manifest contradiction between the two state-

---

[2] St. Thomas, i. 39. 4. ad 3m. "Unitas autem sive communitas humanæ naturæ non est secundum rem, sed solum secundum considerationem. . . . Sed forma significata per hoc nomen, Deus, scilicet essentia divina est una et communis secundum rem." Neither St. Thomas nor we ourselves must be understood to mean that there is no objective foundation for the *oneness* of our conception of human nature. There is indeed an objective foundation for it; but it does not consist in the *real identity*, but in the *real similarity* of human nature as considered in many human subjects. It is this which St. Thomas teaches (*Sum. Theol.* i. 13. 9), saying: "Natura humana communis est multis secundum rem et rationem." He implies thereby that the meaning of the abstract term "human nature" is really verified in each of many human individuals. Yet as each individual verification of that term differs from any other individual verification *considered as individual*, there is no objective identity, but only objective similarity. For further information on this subject, cf. Clarke's *Logic*, pp. 140—162.

ments, *God is One in Essence, God is Three in Persons.*
We have to prove only the former of these statements.

59. We may commence by appealing to the unity
of the universe as testifying to the unity of its
author. It is true that a two-fold objection may be
taken to the validity of such an appeal. It may be
urged that in addition to the universe in which we
are placed, there may possibly be other universes, one
or more, in the remotest regions of space, so far off
as to enter into no relations whatever with any even
the most distant of the constellations which belong
to our cosmos. Whatever unity we discern in our
own cosmical environment, however it may point
to a single Creator of itself, is quite consistent, it
may be urged, with the co-existence of other self-
existing creators for other universes of the kind
suggested. This is the first objection. Another is
that unity of result need not imply more than unity
of action in the cause. Thus the unity even of our
own universe might be satisfied by the hypothesis of
several self-existing Gods acting in friendly combination.

It must be conceded that in view of these
objections an appeal to the unity of our universe as
evidence of the oneness of God falls short of absolute
validity. In other words, it can only establish a
presumption, predisposing our minds to the acceptance of the metaphysical arguments presently to be
propounded. The presumption, however, is entitled
to be regarded as exceedingly strong. The two
possibilities mentioned as depriving it of full cer-

tainty are not of a very solid character. Only captiousness could accept them as in themselves probable solutions of the problem of cosmical unity. On this point we may hear Mr. John Stuart Mill, a man not too given to assent to the conclusions of Natural Theology. He says:[3]

"The specific effect of science is to show by accumulating evidence, that every event in nature is connected by laws with some fact or facts which preceded it, or in other words, depends for its existence on some antecedent; but yet not so strictly on one as not to be liable to frustration or modification from others: for these distinct chains of causation are so entangled with one another, the action of each cause is so interfered with by other causes, though each acts according to its own fixed law, that every effect is truly the result rather of the aggregate of all causes in existence than of any one only, and nothing takes place in the world of our experience without spreading a perceptible influence of some sort through a greater or less portion of Nature, and making perhaps every portion of it slightly different from what it would have been, if that event had not taken place. Now, when once the double conviction has found entry into the mind —that every event depends on antecedents; and at the same time that to bring it about many antecedents must concur, perhaps all the antecedents in Nature, insomuch that a slight difference in any

[3] Mill, *Three Essays on Religion*, pp. 132, seq. We give Mill's words in full, without committing ourselves to every statement he makes on the subject.

one of them might have prevented the phenomenon, or materially altered its character—the conviction follows that no one event, certainly no one kind of events, can be absolutely pre-ordained or governed by any Being but one who holds in his hand the reins of all Nature and not of some department only.   At least if a plurality be supposed, it is necessary to assume so complete a concert of action and unity of will among them that the difference is for most purposes immaterial between such a theory and that of the absolute unity of the Godhead. . . . The reason, then, why monotheism may be accepted as the representative of theism in the abstract, is not so much because it is the theism of all the more improved portions of the human race, as because it is the only theism which can claim for itself any footing on scientific ground."   We agree fully with Mill's last statement, and would refer the reader to Ch. Pesch,[4] who argues that the result of the best modern archæological researches is to show that monotheism and not polytheism was the primitive form of religious belief.

60. Let us now pass on to the metaphysical argument, for which we must claim certainty, although it has to be acknowledged that it is some-what subtle and requires careful reflection for the perception of its full force.   But this, after all, is only what must be expected when we have to deal with so sublime a subject.

With St. Thomas we may introduce the argument

---

[4] Cf. Ch. Pesch, *Der Gottesbegriff*, i. and ii.   Freiburg : Herder, 1885 and 1888.

thus: If the reality expressed by the concept of *Socrates* did not comprise more notes than the reality expressed by the concept of *man*, the extension of both concepts would be the same: in other words, there would be only one *man*, as there is only one *Socrates*. Now the reality corresponding to the concept of *this God* does not contain more notes than the reality corresponding to the concept of *God* or of Divine Nature: because God has not a nature produced by another being, but is His nature, being a cause without cause.[5]

In other words, when there are diverse beings sharing the same common nature, as there are distinct men sharing the common nature of man, there must be a principle of diversity as well as a principle of unity. The diversity cannot be without its *raison d'être* any more than the unity. In the case of God there is not this double principle.

It will help to the understanding of this argument, which we acknowledge to be very abstract, if we put it also in another way. If there are several self-existing beings, the reason of the distinction between them must either be self-existence *as such*, or something *necessarily* connected with self-existence *as such*, or something *accidentally* connected with it. Manifestly, however, self-existence *as such* cannot be the ground of the distinction in question. Nor can the distinction

---

[5] Cf. St. Thomas, *Sum. Theol.* i. 11. 3. "Si ergo Socrates per id esset homo per quod est hic homo, sicut non possunt esse plures Socrates, ita non possent esse plures homines. Hoc autem convenit Deo: nam ipse Deus est sua natura. . . . Secundum igitur idem est Deus et hic Deus. Impossibile est igitur esse plures Deos."

proceed from anything *necessarily* connected with self-existence *as such;* for that must be wherever self-existence is.   Nor can anything accidentally connected with self-existence be said to constitute a reason for the said distinction; because a self-existent being is necessarily unchangeable, change implying possibility of successive states of existence, and such possibility is incompatible with self-existence, which must be as constant as the essence with which it is identical.

Section 2.—*The Simplicity of God.*

Thesis VIII.—*God's Being is physically and metaphysically simple.*

61. What is one is undivided in so far as it is one; what is simple, is not only undivided but indivisible.   Oneness does not exclude composition, although it excludes division; with simplicity all composition is incompatible.   Every man is *one* natural being, but he is not one *simple* being, because he consists of two substantial principles, body and soul, united with one another.   Man therefore is composed of substantial parts; in him there is substantial composition.   If we consider the immaterial soul of man alone, we have a being not composed of substantial parts, and therefore rightly called a simple substance.   Nevertheless, even the soul is not exempt from all composition. It is liable to accidental composition.   For it is changeable in regard to its thoughts and volitions, so that we can distinguish these and it as com-

ponent parts of a whole. Both these kinds of composition are found in existing things, and we call them *real* or *physical* composition. In God neither of them exists, consequently He is physically simple in the strictest sense.

The proof of the physical simplicity of God rests upon His self-existence. Whatever is substantially compounded, depends in its essential constitution upon the union of parts, each of which differs from the compound substance. But since the self-existent owes nothing to what is different from itself, its essential constitution cannot depend upon the union of parts different from itself. Therefore God, being self-existent, cannot be *substantially* compounded. Nor is *accidental* composition conceivable in the Divine Being. How could it be? An accident is a perfection or modification added to the nature of a substance. But to the nature of the Divine Substance no perfection or modification can be added. Any addition made could not be the addition of anything self-existent, because what falls under the conception of self-existence belongs to the Divine Nature itself. Nor, again, could it be the addition of anything not self-existent: because what is not self-existent cannot be found in the Divine Nature.

The same follows from the infinity of God which, as we shall see, is a corollary of God's self-existence and unity. This infinity supposed, we argue thus: What is infinitely perfect can receive no addition. But every accident is an addition to the substance in which it inheres. Therefore a being infinitely perfect, as God's Being really is, can receive no accident.

62. Moreover God is not only *physically* simple, but also *metaphysically*. As *physical* simplicity excludes *physical* composition, so *metaphysical* simplicity excludes *metaphysical* composition. The difference between *physical* (real) and *metaphysical* (virtual) composition may be thus expressed : *Physical* composition means union of diverse *realities* completing one another to constitute one really existing being, as for instance, man is a physical compound of body and soul; *metaphysical* composition means union of diverse *concepts* referring to the same real being in such a way that none of them by itself signifies either explicitly or even implicitly the whole reality signified by their combination; man, for instance, is a metaphysical compound of *animal* and *rational*. This *metaphysical* composition belongs to all creatures, even to such as are *physically* simple. The reason for this assertion is obvious enough. That which is signified by the definition of a created thing, its essence as we call it, depends for its existence, not upon itself, but upon its creating cause. Without the influx of the creating power of God the creature is nothing but an objective idea of the Divine Mind, something known only as capable of existing under the condition that God wills its existence. In other words, the essence of every creature is in itself a mere possibility; not a real, but a conditional existence. In conceiving its essence, or the contents of its definition, we thereby neither express nor imply its

existence. Consequently the objective concept of the real existence of a creature is metaphysically compounded of the two concepts of its essence and existence.[6] That this first kind of metaphysical composition cannot be predicated of God is evident; for its only foundation is the contingency of created being; therefore it must be alien to the Divine Nature, which exists with absolute necessity.

63. Another sort of metaphysical composition in creatures is that contained in the objective concept of their specific nature. The species *man* or *rational animal* includes what is meant by the two concepts *animal* and *rational*. As the former is equally applicable to irrational beasts and to men, it evidently neither expresses nor implies the meaning of the concept *rational*. Therefore we say that human nature is metaphysically composed of the genus *animal* and the specific difference *rational*. Now this sort of metaphysical composition is incompatible with the Divine Nature; because God cannot be included in any genus of beings. Beings can be classed as one genus, only so far as under some one aspect their essences are *perfectly* similar, occupying in this respect a perfectly equal position in the scale of beings. But God cannot be perfectly similar to any order of beings diverse from Himself under any aspect whatsoever; because all other beings are dependent upon Him; they are, as it

---

[6] St. Thomas and the scholastics expressed this briefly by saying that in no created thing are essence and existence the same; and that every created thing is composed of essence and existence, or of potentiality and actuality (*potentia* and *actus*).

were, an outflow of His unchangeable simple self-existence. His justice cannot be perfectly similar to any sort of created justice, nor His mercy to any mercy belonging to any of His creatures. Borrowing a beautiful, although necessarily inadequate illustration from the Angelic Doctor,[7] we may say: As the sun by his light and heat is the unapproachable principle of millions of forms of life and growth, so God by His wisdom and power is the unapproachable principle of all kinds of beings, surpassing in His simplicity the manifold perfections of all and each of them by an infinite distance. It is this which Mr. Herbert Spencer has in view when he rightly maintains that those who admit a first self-existing unconditional Being must admit that this Being cannot be classified. "Between the creating and the created," he says,[8] "there must be a distinction transcending any of the distinctions existing between different divisions of the created. . . . The infinite cannot be grouped along with something that is finite; since, in being so grouped, it must be regarded as not-infinite. It is impossible to put the absolute in the same category with anything relative, so long as the absolute is defined as that of which no necessary relation can be predicated. . . . There cannot be more than one First Cause. . . . The unconditioned therefore as classable neither with any form of the conditioned nor with any other unconditioned cannot be classed at all." So far so good. But when the same author goes on to say of the unconditioned First Cause: "To

[7] *Sum. Theol.* i. q. 4. a. 2. ad 1m.   [8] *First Principles*, p. 81.

admit that it cannot be known as of such or such kind, is to admit that it is unknowable," he certainly is wrong. It is true, from the impossibility of classifying God with any creatures, it follows that no creature can know Him *adequately* as He is knowable and known by Himself; that no creature can *comprehend* Him. But our inability to comprehend God does not imply that we cannot predicate of God whatever real perfection there is in creatures. Later on we shall give reasons to show that we have a real and true knowledge of God, however utterly inadequate it may be.

64. For the present we may add that not only the metaphysical composition mentioned above, but any conceivable sort of metaphysical compositions are all inapplicable to God. The general reason for this may be stated thus: Concepts which in their application to objective reality are absolutely inseparable, so that none of them can have a real foundation different from the real foundation of the rest, cannot be metaphysically compounded. For though none *expresses* what is *expressed* by the others, yet each of them *implies* all the rest. But the concepts which we form of the Divine attributes are in their application to objective reality absolutely inseparable. Each of the Divine attributes in its objective reality coincides with the one self-existing Divine substance, which we have proved to be a simple unchangeable essence. Consequently none of the Divine attributes has any objective foundation except in so far as it is one with the rest; which is evidently the same as to say that the Divine

H

attributes are absolutely inseparable in their application to objective reality. Divine justice, for
instance, without Divine mercy is impossible; and
so is Divine power without Divine wisdom. Therefore these attributes are not metaphysically *compounded*, although they must be said to be metaphysically or virtually *distinct;* the concept of justice
does not *express* what is *expressed* by the concept of
mercy, although it *implies* the same.[9]

SECTION 3.—*The Infinity of God.*

Thesis IX.—*God is infinitely perfect.*

65. *Infinite*, according to the etymological meaning of the word, is that which has no limits. Now
a thing may be said to have no limits, either because
we are not able to assign its limits, or because it
is really unlimited. We speak, for instance, of an

---

[9] *Real distinction* does not necessarily mean *real composition*, nor
does *virtual distinction* necessarily mean *virtual composition.* For
things to be compounded they must first be distinct ; but, given the
existence of distinct things, it is not necessary that they should be
compounded together into a unity. Catholic Theology recognizes
a real distinction between the three Divine Persons, because They
are, as "substantial" relations within the One Godhead, opposed
to one another; but it is not constrained in consequence to admit
that the Godhead is really compounded of Them, because it teaches
that each Person is not really distinct from, but really identical
with, the Essence of the Divinity. Again, Catholic Theology
recognizes a virtual distinction between the Divine Essence and
each Divine Person, but it does not teach us that the Divine
Essence is virtually compounded of the three Persons, because the
concept of each Divine Person does not prescind from, but involves
the concept of the Divine Essence. These observations show us
that the mystery of the Blessed Trinity is opposed neither to the
physical nor to the metaphysical simplicity of God.

infinite number, of infinite space. These expressions do not imply that number and space do or can exist without limit. That is repugnant to reason. For what is number in reality but a collection of units, all of which are equally conceivable by one general concept? But no collection of such units can be so great that the addition of another unit would be inconceivable; on the contrary, however much it may be increased, it must remain a limited number. If it ever became really unlimited or infinite, the taking away of one unit would make it finite; and its infinitude would be made up of a finite number and a finite unit, which is evidently absurd.[10]

66. Nor can space be actually unlimited, because its real foundation consists in the dimensions between the extreme surfaces of *one* body, or of *many* bodies taken together, or of *all* bodies forming the one universe, as we call it. Now such dimensions cannot become so large as not to allow of a larger one. If space ever were actually infinite, a certain part of it, say a cubic inch, would be contained in the whole a really infinite number of times, the impossibility of which is clear from what we have said about infinite number.[11]

67. A so-called infinite number, therefore, can only be a number so great that every number assignable by us is next to nothing in comparison with it. In the same way, infinite space can exist only so far as there can exist a space so great that any corporeal magnitude assigned by us is next to nothing when compared with its dimensions.

---

[10] Cf. St. Thomas, *Sum. Theol.* i. 7. 4.   [11] *Ibid.* 7. 3.

These remarks about infinite number and space will serve to illustrate the meaning of the word "infinite" when applied to God. We do not intend thereby to suggest the idea of a being containing infinite extended parts, or compounded of any sort of infinite entities. Such notions not only suppose the possibility of infinite extension and number, but are also opposed to the simplicity of God, as already proved.

68. Infinity, then, when predicated of God, means that He is unlimited in His perfection, that is to say, that every perfection conceivable belongs to Him. The proof of this statement is based on the truth that God alone is self-existent, and everything else contingent. This truth supposed, we may argue thus: All perfections conceivable fall either under the heading *self-existent* or under the heading *contingent*, in other words, they are either uncaused or capable of being caused. The former class God possesses *formally*, that is, He possesses them as they are in themselves according to their own proper nature. The other class, since He, as the only First Cause, is able to produce them, He must have *equivalently* and *eminently:* that is, in some manner superior to the manner in which they exist outside Him, and at the same time enabling Him to realize them in their own proper nature.

Thus God is infinite in all perfections. For it is no limitation to His perfection that He does not contain contingent perfections *formally*. To contain hem *eminently* is more than to contain them merely *formally.* It is, in fact, to contain them in an infinite instead of a finite manner.

69. This truth of the infinite perfection of God must be our guide in deciding whether any given attribute can be predicated of God or not. There is a truth underlying the error of the agnostic, namely, the fact that our knowledge of God, although evidently true as far as it goes, must necessarily be *inadequate.* From this, however, it by no means follows that no name expressing a created perfection can be given to the Most High. On the contrary, we say that *all nouns and verbs applied to creatures, so far as their objective meaning expresses pure perfection without connoting imperfection, must be true of God before they can be true of creatures.* Indeed perfection, as such, signifies something actual ; and everything actual, so far as it can be conceived without the limitations and privations which accompany its existence in created beings, must be eminently in the Infinite Being.

70. The preceding observations enable us to lay down the following three canons for the predicates to be given to God in common with creatures in general and with man in particular.

I. *Although no predicate given to creatures, and expressing a perfection, attributes this perfection to them without limit; yet the meanings of some predicates, taken by themselves, do not connote imperfection, whereas the meanings of others always connote it. The former must be applied to God in the proper sense of the words, the latter not.* Thus we may say of God that He is infinitely *mighty*, infinitely *wise*, has infinite *know-*

ledge, is infinitely *just*, infinitely *benevolent*, and so on.
But we cannot say that He is infinitely *extended* like
a body, that He *reasons* with infinite perfection, that
He possesses infinite *courage*, &c.   To illustrate the
difference by an example, let us take the two
adjectives *wise* and *courageous*. I may say and must
say of God that He is *wise* in the proper sense of
the word.   And why so?   Because the word *wise*
denotes the perfection of knowing the causes of
things, and this perfection can be conceived without
the addition of any imperfection.   But it is quite
otherwise with the word *courageous*.   This connotes
the condition of having to face danger, whereas
a being which can be threatened with danger
necessarily must be limited in its perfection ;
only things weak and not wholly self-sufficient
can be brought into danger.   And thus the infinitely perfect God cannot be properly said to be
courageous.

71. II. *Although certain predicates are in the most
proper sense applicable to God and to creatures; yet they
are true of God in an infinitely higher sense than of
creatures.* In God they are found without limit and
independently, in creatures they are found under
limitation, and with entire dependence upon the
power of God.   Consequently, the relation of these
predicates to God and to creatures is not equal,
but most unequal, although their meaning is
realized in both : and, in consequence, when we
ascribe them to God, our intention is to ascribe
them to Him with the understanding, implied or
expressed, that there is this inequality of relation

between the mode in which the reality signified exists in Him and in creatures. This may be illustrated by our parallel procedure when in propositions worded in exactly the same terms, we ascribe beauty of countenance to a portrait and to its living original. In each case we say, " What a beautiful face," and by employing in each case exactly the same language, we signify that the same reality finds a truthful concrete expression alike in the original and in the portrait; but we are quite aware of the great difference between the mode in which beauty of countenance is realized and predicable in the two cases. If we do not call attention to the difference by the wording of our proposition, this is partly because when a reality is predicated of a subject in a simple proposition, the predication asserts only the fact of the subject possessing the reality, not the mode in which it is possessed, partly because the difference of mode is sufficiently clear to the persons addressed without formal statement, or at all events can be left to stand over till another time, as one cannot be always explaining. As it is always an advantage to have technical terms to fix distinctions like this, predication is said to be *univocal* when the reality predicated is not only found in all the subjects of predication, but found in each of them in the same manner, and *analogical* when it is found in them, and thereby founds an analogy between them, but is not in them all in the same manner.

To apply this doctrine to the case of God, we say that attributes like " being," " goodness,"

"power," "wisdom," &c., are predicable of God
as well as of creatures, meaning thereby that the
meaning of these terms has a true realization in
Him, although we are quite aware, and on fitting
occasions explicitly declare, that the manner in which
they are realized in Him differs widely from the way
in which they are realized in His creatures: that
His Being, Goodness, Power, Wisdom, &c., are
necessary, uncaused and self-existent, and without
limit; whereas the being, goodness, power, wisdom,
&c., of creatures is contingent, caused, and finite.
We say, therefore, that these terms are predicable
of God and creatures, not *univocally*, but *analogically*. [12]

From this second canon there follows the very
important corollary:

*The application of the same predicates to God and to
creatures does not imply co-ordination or classification of
God with creatures.*

Wherever two things are co-ordinated or classified together there must be not only *likeness*, but,
under *one* aspect at least, *perfect likeness*. Now
creatures, though imitations of the Divine Essence
in all their perfections, are under *no* aspect *perfectly*
like that Essence. What we mean, when we speak
of created perfections, *is in God really;* but the way
in which it is in Him, differs *under all aspects* from

[12] "Quantum igitur ad id quod significant hujusmodi nomina,
proprie competunt Deo et magis proprie quam ipsis creaturis, et
per prius dicuntur de eo. Quantum vero ad modum significandi
non dicuntur proprie de Deo." (*Sum. Theol.* i. 13. 3. c. Cf. *ibid.*
ad 2dum.: "Id quod significatur per nomen non convenit eo modo
ei (Deo quo nomen significat sed excellentiori modo. '

the way in which it is in creatures, not only *in degree* but *in kind.*

Thus, for instance, wisdom, or the knowledge of the nature of things and their causes, is truly in God, and can to a certain extent be truly in man. But in God it is identical with the simple and infinite Divine substance; consequently God *is* His wisdom, and His wisdom is an eternal all-comprehensive act of knowledge, including (as identical with it) an infinitely perfect Will, which never can act against the practical corollaries of theoretical wisdom. In man, on the contrary, wisdom exists as an acquired accidental quality, now as actual knowledge, now as an habitual disposition to actual knowledge ; and so far as it is actual knowledge in the mind, it is composed of many successive mental acts, all of which are more or less inadequate expressions of their objects. In a word, a wise man *is* not his wisdom, but *has* wisdom, and has it only in a *very small degree.*

72. III. *Predicates, the meaning of which expresses perfection with connotation of imperfection, though they cannot be true of God in their proper sense, may be true of Him when used metaphorically.*

As man belongs to the order of sensible things, he is fond of clothing his thoughts in impressive imagery drawn from the objects of sense. A hero is a *lion ;* a discoverer a *luminary* of science ; and so forth. This use of metaphors, provided it be in taste and moderation, is a great aid to human language, even in speaking of God Himself. Instead of *naming* a perfection of His directly, we may *suggest* it indirectly by expressing something which bears a resemblance to it *at least under one or other aspect.* Thus we may attribute *eyes* to God to signify His knowledge, *ears* to express His acceptance of our prayers. We may speak of Him as *angry* with sinners, when we would point to effects of His justice.

73. This subject of the application of terms of human thought to the Deity is treated by St. Thomas,[13] whose doctrine is the doctrine of all Catholic philosophers. It could therefore only be want of familiarity with their teaching which led Mr. Herbert Spencer not to except them from the charge of anthropomorphism which he launches against even the most civilized believers in a knowable Deity. These are his words:[14] "From the time when the rudest savages imagined the causes of all things to be creatures of flesh and blood like themselves, down to our own time, the degree of assumed likeness has been diminishing. But though a bodily form and substance similar to that of man, has long since ceased among cultivated races to be a literally-conceived attribute of the Ultimate Cause; though the grosser human desires have been also rejected as unfit elements of the conception; though there is some hesitation in ascribing even the higher human feelings, save in greatly idealized shapes; yet it is still thought not only proper, but imperative, to

[13] St. Thomas, *Sum. Theol.* i. q. 13. Especially, art. 3. art. 5. and art. 6. are to be noted.

[14] *First Principles,* pp. 109, 110.

ascribe the most abstract qualities of our nature. To think of the Creative Power as in all respects anthropomorphous, is now considered impious by men who yet hold themselves bound to think of the Creative Power as in some .respects anthropomor- phous, and who do not see that the one proceeding is but an evanescent form of the other."

Certainly it would be great irreverence to enter- tain an anthropomorphous conception of God, so as to attribute to Him human perfections, *as such*, in the limited and imperfect way that those perfections exist in ourselves. But no instructed theist will do so. It is true that we attribute to God what Mr. Spencer seems to call *the most abstract qualities of our nature,* understanding, free-will, wisdom, bene- volence, love of justice, &c. Yet at the same time we explain that only the abstract meaning of these perfections is objectively real in God, not the dependence and limitation which attend the realiza- tion of that meaning in man. Instead of co- ordinating God with man in any of these attri- butes, we prove that all of them in Him are identical with His self-existing nature in a way infinitely perfect, and therefore infinitely exceeding our experience and our comprehension. But the fact that we are unable to *comprehend* God's infinity is no proof that we can *know nothing definite* about Him. On the contrary, as we have shown, His very infinitude compels us to predicate of Him whatever created perfection is, by way of abstraction and exclusion of limits, conceivable without in- cluding objective defect or imperfection. Moreover, after having predicated all this, as far as we can, we must confess that all the predicates by which we have tried to describe the infinite Majesty of the Most High, *though they express what is truly proper to His Being,* nevertheless fall *infinitely* short of an *adequate* representation of that Being.

The final practical conclusion, therefore, to which we are led by reasoning from creatures to their First Cause, is not that of the agnostic who says, " We ought to be silent about the attributes of God," but that of the Psalmist: "Great is the Lord and exceedingly to be praised ;"[15] "Magnify the Lord with me, and let us extol His name together."[16]

[15] Psalm xlvii. 1.   [16] Psalm xxxiii. 4.

CHAPTER IV.

Introductory Remarks.

74. OUR inquiries about the First Cause of things have led us to the conclusion that there exists one self-existent, simple, infinitely perfect Being, the personal God of monotheism. We now have to show that this personal God is the First Cause of all that is not God, by creation of it all out of nothing. We will first explain what is meant by creation out of nothing, and then show that the world owes its origin to a Divine act of creation.

SECTION I.—*Definition of Creation.*

75. *Creation, in the wider sense of the word*, signifies a change produced in things already existing, or in the relations between them. Thus we say, that men of genius *create* works of art; that the Pope *creates* Cardinals, that a speech *creates* a sensation. It is evident that in the production of every such change something is originated which did not exist before; for if nothing at all resulted but what there

was already, there would be no change. On this
ground we might be tempted to say that every
production is creation out of nothing. However,
this is true only in a limited sense, inasmuch as
the *result of the change* was previously nothing and
has now become something. It is not true that
there was no substratum or subject pre-existing
which underwent the change. More strictly speaking, the change of a thing is not produced *out of
nothing*, but out of *something changeable*.

76. *Creation in the strict sense* may be defined as
follows with St. Thomas: "Creation is a production
of a thing according to its whole substance, nothing
being presupposed, whether created or increate."[1]

In explanation of this definition we may remark:

(*a*) Creation is *production*. Consequently, what
is created is not without cause, but is the effect of
an existing cause.

(*b*) Creation is *the production of a thing according
to its whole substance*. In other words, by creation is
originated the whole of *a thing existing in itself.*
The phrase, "according to its whole substance,"
distinguishes creation from accidental and substantial changes. An accidental change takes place
when a thing is modified and yet remains specifically the same thing. Thus a child is accidentally
changed by growing bigger, by receiving sense-
impressions, by moving about, by developing his
intellectual faculties, &c. A *substantial* change

---

[1] St. Thomas, *Sum. Theol.* i. 65. 3. c.: "Creatio autem est productio alicujus rei secundum suam totam substantiam, nullo præ-
supposito, quod sit vel increatum vel ab aliquo creatum."

supposes a substance to be specifically changed.
As simple immaterial substances cannot change
their kinds, only corporeal substances are capable
of substantial changes. We have a substantial
change in an individual body, when it manifests
forces differing not only in degree but in kind from
those which it had before. Thus it is probable that
every chemical composition involves a substantial
change of the elements combined, and it is certain
that the change of inanimate matter into a living
plant or animal is a substantial one.

(c) The terms of our definition explained under
(a) and (b), constitute its essence; the rest is added
by St. Thomas in order to illustrate the meaning of
creation out of nothing more fully by opposing it to
certain false theories.

a. By adding that to the production called
creation nothing *uncreated* is presupposed, St. Thomas
opposes the pantheistic error, according to which
the world is an emanation from the Divine Substance.[2] By the same addition, creation out of
nothing is contrasted with the Platonic notion of
an uncreated matter, an error which pervaded also
the philosophy of the Ionians.[3]

β. By adding that creation is a production where
nothing *created* is presupposed, it is explicitly marked
as something altogether different from the change of
existing things.[4]

[2] Cf. St. Thomas, *Sum. Theol.* i. q. 90. art. 1.
[3] Cf. St. Thomas, *Sum. Theol.* i. q. 44. art. 2; *De Potentia*, q. 3.
art. 5.
[4] Cf. *Contra Gent.* ii. 17; *De Potentia*, q. 3. art. 2.

77. Another scholastic definition of *creation taken in the strict sense of the word* is the following, not easily expressed in English : *Creatio est productio rei ex nihilo sui et subjecti*. We may perhaps paraphrase it thus: "Creation is the production of a thing from a previous non-existence as regards itself, and also as regards any being on which the creative act was exercised." After the explanation we have given of St. Thomas' definition, this other will be sufficiently understood, if attention be paid to these two points:

(*a*) That is said to be produced *ex nihilo sui*, which is *really* produced. Every effect therefore is a *productio ex nihilo sui*, even if it consists only in the accidental or substantial change of a pre-existing thing.

(*b*) That is said to be produced *ex nihilo sui et subjecti* which is not merely the result of a change, but a whole new being, a whole substance, which exists by the power of an efficient cause, and of which nothing existed before. We have now to prove that the world originated through creation in the sense explained, and we commence by excluding the alternative suppositions.

Section 2.—*Pantheism.*

78. Thesis X.—*The world and its component elements are not affections of the Divine Substance and inherent in it, but are altogether distinct from it. Pantheism, therefore, is repugnant to reason.*

This assertion is directed against the pantheists or monists, who maintain that the assemblage of things which we call the *world* is really the one Divine Absolute Being under various aspects; these aspects they are pleased to call sometimes *moments*, sometimes *determinations*, sometimes *modes*. We are not here concerned with the semi-pantheistic theories of emanation, according to which creatures are particles separated from the Divine Substance.[5] Our proposition is directed against Pantheism in its perfect form. We shall consider it only in its most general outlines, as it manifests itself in some fundamental theorems common to the well-known pantheistic systems of Spinoza,[6] Fichte,[7] Schelling,[8] and Hegel.[9]

These authors, though starting from very different principles, agree with one another in these two assertions:

I. Properly speaking, there exists only one Being. This one Being is called *Substance* by Spinoza, *the Pure Ego* by Fichte, *the Absolute* by Schelling,[10] *the Logical Concept* by Hegel.

II. The one Being evolves itself by a necessity of fate into forms of being, diverse from and opposed to one another, inasmuch as they are so many several determinations under which the First Being manifests itself; and yet at the same time all one and the same, inasmuch as it is the same First

---

[5] Concerning these theories, see § 84 below.

[6] *Ethica*, Pars I. Prop. vi.

[7] *Grundlinien der gesammten Wissenschaftslehre* (Leipzig, 1794), pp. 10, seq.

[8] *Philosophie der Natur* (1803), p. 67.

[9] *Encyclopädie*, Band. i. §§ 9, 21.

[10] Schelling considerably modified his system in his later works.

I

Being that manifests itself under all these diverse determinations.

79. Against these assertions we say:

(*a*) The attributes of the First Being, demonstrated by us in the preceding theses, compared with our external and internal experience, forbid us to admit that the same being is really common to God and to the things of this world.

We have seen that the First Being, called God, is one undivided essence, in no way composed of parts, and that He unites all perfections in the identity of His unchangeable existence. On the other hand, external and internal experience bear witness to the fact that the world round about us, and human beings themselves, form not really one undivided substance, but many separate individuals, each complete in its own being, differing from and not seldom opposed one to another in natural or voluntary tendencies. Is it not ridiculous to say that a cat is the same real being with the mouse which she devours, and with the dog that worries her, and that cat and dog alike are the same being with the master who with his whip restores peace between them? Is it not absurd to maintain that the criminal to be hanged is really the same being with the Judge who pronounces sentence of death against him, and with the executioner who carries out this sentence? And who can accept the statement that the atheist is substantially the same Being with God, whose existence he denies and whose name he blasphemes?

Moreover, experience tells us that there is

nothing in the material world known to man which is not either composed of parts, or a part itself; and that, consequently, nothing is complete and perfect in its simplicity. How then can this world be really one Being with God, of whom we have proved that He is in the highest degree simple?

Finally, reason based on experience teaches us that the purely corporeal world lacks altogether the faculties of understanding and free-will, and that these faculties, even in the most gifted of the human race, are in a state of imperfection and perfectibility. It is therefore absolutely impossible that either the corporeal or the spiritual world known to men should be one with God, who, as we have proved, is infinitely perfect, and therefore under all aspects without defect, and incapable of evolving new perfections or new modes of perfection in His own Being.

80. (*b*) The evolution of the Deity, as stated by pantheists, is not only opposed to God's attributes, it also involves a contradiction. There is nothing by which it could be caused but the internal activity of the First Cause. Now an activity, by which the First Cause should produce in itself what it does not already possess, is inconceivable. Such production would result in effects contained in their total cause neither *formally* nor *eminently :* that is to say, neither in the same way in which they exist when produced, nor in a higher way more than equivalent to the existence of them all. The total cause of the determinations of being into which the pantheistic Deity evolves itself, is supposed to

be this Deity itself, without the determinations to be evolved. For these cannot be in that Deity *formally*, before their evolution takes place, otherwise there would be no evolution. Nor can they be said to exist in it *eminently*, before they are *formally* actuated; because on this supposition the First Being, so far from tending by its evolution to unfold its own essence, as pantheists would have it, would tend rather to corrupt that essence and to make a monster of it.[11]

Consequently, on the pantheistic hypothesis, the First Cause is less perfect before it determines itself than it becomes by such determination: and yet this lower perfection suffices to effect the determination and raise it to a more perfect state. In other words, it is in itself the total cause of successive advancements in perfection, without previously possessing those superadded perfections either formally or eminently. Thus the pantheistic God continually violates the inviolable principle of causality. Either the principle of causality must go or pantheism.

81. (c) Finally, what becomes of morality in the pantheistic hypothesis? Is there still room for a distinction between actions really good and really bad? If pantheism be true, all actions are good. The coward and the hero, the miser and the philanthropist, the tyrant and the martyr, all are deserving

---

[11] Indeed, Hegel says: "What kind of an Absolute Being is that which does not contain in itself all that is actual, even evil included?" (*Geschichte der Philosophie*, Werke XV. p. 275; cf. Mansel *Limits of Religious Thought*, p. 46.)

of praise; for they all do what the supreme law, which rules the evolution of the Absolute, inexorably demands: their actions are nothing but a manifestation of the pantheistic God *as He necessarily must be according to a law of fate inherent in His nature.*[12]

SECTION 3.—*The Contingency of the World.*

Thesis XI.—*Neither the matter of the universe, nor the human soul, nor anything else except the one simple infinitely perfect God, can be self-existent. Therefore all things except God are contingent.*

82. The first two parts of this proposition are contained in the proposition just established. If nothing in the world known to us is inherent in the Divine substance, then neither matter nor human souls can be inherent in that substance. But outside the Divine substance there can be no self-existent substance, because self-existence is, as we have seen (Th. VII.—IX.), restricted necessarily to one simple infinitely perfect substance. Therefore the matter of the universe and human souls can have only conditioned existence, and are contingent substances.

The same argument proves that nothing outside of God can be self-existent. For if you assume

[12] Spinoza does not seem to shrink from a barefaced acceptance of this necessary inference from his pantheistic system. Thus, for instance, he expresses himself in his *Ethics*, Part IV. Prop. 59, at the end of the proof: "No action considered in itself is either good or bad." And Part IV. Prop. 45, Schol. 2, he bases upon the moral principle just mentioned this practical maxim: "To enjoy ourselves in so far as this may be done short of satiety or disgust—for here excess were no enjoyment—is true wisdom."

anything else but God to be self-existent, for instance, if you assume with the Manichæans a supreme principle of evil, you thereby destroy the unity, simplicity, and infinite goodness of self-existence clearly demanded by reason.

We need only remark that by "things" we mean realities in some way complete in themselves, endowed with an internal principle of action; such realities, for instance, as men and every living being that leads its own distinct life. All other realities diverse from the Divine substance are either parts of contingent things or accidental determinations of the same. In this way the human body is a *part* of the human substance, and the hands and feet of a man are *parts* of his body, whereas his sensations, thoughts, and volitions are accidental determinations. Since matter is contingent, and since only material substances can consist of parts, it is evident that all parts of substances are contingent. That accidental determinations of whatever contingent substances must be contingent, is implied by the very term "accidental," and follows, moreover, from their natural dependence upon contingent substances.

SECTION 4.—*The Dependence of all things on God.*

Thesis XII.—*All things in this world owe their origin either immediately or mediately to an act of Divine power.*

83. According to the preceding proposition, all things in this world are contingent. Consequently

there is none among them which exists by its own nature. They all demand a cause for their existence. For the present we will not inquire whether this cause could not itself be a contingent substance, say a spirit other than God and distinct from all things comprehended under the term "this world." Whatever power of production may be communicable to a contingent being, that power must be derived from the same source whence is derived the contingent being itself, namely, from the self-existent First Cause. Consequently, before any further inquiry, we are right in ascribing the origin of all things in this world to the power of that Cause.

SECTION 5.—*Proof of an Immediate Influence of God.*

Thesis XIII.—*At least our substance distinct from God, has been immediately produced by God Himself.*

84. From Thesis XI. it is evident that everything else save God is contingent. In other words, nothing exists with absolute necessity but God alone; everything which is not God exists only so far as He by His power originates its existence. But God cannot have originated the existence of things purely possible in themselves, unless *at least one* of all possible substances that ever came into existence has been *immediately* produced by Him.

SECTION 6.—*Proof of Creation.*

Thesis XIV.—*God's immediate action in the production of contingent being was not a production out of His own substance; nor can it be, strictly speaking, called change of possible being into actual being, but it is creation of actual being out of nothing.*

85. The first part of this thesis is directed against the semi-pantheistic emanation theories now obsolete. According to these, creatures are as it were particles emitted from the Divine substance. The absurdity of this opinion is evident; for God, being simple, as we have proved (Th. VIII.), is absolutely unchangeable. Therefore it is impossible that He should produce new substances out of His own by causing particles to emanate from it.

The second part of the proposition is necessary in order to warn the reader against a misconception easily arising from the way in which we imagine possible things. Of course we cannot imagine them except by forming pictures of existing things in our imagination. We fall into no error by forming to ourselves such pictures, as long as we recognize them to be mere pictures of things which by their own nature are nowhere until God causes them to exist. We must not, however, forget this, and attribute to purely possible things some sort of real existence distinct from God. If we look at pure possibility in the light of the truth already demonstrated, that all being except God alone owes its reality to the Divine action, we see that the interval traversed between possibility and actuality is a purely imaginary interval, and that consequently no real change takes place when a possible thing becomes actual. In every real change the thing which changes passes from one state of existence to another. The purely possible thing does not exist at all: it has no state of existence. Therefore it cannot really pass from one state of existence to another; its actuation cannot be called *change* in the proper sense of the word.

We shall have other occasions later on for showing that the existence of other substances distinct from the one Divine Substance and created by it implies no limitation of the Infinity of the Divine Substance. It is enough for the present to observe that the infinity of an infinite being is not limited by the existence of other finite beings derived from it and dependent upon it, provided these do not contain, as they cannot contain, any perfection which is not in the Infinite Substance equivalently and "eminently," with absolute unity and simplicity.

SECTION 7.—*Possibility and limitation of the world accounted for by the Divine Infinity.*

Thesis XV.—*From the infinite perfection of God it can be safely inferred that* (1) *creation is possible,* (2) *that the successive or simultaneous creation of all possible substances is not possible,* (3) *that the creation of an infinite substance is impossible. Consequently the actually existing world is not absolutely the best possible world, although it is certainly the relatively best possible world.*

86. (1) We have already explained the meaning of creation out of nothing, and have, moreover, proved the fact of creation. But the way in which creation

.

has taken place we never can fully understand; we have nothing analogous in nature by which to illustrate it; for all actions within our experience are changes of existing things. However, though we cannot comprehend creation, we are able to give some explanations which will serve to make belief in creation easier. We have then to bear in mind that God is infinitely perfect (Th. IX.); and that His Essence possesses the perfections of all possible creatures in a higher and better way; and is therefore, as theologians say, "eminently" equivalent to an indefinite number of possible substances. It follows that seeing His Essence as it is, by His infinite Intellect, He knows by this act of cognition at the same instant all possible things. Since also His Will is infinitely powerful, He can by a mere act of will give existence to whatever possible substance He knows.

The same truth may be expressed also in the following way. An infinitely powerful Will can by its sole act originate whatever is not intrinsically repugnant. But no possible substance is intrinsically repugnant; otherwise the concept of it would mean nothing. Therefore, every possible substance can be originated by the sole act of an infinitely powerful Will. Now, as God is infinite, His Will is infinitely powerful. Consequently, by an act of His Will alone, He can call into existence any possible substance, that is, He can create it out of nothing.[13]

---

[13] It is highly gratifying to find that two of the foremost champions of modern thought have nothing to object against the possibility of creation. Mill says: " There is nothing to disprove

(2) Although God by His infinite power can create *any* substance conçeivable, yet He cannot

the creation and government of nature by a sovereign will." (*Three Essays on Religion*, p. 137.)

Professor Huxley is more explicit, and as his statement *on this subject* agrees marvellously with the doctrine of St. Thomas and Catholic philosophers in general, we will give it in full: "Some say that the Hebrew word *bara* which is translated 'created,' means 'made out of nothing.' I venture to object to that rendering, not on the ground of scholarship, but of common sense. Omnipotence itself can surely no more make something out of nothing than it can make a triangular circle. What is intended by 'made out of nothing,' appears to be 'caused to come into existence,' with the implication that nothing of the same kind previously existed. It is further usually assumed that 'the heaven and the earth' means the material substance of the universe. Hence the 'Mosaic writer' is taken to imply that where nothing of a material nature previously existed, this substance appeared. That is perfectly conceivable, and therefore no one can deny that it may have happened. . . . It appears to me that the scientific investigator is wholly incompetent to say anything at all about the first origin of the material universe. The whole power of his organon vanishes when he has to step beyond the chain of natural causes and effects. No form of nebular hypothesis that I know of is necessarily connected with any view of the origination of the nebular substance." (*Nineteenth Century*, Feb. 1886, pp. 201, 202.)

To sum up the Professor's view on creation. He asserts : 1. To conceive creation as the *change* of nothing into something is tantamount to conceiving an absurdity. 2. There is no objection to creation, if you conceive it as the starting into existence of the whole of the material universe by competent power. 3. Natural science has even in our nineteenth century nothing to say against the possibility of creation. The first two of these assertions agree perfectly with the doctrine St. Thomas expounds, *Sum. Theol.* i. 44. 2. and 45. 1. The third assertion has the approval of all sound metaphysicians. However, the objection to the translation of *bara* is not very strong, because the term "to make out of nothing" is according to common parlance equivalent to "to make something in such a way that it exists without having been made out of anything." The reader may compare the phrase in question with phrases like these : "I see nothing," "He knows nothing," &c.

create *all* intrinsically possible finite substances so that they all should exist at the same time; nor can He exhaust the category of possibilities by successive creations.

The *successive* creation of all conceivable finite substances would mean that God's power of creating had at length become, or was destined at length to become, exhausted. This is clearly incompatible with His infinity. A like inference proves also the impossibility of *simultaneous* creation of the entire category of possible substances. When that creative act was complete, God would be in the position of being unable to go on creating. There is also a further impossibility involved in simultaneous creation of all the possible substances; for it would involve the existence of an infinite number. (Cf. § 66.)

(3) The creation of an infinite substance is no less inconceivable. To be infinite and to be created are contradictory notions. The first involves the most supreme and entire independence, the other is the most intimate and absolute mode of dependence.

87. It follows that this world cannot be *absolutely* the best, if by "absolutely the best" we mean "so perfect that nothing could be more perfect." Whatever God may create is finite, and therefore infinitely distant from God Himself, the one absolutely perfect Being. But it may be asked: Why cannot this world be absolutely the best possible world in this sense, that no creatures can be more perfect than those which exist in it? To understand the impossibility of such optimism we must go back once

more to God's infinite wisdom and power. Having infinite knowledge, He cannot devise a creature, so perfect an imitation of His immense perfection, but that possible imitations innumerable and indefinitely more perfect should remain within the scope and view of His Essence. Having infinite power, He never can create a being so perfect that the production of a better one would transcend His power. Among all created beings, therefore, there is to be found none which is absolutely the best possible.

88. Nevertheless, creation as a whole is *relatively* the best. For that is relatively best, which is best for the end for which it is meant, so far as it is meant for it. Now as God's wisdom is infinite, He cannot be unaware of whatever means are best suited to the end, which He wills His creatures to aim at in so far as He wills it. Moreover, being infinitely good, He cannot act but in perfect harmony with infinite wisdom. Therefore His creatures must reach their end in the most perfect way so far as He intends it. We add *so far as He intends it* in view of the necessary distinction between what God wills *absolutely* and what He wills only *conditionally*. A creature endowed with freedom of will may not reach its end in that way in which God intends it *conditionally*, namely, on the hypothesis of its co-operation with the benevolent intention of its Creator. But it is evident that every creature must reach that end which has been put before it *absolutely*, and to that extent must perfectly conform to the standard fixed by God's infinite wisdom.

89. This doctrine, according to which the world is not absolutely but only relatively the best, may be called *Moderate Optimism.* It is upheld by St. Thomas[14] and his followers. It is opposed to the *Exaggerated Optimism* of Leibnitz,[15] of Malebranche,[16] and of Rosmini.[17] According to Leibnitz this world is the absolutely best possible; because if it were not, there would have been no sufficient reason for God to prefer it to the rest. Malebranche believed it to be the very best conceivable; because God would not have acted in the most perfect way, as it behoves His infinite perfection to act, if He had produced a world less perfect than it might have been. Rosmini thought that no world except the existing one would have been worthy of God; because in this alone there is with the least means the greatest good effected, and thus it alone is worthy of God's goodness. We shall answer the reasons of these authors later.

Having now explained how far creation is possible to God Himself, we shall pass on to the question whether God alone can create, or whether a creature may possibly be endowed by Him with the power of creating. The solution of this question will enable us to state whether God is the immediate Creator of all things existing.

[14] Cf. *Sum. Theol.* i. 25. 6.
[15] Cf. Opp. Leibnitz (Edit. Erdmann), p. 506.
[16] Cf. Malebranche, *Traité de la Nature et de la Grâce,* 2, 51.
[17] Cf. Rosmini, *Teodicea,* n. 651.

SECTION 8.—*Proof that God alone can create.*

Thesis XVI.—*Creation out of nothing involves the exercise of infinite power. Consequently God alone can create out of nothing.*

90. It is evident that there must be a certain harmony between the natural perfection of efficient causes and the perfection of their activity. In proportion as the natural perfection of their substantial being is greater, must their competence as efficient causes increase; for action is a manifestation of being, and consequent upon it. Therefore, a being whose nature infinitely transcends the nature of other beings must be able to produce effects in a way infinitely transcending that in which other things produce their effects. Now between the infinite perfection of God and the perfection of any creature whatever, there is an infinite distance. God therefore must be able to produce effects in an infinitely more perfect way than creatures.

Hereupon we argue thus : If we find in the series of effects one which is out of proportion with all the rest, so that in it an efficiency is manifested with which the efficiency manifested in others cannot be compared—that effect is the work of the infinitely powerful God alone. But a substance created out of nothing is such an effect. All other effects are mere changes of substances already created. All other effects are conditioned not only by the influence of their efficient cause, but also by the nature of the subject in which they are produced. This

subject was originally a work of creation, wholly
dependent upon its creating cause alone.   In
other words, every effect which is not creation
is dependent upon creation for its support, whereas creation is not dependent upon any other
effect.   Under this aspect creation appears as
the *primary action*—to use the words of the great
Aquinas—and we must therefore conclude that it is
feasible to the *primary agent* alone.[18]   Creation is
the *primary efficient action*, inasmuch as some creation
precedes every other efficiency; as also because no
other efficiency can be compared with it in excellence.   Therefore that Being alone, with whose
infinite excellence no other being can be compared,
is able to create substances out of nothing.

91. St. Thomas suggests to us another argument.[19]   The greater the disproportion between the
state before the exercise of efficient causality and the
state after it, the greater must be the perfection of
the causality exercised.   More skill is required to make
a statue out of a piece of marble than a tomb-
stone, to make a cathedral out of building materials
than a factory.   To make the letters of the alphabet
subservient to the prosaic expression of daily occur-
rences is an achievement incomparably easier than

[18] *Contra Gent.* ii. 21.   "Cum enim secundum ordinem agentium
sit ordo activorum, eo quod nobilioris agentis nobilior est actio,
oportet quod prima actio sit primi agentis propria.   Creatio autem
est prima actio, eo quod nullam aliam præsupponit et omnes aliæ
præsupponunt eam.   Est igitur creatio propria Dei solius actio, qui
est agens primum."

[19] St. Thomas, *Sum. Theol.* 1a. q. 45. art. 5. ad 2. et 3.

to weave them into the tissue of a tragedy like *Hamlet.*

This being so, if between the state before the exercise of causality and the state after it there is ever an infinite disproportion, then the causality exercised must be infinitely perfect, and therefore can belong to God alone. Now this is precisely the case in creation. The individual substance created out of nothing is void of all actual existence before the Creator calls it into being. It is nothing by its own nature ; whatever it is, has been produced by the power of the Creator. Now between nothing and any kind of existence there is an infinite dispro-portion. The power, therefore, which creates things out of nothing must be infinite ; it must be the power of God alone.

92. But here it may be objected : True, the preceding arguments seem to prove that no creature can have a power adequately proportionate to the creation of another creature. This, however, does not show that a creature cannot co-operate with God as His instrument in creation. How will you show that God cannot create one creature by the instrumentality of another ?

To solve this objection, we must distinguish between *instrument* in the proper sense, and *instru-ment* in the wider sense. An instrument, strictly speaking, is only that which produces the very effect in reference to which it is said to be instrumental, under the guidance of a higher cause. In this sense, the brush of the painter is his instrument in the pro-duction of a picture, and the sewing-machine is the

J

instrument of the tailor in the making of a coat. They make the picture and the coat respectively, although under guidance from the human hand. Moreover, it is the part of an instrument to concur in the action of the principal agent by some action proper to itself which disposes something already existing to the effect of the principal agent. Thus the saw cuts, which is an action proper to itself and exerted on some already existing material, and therefore concurs to the production of, say, a circular plate, which is the effect after which the principal agent is striving. Hence only those effects can be wrought with the help of instruments which consist in the gradual change of some subject-matter, disposing it to a purpose. But creation, as we have seen, does not consist *in the change of a subject already existing;* it is rather the *effecting of a subject* by the power of will. Therefore instrumentality, properly speaking, cannot come into play, when creation out of nothing is to take place.[20] However, if we use the word *instrument* in a wider sense, to signify a cause which produces an effect, intended by God to be the condition under which He Himself will create a new substance that stands in a certain relation to the effect produced : we may then say that a creature can be the instrumental cause of a new creature. Thus parents may be said to be the instrumental causes of the souls of their children, although these souls are created by God alone, as we shall see in the following section.[21]

---

[20] Cf. *Sum. Theol.* i. 45. 5. c. § " Sed hoc esse non potest."
[21] Cf. *Sum. Theol.* i. 118, 2. ad 3m.

SECTION 9.—*Proof that God is the immediate Author of Mind and Matter.*

Thesis XVII.—*Every individual human soul, and every element of matter considered in its original state, is an immediate effect of Divine creation.*

93. As we have proved above (§§ 30—39), the human soul is an immaterial substance, a spirit, although a spirit united to matter. Upon this we argue as follows: If the human soul cannot be evolved out of matter, nor be taken from the substance of a spirit, it owes its existence immediately to creation. But it is evident that a material being cannot be changed into an immaterial being; and it is absolutely impossible that a spirit should be divided. (§ 34.) We must then conclude that every human soul comes into existence by creation out of nothing, and as God alone can create things of nothing (Th. XVI.), every human soul is immediately created by God Himself.[22]

94. As regards the origin of matter, in whatever state it may have been originally, it is certain that its existence is due to an exercise of Divine Power, for it is not self-existent, but contingent. (§§ 81, 82.) The question still to be answered in regard to its origin is this: Was matter produced by Almighty God immediately or mediately? Now it must have been immediately created, because mediate production of matter is impossible. For on two suppositions only could it be possible; first, that God could change a spirit into matter, or secondly,

[22] Cf. *Sum. Theol.* i. 90. 2. et i. 181. 1—3.

that He could communicate to a spirit the power of creating matter. But on the face of them, neither of these suppositions can be held : it is incompatible with the simplicity and characteristic being of a spiritual substance that a spirit should be transformed into matter, and it has been proved already, that the power of. creation belongs exclusively to God. (Th. XVI. §§ 90, seq.) We see, then, that the origin of matter is due to immediate Divine creation. In what state it was created, whether in the state of elementary matter, or of substances compounded of elementary matter, our *reason* cannot tell. We must be satisfied with knowing that at least every part of matter considered in the most simple form in which it can exist—in other words, every element—has been created by God immediately.[23]

Scholion. The doctrine of creation in its relation to the theory of evolution.

95. From the proof given above it follows that all creatures of the universe are under a certain aspect the immediate handiwork of God. They are all made up of material elements immediately created by Him. It is true, these elements are not now in that state in which they were when they came forth from the abyss of their nothingness. Under the influence of destructive and generative forces put into matter by the Creator, its elementary parts

---

[23] *Sum. Theol.* i. 44. 2. et i. 65. 3. et *Compendium Theologicæ*, c. 95. "Elementa secundum se tota non sunt ex aliqua materia præjacenti, quia illud quod præexisteret haberet aliquam formam . . . oportet igitur etiam ipsa elementa immediate esse producta a Deo.'

circulate through immeasurable space, and form the substratum now of this, now of that, species of inanimate or animate matter. But however great may be the changes which matter thus undergoes, its amount is neither diminished nor increased, its original potentiality for the reception of various principles of force (or *forms*, as scholastics call them), remains always the same. A part of matter determined to a certain mode of being and action by an internal principle of force constitutes a body, or an individual corporeal substance. Under the influence of created forces, the state of matter in an individual body can be so disturbed that the principle of force by which it is determined can no longer continue to maintain its existence. Thus the body loses its existence as this or that individual substance, but it never drops out of existence altogether. The extinction of one principle of force is accompanied by the production of another, the natural result of a new combination of matter. Each body, then, considered in its basis, is God's work ; whereas the principles of force, or the *forms*, through which bodies now existing receive their specific character, are due to the destructive and generative activity of created agents, with the single exception of that principle from which the human body receives its specific determination, namely, the rational soul, the source not only of the intellectual, but also of the sensitive and vegetative, life of man.

96. How far observation has justified, or will justify the theory of evolution, we leave it to biologists to decide. From a mere philosophical point

of view we are unable to discover anything in
it which would be out of harmony with reason,
if only the following principles are kept strictly in
view :

(1) There is no evolution but of matter created
by God, through principles of force set to work by
Him originally, and working throughout all ages of
their operation according to laws determined by His
infinite wisdom.

(2) A lower principle of force is never by itself
alone the *total* cause of the production of a higher
one. Consequently the more perfect offspring of an
imperfect species of living beings is not due only to
the generative force of that species, but other causes
must help to produce it.

(3) A human person is never the effect of evolution.

The generative power of a created agent can pre-
dispose matter for the reception of a human soul:[24]
but the soul being spiritual, God alone can create it,
and join it to matter, from which union there results
a man.

These three principles, which are simple corollaries of the theses proved above, contain the most
fundamental truths about Divine creation as the
cause of this world.

We shall now proceed to answer some questions
connected with creation, the solution of which will

---

[24] St. Thomas, *Sum. Theol.* ia. q. 118. art. 2. ad 4. " Homo generat
sibi simile, in quantum per virtutem seminis ejus disponitur materia
ad susceptionem talis formæ," *i.e.* of the " rational soul." (Cf. *ibid.*
art. 3. et q. 76, art. 1.)

throw still more light upon the total dependence of all things upon God.   These questions are :

1. Is creation the result of a necessary, or of a free volition of God ?

2. Could God have created without creating from eternity ?

3. If eternal creation be not necessary, is it at least possible ?

4. Can a world like ours exist from eternity ?

What we have to say upon these questions will form the subject-matter of the five following propositions :

SECTION 10.—*Creation a free act of God's will.*

Thesis XVIII.—*God has freely chosen to produce creatures.*

97. Victor Cousin [25] says : *Dieu s'il est cause peut créer; et s'il est cause absolue, il ne peut pas ne pas créer*—" If God is a cause, He can create, and if He is an absolute cause, He must create."

According to this philosopher, the act of creation is under different aspects both free and necessary. It is free, not because God could determine whether He would exercise His creative power or not, but only because there is not any external force constraining Him to the exercise of that power.   The necessity of creation, on the other hand, is to be sought in the nature of God Himself; it is this nature which irresistibly impels Him both to desire and to produce creatures.   " The creative act is a necessary act, because it results from the

[25] *Introd. à l'Histoire de la Phil.* Leçon 5.

nature of a cause, which must needs act ; and it is free, for it proceeds from the proper, independent, primitive spontaneity of a cause which acts by itself, which determines itself, so that its determination, though necessary, is nevertheless entirely its own, and is not under any influence from without."[26]

Against these assertions we maintain that God has created only because He freely willed the existence of creatures, being equally free not to will it had He pleased ; as again to will the existence of creatures other than those actually created had that been His choice.   This is the only legitimate inference from the infinitude of the Divine perfection.   Had God been compelled by necessity to create, He must have been so compelled, because His infinitely perfect intellect represented to His infinitely perfect will that creation was a necessity required to supply some deficiency otherwise discernible in His Being.   But creation could not have this effect.   To infinite perfection nothing further in the way of perfection can be added, and again, to view the same truth in a different light, created perfection is derived perfection.   It is derived from that of God in which it is precontained *eminently*.[27]

[26] " L'acte créateur est un acte nécessaire, puisqu'il resulte de la nature d'une cause, qui ne peut pas ne pas agir ; et il est libre, parcequ'il émane de la spontanéité propre, indopendante, primitive, d'une cause, qui agit d'elle même, qui se détermine elle même, sans que sa détermination nécessaire, mais toute sienne, subisse aucune influence du dehors." (T. E. Allaux, *La Philosophie de M. Cousin*, pp. 19, 20.)

[27] This technical term has been explained already. See pp. 100, 101.

What is here meant will be more easily realized by the reader if he considers the relation of the supreme to the subordinate authorities in the body social. Under the absolute monarch many lower officials are constituted, each endowed with a measure of power and authority derived from his. Now their authority cannot be *added* to his so as to form a total authority of larger dimensions than his is by itself. Whatever they have they hold under him, and he possesses it in a higher and more independent manner. Substitute God for the absolute monarch, creatures for the subordinate powers, perfection for authority, and then we have set before us exactly the relation of the Divine perfection to that imparted by creation to creatures. And we see clearly that creation *adds* nothing to the Divine excellence which it did not already possess. There can, then, be no motive presentable to the perfect will of God necessitating creation. On the other hand, although creation is seen to be an act which does not increase the Divine perfection, it is also seen to be an act good in itself, and therefore, though not necessary, still worthy of election should God so please. For creatures, as being imitations of the Divine perfection, are worthy of existence and consequently of love.[28] Their existence need not be, but it may be if it please God to choose it.

[28] Cf. St. Thomas, *Sum. Theol.* i. 20. 2. c. et ad 2dm et 4tm.

SECTION 11.—*Creation not necessarily Eternal.*

Thesis XIX.—*The decree to create is necessarily eternal, but its effect, or the resulting existence of creatures, is not necessarily eternal.*

98. The way in which an eternal and yet free decree can exist in God is incomprehensible to our limited intellects; nevertheless we can understand the reason why the free decree to create must be eternal. A free choice cannot be reasonably delayed without a sufficient motive. But in God there was no sufficient motive to delay the decree to create. The reason for which free beings reasonably suspend their choice is either the fact that for the present they are not in need of an action, which later may be useful to them, or the consciousness that choosing at once may cause them unforeseen inconveniences. But God could not suspend His decree for either of these reasons.

He is by His very essence independent of creatures; they never can be useful to Him, nor augment His infinite perfection. Moreover, whatever motives there may be to create or not to create, these motives are *always* and *fully* perceived by His infinite intellect. In the same instant in which He sees them, He sees also the result of whatever line of action He may choose. It is, therefore, inconceivable that He ever should have existed without the decree to create.

99. As to the second part of our thesis, we do not state therein that God cannot create anything

from eternity; we say only that it cannot be proved that anything has been created from eternity. Our proof of this statement is as follows: The reason for which God is said to have necessarily created from eternity must lie either in the nature of His essence, or of His free decree, or in the nature of creatures, or in some combination of these motives one with another.

In God's own essence there cannot possibly be a reason why He must create from eternity if He chooses to create at all, since His essence is quite sufficient for His infinite love of good without the addition of any creatures—*a fortiori*, without the addition of them from eternity. Nor can it be admitted that the existence of creatures must have the same eternity as the Divine decrees by which it is determined. As the power of Divine volition is the only efficient cause of their existence, they must exist with all the determinations and assignments with which God from eternity wills them to exist. Suppose a sovereign to make a decree ordaining that certain authorities shall come into being at certain fixed times, one a week hence, another a year hence, &c., then they would come into being according to their assignments, and not at the date of the decree. Consequently it cannot be inferred from the eternal decree of creation that the existence of creatures is from eternity, unless it be proved that God in His eternal decree has resolved to grant to creatures an existence coeternal with His decree. But this cannot be proved.

Is there, then, anything in the nature of creatures

to require that their existence, if realized at all, should be eternal? None can be given. All creatures are of themselves nothing; their existence or non-existence makes not the least alteration in God's infinitely perfect Being. It depends, therefore, upon the free choice of God to fix the limits of their duration as He pleases.

Nor does the necessity of eternal creation arise out of the relation of the Divine essence to the creative *fiat* or to the nature of creatures or to both.

In the relation of this decree to the Divine essence we find a reason for the eternal existence of the decree itself, but not of the creatures decreed; in the relation of the nature of creatures to the Divine essence we have a reason for affirming that God must love creatures if they exist, but no reason for the necessity of their eternal existence. If, however, we turn to the relation existing between the creative *fiat* and the nature of creatures, we may be tempted to think that here there is really a reason for the necessity of eternal creation. We might seem justified in arguing thus: The total cause of every creature is the free decree of God, which free decree has existed from eternity. But the total cause of an effect cannot exist without the simultaneous existence of the effect. Every creature, therefore, which really is a creature in the strict sense of the word—that is to say, every being immediately produced out of nothing, must have existed from eternity. However, it is not at all evident that in every case without distinction the total cause of an effect cannot exist without the simultaneous existence of the effect. It is true that a cause as such bears a necessary relation to an effect. It is also true that a cause from which an effect proceeds, according to a natural law to which the cause is subjected, cannot be in the state sufficient for the production of the effect without producing it at once. But, given an infinite will able by the mere expression of its purpose to call things out of nothing into existence, it is not at all evident that it cannot remain unchangeable, and yet freely determine when the effects shall begin, of which its own infinite power is the only efficient cause. Certainly no one can discover an intrinsic contradiction in this proposition : Although the free decree to create, which is the only efficient cause of the existence of creatures, has existed from all eternity, nevertheless the creatures decreed from eternity have had a beginning, because a beginning has been fixed from eternity by this free decree.

SECTION 12.—*On the possibility of Eternal Creation.*

Thesis XX.—*It is not evident that no creature whatsoever can exist from eternity.*

100. The great doctors of the middle ages agreed that eternal creation was not a necessity; they differed from one another on the less important point whether eternal creation is or is not intrinsically impossible.

St. Thomas Aquinas considered the controversy hopeless, at least in its most general form, not descending to the particular inquiry whether this or that given creature—man, for instance—could possibly have existed from eternity.[29]   We say only that the impossibility of a creature which had no beginning cannot be demonstrated.   In order to prove this statement, it will be enough to show that the arguments against the possibility of eternal creation are by no means decisive.   The most forcible are the following four, to each of which we will reply—

101. *First Argument.*   Every efficient cause must exist before its effect.   But if eternal creation is admitted, God, the efficient cause of the being created from eternity, does not exist before His effect.   It is, therefore, against reason to admit eternal creation.

Answer.   It is not to be denied that an efficient cause which produces its effect *gradually* must exist before its effect exists; whence it follows that the existence of all effects produced by corporeal substances is posterior to that of their causes.   It is also to be granted that an efficient cause, which is not by its very existence always ready for the production of an effect, must exist before its effect.   But it is in no way evident that cause and effect cannot be simultaneous, when the cause by its mere existence is ever ready to act.   Now creation is an instantaneous effect, and God by His unchangeable and infinitely powerful Will is always able to

---

[29] St. Thomas, *Sum. Theol.* 1a. q. 46. art. 2.   To understand St. Thomas properly, the reader must *ponder* what he here says in answer to the eighth objection.

produce every effect conceivable. The conclusion, then, of this first argument cannot be granted as evident.

102. *Second Argument.* Creation is production out of nothing. But a creature which exists from eternity has been always something. Consequently such a creature cannot be said to have been produced out of nothing ; in other words, it cannot really be a creature.

Answer. The meaning of the phrase, " Creation is production out of nothing," is this: the created being is nothing in itself, but owes its whole existence to the will of its Creator, who has not produced it by the change of any substratum, but has called it into existence by a free act of His omnipotent Will. From this it does not follow that the created being cannot have been called into existence from eternity. If a creature has existed always, it has always been something through the exercise of creative power, but it has never been something in virtue of its own essence.

103. *Third Argument.* Every finite being must be under all aspects infinitely distant from the perfection of God, the one infinite Being. But on the hypothesis of an eternal creation this is not true, because a creature produced from eternity is equal at least in duration to God.

Answer. We grant the major, but deny the minor of this argument. By the very fact that the duration of a creature is contingent and continually dependent upon God's free-will, it is infinitely less

perfect than the duration of God, who continues
in existence with absolute necessity by virtue of His
own essence.

104. *Fourth Argument.* Succession from eternity
is impossible. But succession belongs to the nature
of every creature. Every creature which exists in
the moment A can cease to exist in the following
moment B. This could not hold if the duration of
the creature in the moment B were not really
different from its duration in the moment A. But
really different durations following one another
constitute a succession of durations.

Answer. We grant that succession from eternity
is impossible. We do not deny that succession
belongs to the nature of every actually existing
creature; but we say that it is not evident that it
must belong to the nature of every *possible* creature.
Though great scholastic philosophers, St. Bona-
venture,[30] the Conimbricenses,[31] and others, held
that even in the duration of a created spiritual
substance there is succession, by reason of the
contingency of all created being; still that position
is open to doubt. The full reason why a spirit
existing now can presently cease to be is not
any tendency to nothingness inherent in the spirit
itself, but it is the absolute dependence of the
creature upon the power of God, who preserves
it in being, and who by withdrawing His preserving
influence could, if He pleased, let it fall back into
nothingness. We have, therefore, no clear evidence

[30] In l. 2. dist. d. 2. a. 1. q. 3.
[31] In l. 4. *Phys.* c. 14 p. 2. Cf. Pesch, *Phil. Nat.* n. 502.

that in the substance of a spiritual creature there is succession.

But it may be asked, Is there not necessarily succession in its operations? Or is any created spirit possible which can operate without change in itself? If that is an impossibility, every created spirit must necessarily have a beginning, for a spirit cannot be wholly without operation. This reason goes a long way to show that the creation of a spirit from eternity, and *a fortiori* the creation of matter from eternity, is absolutely impossible, because an existence from eternity can hardly be other than a changeless existence ; and we cannot conceive either matter or spirit to have existed from eternity without change. We are not inclined to think that such a created existence is possible ; but neither have we a certain reason for saying that it is intrinsically repugnant. We must, then, conclude by saying that the impossibility of eternal creation is not certainly proved.

SECTION 13.—*The beginning of this World.*

Thesis XXI.—*The universe, considered in its chief processes, had a beginning.*

105. Having stated our opinion about the possibility of eternal creation in the abstract, another question remains to be answered. Can the particular world in which we live have existed from eternity ?

The meaning of this question is not whether the innumerable species of creatures which constitute

K

the world known to man can have been created without a beginning. Even the conclusions of natural science indicate that all living beings which people the earth, if considered not in the germ of their species, but in their specific nature itself, had their origin long after the creation of matter. We intend only to ask: Was it intrinsically possible, and consequently in the power of the Almighty, to decree that the chief processes of nature should go on without ever having had any beginning? This question may be resolved into the following three:

1. Can there have been motion of matter without a beginning of motion?

2. Is evolution of vegetable and animal life possible without a beginning of evolution?

3. Can the generations of mankind have succeeded one another for all ages without there being any first parents or first children?

To each of these questions we answer in the negative.

106. And first as regards motion of matter. Motion is not an instantaneous act, but involves really different successive phases. There is no motion of matter without continuous changes of position of material particles. The concept of motion and the concept of succession are inseparable from one another. But succession cannot have existed from eternity. In it a " sooner " and a " later " are necessarily involved. Every " later " had evidently a beginning, and consequently every " sooner," which is essentially related to a " later "

—in other words, every "sooner" which constitutes a part of succession must have had a
beginning. Bearing now in mind that succession
is involved in motion so as to be necessarily connected with the movements of material particles,
we must pronounce it metaphysically impossible
that motion of matter should have been without
a *first* start or beginning of motion.

This conclusion opens the way to the other,
that evolution of life, the processes of assimilation
and decomposition, of generation and corruption
in animate matter, are inconceivable unless they
have had a beginning. They all imply succession,
and consequently can have had but a limited
duration.

107. Coming now to the human race, it must
have had a beginning not only for the reasons just
given, but also because the number of human souls
that possibly can exist can never be actually infinite.
Such a number is intrinsically impossible, as we
have shown in our chapter on infinity. (§ 66.) But
if mankind had existed from eternity, the number of
human souls that existed at any given moment, if
we suppose that none of these naturally incorruptible
beings is annihilated by the absolute power of God,
would really be actually infinite. Whatever therefore may be our opinion on the absolute possibility
of an eternal creature, there can be no doubt that
a universe like ours, in which there is motion
and organic life, and in which one generation of
men follows another, cannot have existed from

eternity, considered even in its most fundamental features.[32]

We have treated here the question of the duration of our world only from a metaphysical point of view. So far as the existence in the past of the present state of our solar system, of organic life and of man is concerned, the theories of modern astronomers, of geologists and paleontologists support our conclusions.

On the other hand, Aristotle opposes them inasmuch as they rest upon the impossibility of motion without a beginning. The arguments by which he endeavoured to prove that motion must be without a beginning, together with modern arguments in favour of eternal creation, will find their solution in the following chapter.

[32] Our thesis is supported by Cardinal Zigliara, who arrives at the same conclusions in a way somewhat different. His words are: "Existimo autem mundum uti nunc est, non potuisse ab æterno creari. . . . Etenim si creatio ista foret possibilis, consequi videtur quod in successione ab æterno usque ad præsens forent, in facta hypothesi, actu infinitæ successiones vel in tempore, vel in motu, vel in generatione, vel saltem in cogitationibus alicujus mentis creatæ." (*Summa Philosophica*, Vol. II. pp. 38, 39.)

CHAPTER V.

SOME of the difficulties urged against the conclusions at which we have arrived have already been
partially considered. It was indispensable to the
course of our argument not to pass them by un-
noticed. But it is necessary to examine them more
fully in the present chapter.

SECTION 1.—*Arguments urged by Traditionalists in favour of
the opinion, that only by faith can we be certain of God's
existence.*

108. (1) *First Traditionalistic Argument.*—The
existence of God is an article of Christian faith.
But articles of Christian faith must be believed
on the authority of God—they cannot be proved
by natural reason alone. Consequently the existence
of God is indemonstrable.[1]

Answer. The term "article of faith" may be
taken both in a wider and in a more restricted
sense. In a wider sense, every truth revealed by
God is an article of faith, even if it is demonstrable
by reason. In a more restricted sense, only those

[1] St Thomas, *Sum. Theol.* 1a. q. 2. art. 2. obj. 1.

dogmas, which, even after their revelation, cannot be proved by reason alone, are articles of faith. Such dogmas are the Mysteries of the Incarnation, of the Blessed Trinity, and others. Many truths of Natural Theology are articles of faith in the wider sense; they form part of the revelation made by God to His Church; but they are not articles of faith, if this term be taken in its more restricted sense. To this class belongs the great fundamental truth of the existence of a Personal God.

If it be urged that from the solution just given it would follow that God had revealed to us His existence and attributes without any need, we answer with St. Thomas,[2] that the revelation even of those truths concerning God and His perfections which can be discovered by reason alone, is a great benefit to mankind. To say nothing in this place of the supernatural graces attached to it, there are three great wants clearly discernible from which, had not these truths been revealed, the human race as a whole would have suffered.

First, without this revelation few men would have a proper knowledge of their Creator. Some would not arrive at it on account of their natural incapacity to inquire into recondite truths, and others could not undertake a satisfactory search on account of the multitude of their occupations. Moreover, a large number would shirk the patient consideration and reasoning without which a more accurate knowledge of the First Cause of all things cannot be attained.

[2] *Contra. Gent.* i. c. 4.

Secondly, if that revelation were not given, the comparatively few, who could and would speculate about Divine things, would take a long time to reach any large or valuable results on account of the difficulty of the speculation. And thus a considerable part of human life would be spent in arduous study of Him, whom we are not created to study so much as to know and love and obey from the dawn of reason.

Finally, on the same hypothesis there would be far more room for erroneous views about God, than there is now, as we may infer from comparing the theories of philosophers with the truths possessed by any child that knows its catechism.

109. (2) *Second Traditionalistic Argument.*—It is impossible that the contemplation of finite things should lead to any certain knowledge of the Infinite God.

Answer. It is true that we cannot leap from finite to infinite by one argument. But we can by a chain of arguments. We have to commence by proving that there is a First Cause, and that this First Cause can be but One. After that, it is to be shown that no perfection conceivable is wanting in that Cause which we call God. Thus it appears that one Infinite God really exists, although the notion we have of Him can only be partially positive.[3] That is to say, we cannot express the fulness of God's perfection by mere affirmation; but having affirmed it under a certain aspect, we must signify the rest by excluding all limits from what we have

---

[3] St. Thomas, *Sum. Theol.* 1a. q. 2. art. 2. ad 3m.

affirmed, saying for instance, God is wise *without limit*, He is *infinitely* wise, and the rest.

SECTION 2.—*Kant's difficulties against the proofs of God's existence.*

110. Kant, in his celebrated work, *Kritik der reinen Vernunft* (*Critique of Pure Reason*), discusses at length the Ontological Argument, the Argument of the First Cause, and the Argument from Design. He finds fault with each of them, and arrives at the conclusion that speculative reason is unable to come to a satisfactory result in the matter.

Answer. 1. What Kant alleges against the ontological proof, we may pass over, as we ourselves do not admit that proof; although we do not approve of all that Kant says in refuting it.[4]

2. Against the Argument of the First Cause, Kant has two principal difficulties. First, he considers that we are not certain of the universal value of the " Principle of Causality," upon which the proof of the existence of a First, Self existing Cause entirely turns.[5]   The answer to this objection is fully given in our proof. (§§ 25, 26.)   It was there shown that Kant's opinion must lead to the denial of the principle of contradiction itself, and to universal scepticism.   But he is armed with another weapon.   He says that those who use the Argument of the First Cause really fall into the fallacy of the ontological proof, while appearing

---

[4] See discussion of Ontological Argument in c. i.

[5] *Kritik der reinen Vernunft*, p. 637 (Dritte Auflage).   In the t anslation by M. Müller, p. 523.

to avoid it. They first demonstrate *a posteriori* a first cause, a self-existing being; and then from the concept of self-existence they infer the existence of an Infinite Being. This conclusion he deems to be invalid. Were it valid, he says, it would be equally lawful to infer by a converse process the existence of an Infinite Being from its concept—and this is the line of the ontological proof.[6] This objection at first sight seems formidable: but in reality its whole force is due to a want of distinction between unlawful and lawful reasoning *a priori*. It is unlawful to reason *a priori* from a concept, the internal truth of which may reasonably be doubted by those whom you would convince. So long as they may reasonably say, we do not know whether an intrinsic contradiction may not be hidden in that concept, your conclusion must remain suspected of error. But should you argue from the concept of a thing, the existence of which you have already proved, no one can reasonably demur to your conclusions. Now those who defend the Ontological Argument follow the former unlawful line of reasoning; while the latter, the lawful line, has been observed by us in the development of our Argument of the First Cause. Those who use the ontological proof, begin with the assumption that the concept of an infinitely perfect being is not self-contradictory. This they have no right to do, as we showed when discussing their argument. Very different is our mode of reasoning. We first prove *a posteriori* that an intelligent, self-existing Being

[6] *Ibid.* p. 639. Apud M. Müller, *ibid.* p. 525.

certainly exists.   This established, we have a right
to maintain that the concept of self-existence is not
self-contradictory; for what *must* exist, *can* exist.
We are, therefore, entitled to argue from that
concept, and to assert as absolutely true everything
that is evidently connected with the truth of self-
existence, to wit, that a self-existing being is
evidently One, Simple, and infinitely Perfect.

3. The Argument from Design is held in higher
respect by Kant.[7] He objects, however, to its
conclusiveness for two reasons.

(*a*) By itself alone it does not lead us to the
knowledge of a Self-existing, Infinite God and
Creator, but only to the persuasion that there exists
an intelligent Architect of this world. To know
something definite about the nature of this Architect,
we must fall back upon the unsound ontological
proof; for, in trying by means of the Argument of
a First Cause to bring the Argument from Design
to a full issue, we commit ourselves to the ontological proof, inasmuch as we reason *a priori* from
self-existence to Infinity.

To this we answer: it is true that the Argument
from Design does not carry us the whole way. We
completed it on the lines of the Argument of the
First Cause.[8] But we deny that this mode of completing it can be justly condemned as a falling back
upon the ontological proof; and the reasons for
this denial we have just given.

(*b*) Kant again doubts whether the supposition

---

[7] *Ibid.* p. 651.   Apud M. Müller, *ibid.* p. 535.
[8] C. ii. § 46, and throughout the whole of cc. iii. iv.

underlying the Argument from Design is valid, "that well-ordered effects of nature no less than well-ordered effects of human art, can only have been produced by the pre-arrangement of an intelligent mind.[9]

Regarding this difficulty we remark that the analogy between order in works of nature and order in works of art *by itself alone* is not an absolutely solid foundation, although, as Kant himself admits, it is *very persuasive.* Consequently, to anticipate Kant's objection, we went deeper down, and laid another foundation, which is solid enough. (Cf. §§ 42—45.)

SECTION 3.—*Difficulties of Spencer and Mill against the proof of a First Cause.*

111. (1) Mr. Herbert Spencer[10] grants that regarding the origin of the Universe three verbally intelligible propositions may be made : the atheistic, the pantheistic, and the theistic, but he maintains that further consideration shows them all three to be inconceivable. The atheist postulates a self-existing actual universe, the pantheist a self-existing potential universe, the theist a self-existing Creator of the universe ; consequently all the three theories rest upon the assumption of self-existence. Self-existence, however, is inconceivable, and accordingly none of the three theories can be admitted as a conceivable explanation of the world's origin.

---

[9] *Ibid.* p. 654. Apud M. Müller, *Ibid.* p. 537.
[10] *First Principles*, pp. 30—35.

To prove that self-existence is inconceivable, he argues thus:[11] "It is clear that by self-existence we especially mean, an existence independent of any other—not produced by any other; the assertion of self-existence is simply an indirect denial of Creation. In thus excluding the idea of any antecedent cause we necessarily exclude the idea of a beginning—to admit that there was a time when the existence had not commenced, is to admit that its existence was determined by something, or was caused : which is a contradiction. Self-existence, therefore, necessarily means existence without a beginning; and to form a conception of self-existence is to form a conception of existence without a beginning. Now by no mental effort can we do this. . To conceive existence through infinite past time, implies the conception of infinite past time, which is an impossibility."

Answer. It is at least consoling to have in this passage a recognition of the old truth that the human mind is forced to admit something self-existing. Mr. Spencer also in another passage says:[12] "We cannot think at all about the impressions which the external world produces on us without thinking of them as caused; and we cannot carry out an inquiry concerning their causation without inevitably committing ourselves to the hypothesis of a First Cause." In these words he himself gives us a clue wherewith to extricate ourselves from the labyrinth of his arguments about self-existence. He confesses in this latter passage

[11] *First Principles,* p. 31.   [12] *Ibid.* p. 37.

that we cannot do without self-existence; and in the very passage which we have quoted above, and in which he has declared self-existence to be impossible, he has given a tolerably clear explanation of self-existence; how then can he uphold his assertion that self-existence is inconceivable? We cannot explain anything without really conceiving it, unless indeed we try to explain what involves an intrinsic contradiction. Can any intrinsic contradiction be suspected in the notions from which we form the concept of self-existence? Far from giving any reason for such a suspicion, Mr. Spencer adduces the strongest motives possible for not entertaining it. He states that the human mind cannot explain the most obvious daily experiences without falling back upon a First Cause. This granted, we must either admit the existence of a First Cause, or assert that our minds have an essential tendency to obtrude upon us a notion that is wholly visionary.

Mr. Spencer's inability to take in the idea of self-existence seems to arise from the views which he holds—erroneous views, we should call them—on the human intellect, and on time, and also from his failing to make any distinction between comprehending a thing thoroughly and conceiving it at all. Were the acts of the human understanding the effects of organic impressions, and were all thinking consequently reduced to the association of pictures in the imagination, the concept of self-existence in that case would be, as Mr. Spencer says, "literally unthinkable," as would also be all other universal and immaterial concepts. We have argued already for the existence of such concepts in expounding the argument of the First Cause.[13]

Mr. Spencer says that the idea of self-existence involves the concept of infinite time. But why? The concept formed by men of a Being uncaused and wholly independent is in reality a concept of self-existence. This concept does not explicitly express the infinite duration of that Being, and is so far forth inadequate; it is not a *comprehensive* concept; God alone *comprehends* His self-existence and infinite duration. This duration is, however, not infinite time, as Mr. Spencer thinks it should be. In God there is no kind of succession; and where there is no succession, there is no time.

Moreover, actually infinite time is self-contradictory; there can be *finite actual* time, and *indefinite possible* time, but not actually infinite time. God's duration is eternity, the unchangeable continuance of His self-existing Essence without possible beginning or end. Being eternal in Himself, He is the source of all existences capable of change, and consequently the real ultimate foundation of all possible time, which He comprehends by knowing fully His own eternity. We can have a *true* concept of indefinite possible time, but not an *adequate* concept. We conceive indefinite possible time, past or future, when we conceive the possibility of an indefinitely long series of successive changes before or after the present moment.

[13] See also the articles, "An Examination of Mr. Herbert Spencer's Psychology," by Professor Mivart, *Dublin Review*, October 1874 till January 1880.

112. (2) Mill, in his *Essays on Religion*,[14] objects against the Argument of a First Cause thus: "The Argument for a First Cause admits of being, and is presented as a conclusion from the whole of human experience. Everything that we know (it is argued) had a cause, and owed its existence to that cause. How then can it be but that the world, which is but a name for the aggregate of all that we know, has a cause to which it is indebted for its existence?

"The fact of experience, however, when correctly expressed, turns out to be, not that everything which we know derives its existence from a cause, but only every event or change. . . . That which in an object begins to exist is that in it which belongs to the changeable element in nature; the outward form and the properties depending on mechanical or chemical combinations of its component parts. There is in every object another and a permanent element, viz., the specific elementary substance or substances of which it consists and their inherent properties. These are not known to us as beginning to exist: within the range of human knowledge they had no beginning, and consequently no cause; though they themselves are causes or con-causes of everything that takes place. Experience therefore affords no evidences, not even analogies to justify our extending to the apparently immutable a generalization grounded only on our observation of the changeable."

Answer. The proof which Mill here puts before

[14] Pp. 142, 143.

his readers as the common proof for a First Cause,
is certainly not the proof given either by us or by
St. Thomas, or any Catholic author of weight and
reputation.

The observations which Mill makes on the proof,
as he has stated it, deserve attention. It is true
that by mere reasoning from the facts of experience
we cannot convince ourselves that the elements of
matter are created out of nothing. But we arrive
at that conviction, if we begin with facts of
experience, and from them reason out the conclusion, admitted even by Mr. Spencer, that there
must be a First Cause of changes, and thence
inquire into the nature of this First Cause and its
relation to the elements of matter. Such was our
mode of reasoning in chapters ii. sect. 2, iii., and iv.

113. (3) Mill brings a second objection against
the necessity of searching for a First Cause. He
says: [15] " It is thus a necessary part of the fact
of causation within the sphere of our experience,
that the causes as well as the effects had a beginning
in time and were themselves caused. It would
seem, therefore, that our experience, instead of
furnishing an argument for a First Cause, is repugnant to it; and that the very essence of causation as it exists within the limits of our knowledge,
is incompatible with a First Cause."

Answer. Mill in this passage fails to see a
distinction between the *circumstances* of causation
to which our experience witnesses and its *essence.*
The natural causes of which we have experience

[15] *Essays on Religion,* p. 144.

have each its own cause; but the dependence of each cause upon another preceding it is neither of the essence of causation nor a necessary adjunct of it. The essence of causation consists in the fact that one being is in some way the reason why something else exists.

Whether the cause which acts is itself caused has nothing to do with the essence of causation; it is a circumstance accompanying the causation of the beings that come under our experience. But from this it does not follow that every cause must be caused. On the contrary, it can be shown that this hypothesis is against evident first principles.[16]

114. (4) Mill objects to the argument by which from the existence of the human mind we prove the existence of a self-existing intelligent Being. He says:[17] "We are then entitled to ask, Where is the proof that nothing can have caused a mind except another mind? From what, except from experience, can we know what can produce what —what causes are adequate to what effects? That nothing can consciously produce mind but mind is self-evident, being involved in the meaning of the words; but that there cannot be unconscious production must not be assumed, for it is the very point to be proved. Apart from experience, and arguing on what is called reason, that is, on supposed self-evidence, the notion seems to be that no causes can give rise to products of a more precious or elevated kind than themselves. But this

---

[16] Cf. Argument of First Cause, c. ii. sect. 2.
[17] *Essays on Religion*, p. 152.

L

is at variance with the known analogies of nature. How vastly nobler and more precious, for instance, are the higher animals and vegetables than the soil and manure out of which and by the properties of which they are raised up! The tendency of all recent speculation is towards the opinion that the development of inferior orders of existence into superior, the substitution of greater elaboration and higher organization for lower, is the general rule of nature. Whether it is so or not, there are at least in nature a multitude of facts bearing that character, and this is sufficient for the argument."

Answer. This objection of Mill rests evidently on two suppositions : 1. Only from experience can we know what sort of causes we must assume in order to explain given effects. 2. Experience bears positive evidence that effects are sometimes more perfect than their causes.

To the first of these suppositions we must reply by distinguishing between the determination of the sort or quality of cause required to produce the effect under consideration, and the identification, from among the number of those possessing the required qualities, of the particular individual, by which the effect has in fact been produced. The latter point can, as a rule, only be determined by experience; but the former can be determined by inference from the nature of the effect, and, in fact, can be determined in no other way. It is only in virtue of a previous inference which gathers from the nature of the effect wrought the necessary qualities and conditions of the agent which produced it, that experience is enabled to detect the actual agent out of the number of others which may happen to fall under observation. Moreover, if study of the effect leads to the conclusion that the adequate cause is one which from the nature of its essential attributes must be the only one of its kind in existence, in that case no further recourse to experience is necessary, and we are entitled at once, on the sole basis of the inference, to identify the actual individual agent.

To the second of Mr. Mill's fallacious suppositions we must give an answer on similar lines. Experience may seem to a superficial observer to bear positive evidence, that effects are sometimes more perfect than their causes: as, for instance, that a mature tree with its foliage and fruit is more perfect than the seed whence it sprang. Nevertheless, more solid investigation is aware that it must be guided to its results not by bare observation, but by observation based on the principles of reason. The principle of causality demands that the cause shall always precontain what it communicates to the effect. The seed, so far forth as it is less perfect than the tree that grows out of it, must be the *partial* not the *total* cause of the tree, and accordingly observation proceeds to discern what are the other contributing factors out of whose union and co-operation the total cause is composed. In the seed itself is a latent virtue which only reveals itself by a gradual process. In order to the evolution of this latent power, nutritive elements must be supplied in due time and manner from without. When all these contributory agents are considered, we discover that the principle of causality has in no sense been violated. Each contributor precontains what it communicates, in equal or higher measure than its correlative portion of the effect; and the assemblage of them all precontains adequately the entirety of the effect.

Thus our reasoning to the existence of God is quite justified. Throughout we keep in view the principle of causality, and find it leads us safely to the conclusion drawn. Applying it to the assemblage of visible things which surround us and are stamped with the characteristics of effects, we conclude that there must be a self-existing Being which is their Cause. This determines the kind of cause postulated. Further study of the idea of self-existence shows that there can only be one self-existent Being; and we are thus, without recourse to experience, enabled to identify our First Cause. The next stage has led us to discern the necessity of creation; since, on any other hypothesis, we should be having two first causes. And lastly, we were able to argue from the nature of the human mind on the one hand, and analysis of the notion of infinite being on the other, to the conclusion that the human soul must have been created by a free act of divine volition.

115. (5) Mill objects further:[18] "If mind, as mind, presents intuitive evidence of having been created,

---

[18] *Essays on Religion*, p. 153.

the creative mind must do the same; and we are no nearer to the First Cause than before."

Answer. It is not *mind* as *mind*, but the *human* mind as *human* mind, that presents evidence of having been created. This human mind manifests itself to us as contingent and finite. From the conclusion, then, that the human mind must have been created, it in no way follows that the creative mind similarly owes its origin to creation. On the contrary, the irrationality of seeking an explanation of the existence of created things in a *processus ad infinitum*, showing that there must be a First Cause, shows likewise that the First Cause could not have been created, but must be self-existent.

Section 4.—*Difficulties of Mill and Lange against the Argument from Design.*

116. (1) Having applied the Argument from Design to the case of the human eye, Mill thus objects to its force:[19] " Creative forethought is not absolutely the only link by which the origin of the wonderful mechanism of the eye may be connected with the fact of sight. There is another connecting link on which attention has been greatly fixed by recent speculations, and the reality of which cannot be called in question, though its adequacy to account for such truly admirable combinations as some of those in nature, is still and will probably long remain problematical. This is the principle of the 'survival of the fittest.'"

Answer. Only if accepted in its most extreme

[19] *Essays on Religion,* p. 172.

form can the Darwinian theory be urged as an
objection against the Argument from Design;
whereas, on the other hand, the extreme form of this
theory is losing in public favour just because it
attributes so much to chance and is absolutely
exclusive of finality. If evolution be the true explanation of the existing order of the cosmos, and
this evolution is due to the gradual working out to
their final issues of laws inherent in matter from
the commencement, then the question whether this
existing order be due to intelligence or not, is not
solved, but merely pushed back. In the achievements of human industry, a self-constructing machine
would be taken to imply not comparative absence
of skill and contrivance in its maker, but a higher
exercise of these qualities; and the same will have
to be said of the machine of the cosmos. The
more its order is due to an evolution which is the
outcome of the action of fixed laws inherent from
the first and tending definitely towards the final
result, the more striking is the manifestation of
intelligence which it bears upon its face. However,
the essence of extreme Darwinism lies in this,
that it seeks to attribute the course of evolution
ultimately to chance. Accidental varieties spring
up among individuals, and out of the vast number
of these, those which are advantageous in some
line to their possessors, are said to perpetuate
themselves in the struggle for existence. They go
to form the *fittest*, and the struggle for existence
being severe and consequently destructive, the fittest
of those born are naturally the survivors, and sur-

viving, transmit their acquired advantages to their offspring, and thereby fix them.

Such a system, no doubt, is directly opposed to the Argument from Design. If the order of the world can be explained by chance, there is no need to refer its origin to intelligence. But then this hypothesis of origin by chance is just that which has to be rejected as inadmissible, because it offends against the undeniable truth that order presupposes finality in the immediate cause and intelligence at all events in the ultimate cause. It is not necessary, again, to justify this statement, as we have done so already (Cf. §§ 42, seq.), when we dealt with the hypothesis of a fortuitous concourse of atoms. There is, in fact, no essential difference, from a metaphysical point of view, between that ancient theory and the modern theory of Natural Selection when taken in its extreme form. However, it is precisely on the ground that it attributes the magnificent order of nature to sheer chance that this extreme form of Darwinism is going out of favour.

We may here notice, without associating it with Mr. Mill's name, another prevalent mode of meeting the Argument from Design, which in some respects is the opposite of that just considered. The Argument from Design, it is said, proceeds from the supposition that the cosmos is like Paley's watch, a machine in which the component parts have no natural tendency towards one another, but have their motion and unity impressed upon them from without. In other words, the ordering impulse is here without the machine, and it is just on this account that the inference to the existence of a designing mind is just. But by what right is it assumed that the ordering impulse in nature generally is of this sort ?

" The thought or design which is at work in the growth and development of organized structures is not a mere mechanical power or cunning acting from without—shaping, adjusting, putting together materials prepared to its hand, constructing them according to an ingenious plan after the manner of a maker of machines. Here, on the contrary, the idea or formative power goes with the matter, and constitutes the very indwelling essence of the thing. Instead of coming in as an after-thought, to give to existing materials a new use and purpose not included or presupposed in their own original nature, the idea or design is present from the very beginning, inspiring the first minute atom or cell with the power of the perfect whole that is to be. Nor for the building up and completing of the structure, is there any call for the interposition of external agency. From first to last it is self-formative, self-developing : the life within resists all merely outward interference and subordinates all outward conditions to its own development. In this case, therefore, we do not need to go beyond or outside of the thing itself in seeking for the explanation of it. The thought or reason that explains it is within the thing itself, nay, *is* its very self: so that to perceive or know the thing at all is to perceive or know the reason and ground of its existence."[20]

[20] Caird's *Introductions to the Philosophy of Religion*, pp. 146, 147.

If we find this to be so in the organisms around us, may we not extend the same idea to the whole finite world and regard its order and the finality of its movements as throughout proceeding from a directing force which is immanent within it rather than from one outside it like the God of Paley?

This objection is easily answered. It is of no consequence, in the first instance, whether the directing principle which imparts finality to the movements of the cosmos be external or internal to it, except, indeed, in so far as the internal principle of vital movement and growth in organisms supplies us with evidence of a much more elaborate and far-reaching finality than we find in the mechanical achievements of human industry. But as long as there is finality, there must be intelligence. For finality involves an operation of the future on the present, determining the course and direction which the present movements are to take in order that they may reach the future goal, and operation of the future on the present is inconceivable except in so far as the future is apprehended by an intelligence which can set the physical forces in corresponding motion and prescribe to them their lines of movement.[21]

Thus it matters not, in the first instance, where we place the thought whence the design and finality of the cosmos proceeds, whether within it as an immanent principle, or without it as a God distinct from it and transcending it. Ultimately, however, the hypothesis of thought immanent in the cosmos,

[21] Cf. §§ 43—45, where the full proof of this statement is given.

of an *anima mundi* in fact, is excluded. For the argument of the First Cause leads us to a First Intelligence which is *self-existent*, and the analysis of the idea of self-existence causes us to perceive that the First Intelligence must be a Pure and Infinite Spirit, whereas the cosmos is finite and material. Only on the hypothesis that cosmical monism or pantheism was irrefutable, would an objection like that just remarked upon, be really strong. We have, however, given ample proof to show the futility of pantheism and any other form of monism. (Cf. c. iv. sect. 2). And if the reader bears still in mind what we have said there, he cannot fail to see that every appeal to immanent teleology against an intelligent Designer is as futile as Mill's appeal to the "survival of the fittest." Indeed it is still more obviously opposed to reason than that appeal, inasmuch as its foundation is more directly repugnant to the attributes of a self-existing Being.

117. (2) Mill thinks that design and omnipotence are incompatible. "It is not too much to say," he maintains,[22] "that every indication of design in the cosmos is so much evidence against the omnipotence of the Designer. For what is meant by design? Contrivance: the adaptation of means to an end. But the necessity for contrivance—the need of employing means—is a consequence of the limitation of power. Who would have recourse to means, if to attain his end his mere word was sufficient? The very idea of means implies that the means have an efficacy, which the direct action of the Being

[22] L.c. pp. 176, 177.

who employs them has not. Otherwise they are
not means, but an incumbrance. A man does not
use machinery to move his arms. If he did, it
could only be when paralysis had deprived him of
the power of moving them •by volition. But if the
employment of contrivance is in itself a sign of
limited power, how much more so is the careful and
skilful choice of contrivances ? Can any wisdom be
shown in the selection of means, when the means
have no efficacy but what is given them by the will
of Him who employs them and when His will could
have bestowed the same efficacy on other means?
. . . No one purpose imposes necessary limitations
on another in the case of a Being not restricted by
conditions of possibility."

Answer. By this way of arguing Mill proves
nothing more clearly than that he has a wrong
notion of omnipotence. Omnipotence is not an
ability to effect things which are intrinsically impossible, but it is the power to effect whatever is
intrinsically possible. A power to produce what is
intrinsically impossible, for instance a philosopher
without a reasonable soul, would be a power for
non-sense in the strictest meaning of the word; it
would be no power at all. Mill thinks that an
omnipotent Being is not "restricted by conditions
of possibility." This is true enough if it merely
means that God can do or make everything which
is not intrinsically impossible ; but it is not true, as
Mill suggests, that an omnipotent Being can by His
free-will make the intrinsically impossible become
intrinsically possible. Now it is intrinsically impos-

sible for all means to suffice for all ends indiscrimi-
nately. If God will, for instance, that the sun's
action on the earth should be precisely what it is
now, and in accordance with the same physical
laws as now obtain, He could not possibly accom-
plish this end by putting the earth where Jupiter is
and Jupiter where the earth is. If He willed that
the innumerable species of living beings that people
the earth should live on nourishment naturally suited
to their organisms, He could not reach this end by
providing food for only a few of them. Finally, if
He willed that men should merit their final happiness by faith, obedience, and patience, He could not
remove all difficulties and sufferings from their path
through life.

If these considerations are borne in mind, it
becomes clear that in selecting certain means
rather than others as being necessary or appropriate to the accomplishment of certain ends, God
displays no want of power. The necessity or appropriateness of the means for the ends is determined
by the laws of intrinsic possibility.

However, Mr. Mill's objection is not yet fully
answered. Why, he may still urge, require any
means at all? Why, if God is omnipotent, can He
not create, for instance, full-grown living beings
at once, by a mere exercise of will? The question
seems specious enough, but it proceeds from failure
to see that the freedom of God is not less infinite
than His omnipotence. Of course, an omnipotent
God could create straight off all the trees in the
world in a state of maturity, and could maintain

them in the perfection of their nature without the
agency of nutritive elements and processes. But
He may also prefer a system such as that in actual
existence, in which results are worked out gradually
by an evolutionary process, various agents com-
bining and co-operating according to their natures
and properties. Surely the present age, which is
so much in love with evolution, ought not to deny
that this latter is in itself an attractive system:
one, therefore, which may reasonably be selected
by a God desirous to manifest the excellences of
His creative power in a high degree. As an
absolutely best world is intrinsically impossible
(Th. XV.), the manifestation of God's omnipotence
in the world can in no system be exhaustive.
Precisely because Omnipotence is infinite power,
its effects cannot reflect it adequately. How far
it shall be manifested, depends entirely upon God's
free choice. God can choose no system in which
the dictates of infinite wisdom and goodness would
be violated. But among the indefinite number of
systems that may be in harmony with the requirements of absolute wisdom and goodness, there is
none of which the preference was not entirely open
to the freedom of the Creator. The answer, then,
to the question, Why require any means at all? is
briefly this: Because God in His infinite freedom
has chosen a universe consisting of beings which
cannot manifest His power, wisdom, and goodness
in that degree which He freely intends without the
adaptation of means to ends in such excellency and
such profusion as our experience witnesses.

118. (3) Lange[23] argues against design from the great waste of living germs recurring constantly in nature. " It cannot possibly be doubted that nature proceeds in a way which has no resemblance with human adaptation of means to ends; nay, that its most essential *modus operandi,* judged by the standard of human understanding, is such as can only be compared with the blindest chance. . . . From the pollen of the plant to the fertilized seed-corn, from the seed-corn to the germinating plant, from the latter to the mature plant which again bears seed, we see a constant repetition of a mechanism which preserves life so far as it is preserved in the present order of things, only by the generation of thousands of beings to destroy them immediately, and by availing itself of fortuitous coincidences of favourable conditions. The destruction of living germs, the failure of what has begun, is the rule; the ' connatural ' (*naturgemässe*) development is a special case among thousands; it is the exception, and this exception is made by that nature which the purblind teleologist admires for its self-preservation brought about by adapting means to ends. . . . What we call chance in the preservation of species, is of course no chance in regard of the universal laws of nature, the grand machinery of which calls forth all those effects; but it is chance in the strictest sense of the word, if we take this term as an expression of what is opposed to the results obtained by an *Intelligence calculating in a similar way to men.*" Similar lamentations about nature's " clumsiness "

[23] *Geschichte des Materialismus* (2te Auflage), Vol. II. pp. 246, 247.

and "cruelty" occur repeatedly in Mill's *Essays on Religion.*[24]

Answer. We have to acknowledge that the eloquent writer of the *History of Materialism* does not advocate blind chance quite so openly as the Epicureans of old. According to him, the preservation of the actually existing world of animals and plants is due to the grand machinery of the laws of nature. Be it so. Where, then, shall we search for the origin of these laws? Proximately, of course, they are founded on definite combinations of the forces of diverse natural beings. But those combinations themselves—whence did they proceed? To this we have given a full answer. (Cf. §§ 43, seq.) After all, therefore, even if we allow for argument's sake that apparent failures result from the collision of various natural laws—as Lange evidently supposes—it must nevertheless be admitted that these laws are designed by an intelligent Mind.

But, it may be asked next: Is it reasonable to believe that this Mind is infinitely perfect? If so, whence so many failures in nature's working? Should not a Creator of infinite perfection have taken care that every one of His creatures reached the end for which it was intended? This evidently is not the case in the present order of things; for what can be the end intended by the production of living germs but that they shall grow and bear seed. Instead of that, the greater part of them is wasted. Does not this one fact alone suffice to justify fully Lange's inference that nature is not subject to the

[24] Pp. 28, 29, 30, 35, 36, &c.

government of a directing Mind in any way similar
to human minds? The answer to this question is not
too difficult. Before we can reasonably pronounce
that there are failures in nature, we must first be
certain that nature's ends go no farther than we
suppose them to go. The weak point in Lange's
argument lies precisely in his taking for granted
that living germs are good for nothing unless
they become full-grown living beings. This, however, is evidently not the case, and Lange himself
practically denies it as often as he eats a piece
of bread or an egg. Who will say that all the
germs of life that are destroyed to furnish a savant's
breakfast-table, are wasted? As we have demonstrated
in chapter iii., God is infinitely perfect, consequently,
infinitely good and wise. The object of His creation
must be worthy of His goodness and wisdom. From
this it follows, as we shall see in the treatise on
Divine Providence, that the *absolutely* last end of all
creation is the manifestation of God's goodness to
His rational creatures, and the *relatively* last end the
happiness of the rational creatures themselves. The
rest of the creation must serve as means to attain
the last end, which cannot be immediately reached
but by the knowledge and love of God, whereof only
rational creatures are capable. Experience proves
that the inferior creation is useful for man in various
ways, and that many of these ways, formerly unknown, are revealed in the course of time. It is,
therefore, unreasonable to say that creatures are
useless because we cannot find out *how far* they are
useful. After it has been demonstrated clearly that

an infinite Mind is the Author of the universe, we cannot without rashness scrutinize the ways by which that one infinite Mind of God leads His creatures to their respective destinies. It is enough for us that we can prove that there is an infinitely good God, who guides His creatures to those particular ends which He *conditionally* intends, as often as the conditions are put, and that in any case He guides them to those ends which He *absolutely* intends, making all things contribute to the last general end of creation.

Lange's objection appeared quite lately in a new form. " I am not saying," says Mr. Mallock,[25] "that the theory of evolution has disproved the existence of a designer, but that it has destroyed the traditional evidence that the designer is good, or indeed that he is even wise and skilful. How it has done this can be explained briefly as follows. Suppose we were told of a certain marksman that every one of his rifle-shots, no matter at what distance, invariably hit the target in the very centre of the bull's-eye, we should say that this was evidence of unrivalled skill. Supposing, however, we were to discover subsequently that for every shot that hit the bull's-eye he had fired a thousand that hit the rim of the target, and fifty thousand that hit the neighbouring haystacks, instead of thinking him skilful for having hit the bull's-eye occasionally, we should be inclined to think him skilful if he contrived always to miss it. Now the old idea of creation was that everything was created suitable to the conditions of its existence; in other words, the bull's-eye was hit each time. The scientific theory is the precise opposite—that most things were created unsuited to the conditions of their existence; and those only have survived which happened accidentally to suit them. In other words, for each time the bull's-eye is hit, it is missed thousands of times; and as the God we are assuming is, *ex hypothesi*, firing eternally, the fact of his hitting the target is no proof of his having aimed at it. If the discoveries of science amount to anything, they amount to this—that the successes of nature are the siftings of innumerable failures; and if there is any force in the argument, that the successes show skill, there is equal force in the argument that the failures show want of it. . . . I am granting that the existence of a designer is not only not disproved by science, but proved by it. The one thing on which I am here insisting is that science does not indeed disprove that the designer is good and wise, but assuredly does destroy every proof that he is."

Answer. We beg our reader not to mistake the proper meaning of this difficulty. Mr. Mallock is far from upholding the cause of agnosticism. All he contends for is that, in the face of modern scientific discoveries, God's goodness and wisdom cannot be proved by reason, although they can be certified by faith.

, For the present we are only concerned about the wisdom of the Designer of Nature. By what arguments does our objector think that science has destroyed the evidence for it? He refers us to the theory of eternal evolution. Science, he considers, has made it certain that evolution has been an eternal process in nature, and upon this assumption his argument is manifestly based. Is, then, this basis solid? If "eternal," evolution is to mean evolution without beginning, it is certain that no cautious thinker would venture to maintain that it has been established with any degree of probability on the grounds of scientific facts. Moreover, we have had occasion to prove that eternal evolution in this sense is intrinsically repugnant (pp. 146, 147). Perhaps by eternal evolution Mr. Mallock only means evolution throughout countless ages. Even if thus explained, can evolution be taken for more than what Mr. Huxley takes it for — viz., "a workable hypothesis"? Whether the true answer be negative or affirmative, we will at all events start from the assumption that evolution existed and went on through unmeasurable geological periods, after the manner in which Darwinians conceive it. On this assumption, if with a view to consider the tenability of the hypothesis, we suppose the laws of evolution to have been instituted by a Personal God, the comparison he makes between a marksman and the arranger of the universe is intelligible enough. As the marksman aims at the target in such a way as to hit, if possible, the bull's-eye, so God, in laying down the laws of evolution for inanimate and animate things, has a certain aim ; and if He is to be taken as wise in any considerable degree, He must reach His aim not only in some cases, but at least in most cases ; He must reach it in each case not only approximately, but with precision. Otherwise He would be like a marksman who misses the target a far greater number of times than he hits it, and who when hitting it strikes only the rim, not the bull's-eye.

But now if we are to judge from the appearance of nature whether God does hit the bull's-eye to this extent, we must first be certain what is the bull's-eye at which He is aiming when He lays down and maintains laws of evolution for matter and life. Mr. Mallock seems to think that according to our doctrine God has intended that every living being should be in complete harmony with its surroundings, and should always be placed in such conditions as would foster and not hinder its connatural development. It is quite true that if this had been the object of the Creator, scientific facts might be said to have destroyed all our evidence for His wisdom, and laid us open to the attacks of agnosticism. But the advocates of the design argument have never imagined that the Divine intention in framing this world was to disregard the inherent tendencies to corruption, and to secure to each form of organic life the completion of its natural development and the fulness of comfort and enjoyment. This has not even been supposed of man, the highest among living organisms. If indeed man's life as a whole to the inclusion of the life to come were meant, we should have to speak differently. But as far as that portion of his life is concerned which is led here below, it was acknowledged many thousand years ago by one whose theism is beyond suspicion that, " Man born of a woman, living for a short time, is filled with many miseries." [26] And the very Founder of Christianity deemed the conditions of life so inadequate to assure absolute happiness and development that among the reasons for which He wished His disciples not to be over-anxious for the future, we find this, " Sufficient for the day is the evil thereof." [27]

Under the heading " Divine Providence " we shall show that God has created the world for the manifestation of His goodness to rational creatures, and for the happiness of the latter, who alone are capable of true happiness. Consequently, in so far as evolution with the restrictions laid down above (pp. 133, 134) may be admissible, this is the final goal towards which its whole course must be directed. And the final goal must be reached only and precisely in that degree of perfection which the Creator intends.

We conclude, then, by saying that the target at which the Designer of Nature is aiming is not the prosperity of corporeal life, and the bull's-eye in the target is not the perfect adaptation of each individual life to its surroundings. The true target is God's glory and the final happiness of those rational creatures who obey the voice of their conscience, and the bull's-eye in the target is precisely that degree of God's glory and man's final happiness which the Creator in the light of His infinite knowledge has fixed absolutely. It will be hard for the champions of natural science to show either that

[26] Job xiv. 1.   [27] St. Matt. vi. 34.

the end of creation thus explained is asserted without sufficient evidence or to prove that it will not
be reached finally.

SECTION 5.—*Darwin's reasons for doubting the existence
of God.*

119. As appears from the *Life and Letters of
Charles Darwin,* edited by his son Francis,[28] that
great observer of Nature never *denied* the existence
of God.   The arguments brought forward to prove
that there is a God, seemed to him sometimes quite
overwhelming; and in such moments he was forced
to be a complete theist.   Yet, after he had lost
his faith in the Gospels, he lost also the habitual
conviction, formerly so strong in him, that the
universe is ruled by a wise God.   His attitude
towards monotheism became that of a non-aggres-
sive agnostic.   Most of the reasons by which he
tried to justify his position, are closely connected
with his biological theory of evolution.   On account
of the great influence which this theory exercises
over many minds, we think it well to give these
reasons in full with Darwin's own words and to
test their force carefully.

The value of the Argument from Design is called
in question by Darwin chiefly for three reasons,
each of which we will state in Darwin's own
words.

(*a*) In his autobiography, written in 1876, he
says :[29] " The old argument from design in nature,

<hr>

[28] Vol. I. viii. " Religion."   [29] *Ibid.* p. 309.

as given by Paley, which formerly seemed to me so conclusive, fails, now that the law of Natural Selection has been discovered. We can no longer argue that, for instance, the beautiful hinge of a bivalve shell must have been made by an intelligent being, like the hinge of a door by man. There seems to be no more design in the variability of organic beings, and in the action of Natural Selection, than in the course which the wind blows. I have discussed this subject at the end of my book on the *Variation of Domesticated Animals and Plants;* and the argument there given has never, as far as I can see, been answered."

The argument to which we are referred in this passage is as follows:[30] "Are we to believe that the forms are preordained of the broken fragments of rock which tumble from a precipice and are fitted together by man to build his houses? If not, why should we believe that the variations of domestic animals or plants are preordained for the sake of the breeder? But if we give up the principle in one case, . . . no shadow of reason can be assigned for the belief that variations . . . which have been the groundwork through Natural Selection of the formation of the most perfectly adapted animals in the world, man included, were intentionally and specially guided."

The doubt expressed in the preceding lines is dwelt upon also in a letter to Miss Julia Wedgwood (written July 11, 1881).[31] He owns in this letter

---

[30] *The Variation of Animals and Plants,* Vol. II. p. 431.
[31] *Life and Letters of Charles Darwin,* Vol. I. p. 314.

that "the mind refuses to look at this universe being what it is, without having been designed." Yet he finds it too difficult to believe that all variations of organic structures should have been designed, for instance, "each variation in the rock pigeon." It seemed to him that to care about such trifles was scarcely worthy of a Being who is the Maker of a universe. "Do you consider that the successive variations in the size of the crop of the pouter pigeon which man has accumulated to please his caprice have been due to "the creative and sustaining powers of Brahma?" In the sense that an omnipotent and omniscient Deity must order and know everything, this must be admitted; yet in honest truth, I can hardly admit it. It seems preposterous that a maker of a universe should care about the crop of a pigeon solely to please man's silly fancies. But if you agree with me in thinking such an interposition of the Deity uncalled for, I can see no reason whatever for believing in such interpositions in the case of natural beings," &c.

In the same sense Darwin expresses himself in a letter to Dr. Gray:[32] "An innocent and good man stands under a tree and is killed by a flash of lightning. Do you believe (and I really should like to hear) that God *designedly* killed this man? Many or most persons do believe this; I can't and don't. If you believe so, do you believe when a swallow snaps up a gnat that God designed that that particular swallow should snap up that particular gnat

[32] *Life and Letters of Charles Darwin*, Vol. I. pp. 314, 315.

at that particular instant? I believe that a man and a gnat are in the same predicament. If the death of neither man nor gnat are designed, I see no good reason to believe that their *first* birth or production should be necessarily designed."

We may put Darwin's argument in concise form as follows: If *some* adaptations of certain antecedents to certain consequents are explained by design of the Creator, *all* must be explained so, however trifling they may appear. But not all can reasonably be explained so; for instance, it cannot be reasonably referred to creative design that pieces of rock tumbling from a precipice are found fit for building houses, or that man turns rock pigeons artificially into fantail pigeons, or that a flash of lightning kills an innocent man, or that a swallow snaps up a gnat. There is consequently no sufficient reason for admitting design at all.

What shall we answer to this? At first sight it might seem reasonable to doubt whether it is necessary to admit design everywhere in nature, if you admit it anywhere. There is indeed no immediate appearance of intrinsic contradiction in the idea of a universe in which only the more important operations should be guided by design.[33] Consider-

---

[33] In a letter to Asa Gray, dated November 26, 1860, the great biologist himself inclines to take this view. He writes: " I am inclined to look at everything as resulting from designed laws, with the details, whether good or bad, left to the working out of what we may call chance. Not that this notion *at all* satisfies me. I feel most deeply that the whole subject is too profound for the human intellect. A dog might as well speculate on the mind of Newton. Let each man hope and believe what he can." (*Life and Letters,* Vol. II. p. 312.)

ing, however, that the first Designer of the world
is self-existent and infinitely perfect, He must
know from eternity not only in general, but in
detail, all conditionally future results of any plan
possible. Moreover, His infinite wisdom necessarily prevents any event from happening, the
occurrence of which would in no way serve His
plan. From this it follows that every effect in
the universe has been designed by God, inasmuch
as He has foreseen it, and has from eternity
decreed not to prevent its happening, but to
make its occurrence serve the end of all creation.[34]
Granting then Darwin's assertion that we cannot
be consistent with ourselves, unless we admit
that all effects in nature have been foreseen and
preordained, we deny altogether that there is
anything repugnant to reason in this admission.
Reason forbids us indeed to admit that each particular event has been designed *by a particular act*
of the Divine mind distinct from the act by which
the whole of the universe was planned. Such an
assumption would clash with God's simplicity and
infinite perfection. But there is nothing intrinsically
repugnant in the statement that God by one act of
His infinite intellect foresaw all events, and by one
act of His infinite will subordinated each of them
to a particular good purpose. On the contrary, this
cannot be denied without denying what is logically
connected with God's infinite perfection, as will
appear in our treatises on Divine knowledge and
providence.

[34] Cf. the solution of Lange's difficulty, § 118.

120. (b) Another doubt against the conclusiveness of the design argument arose in Darwin's
mind from the consideration of the so-called
"rudimentary organs" in man. He thus expresses
it in a letter to Asa Gray •(December 11, 1861):[35]
"With regard to Design I feel more inclined to
show a white flag than to fire my usual long-range
shot. I like to try and ask you a puzzling question,
but when you return the compliment I have great
doubts whether it is a fair way of arguing. If anything is designed, certainly man must be: one's
'inner consciousness' (though a false guide) tells
one so; yet I cannot admit that man's rudimentary
mammæ . . . were designed."

The difficulty in conceiving "rudimentary"
organs as designed, expressed in the above passage,
has often been repeated by Darwinists. It rests
upon their not seeing the particular purpose those
organs should serve. But from the fact, that
the immediate object of an effect in nature cannot
be discovered by us, it certainly does not follow that
such an effect was not designed for some immediate object. As we have remarked already, when
solving Lange's difficulty, there are many things apt
to further the attainment not only of one but of
several particular ends. Granting then for argument's sake, that a "rudimentary" organ may be
useless to the organism in which it is found, this
in no way justifies the inference that it is altogether
useless; or that it is out of harmony with the final
end an infinite Creator must intend by decreeing the

[35] *Life and Letters*, Vol. II. p. 382.

existence of the universe. We have touched upon
this final end above (§ 118). We have explained
there that God creates in order to manifest His
perfection to His intellectual creatures. But does
it follow from this that each fact in nature must be
understood by man? No one can reasonably deny
the possibility of the existence of intellectual creatures
whose minds are far more penetrating than the
mind of man. Supposing then that there exists
a world of created spirits, is it not very probable
that they see perfectly the rationale of the rudimentary organs, and recognize in them a vestige
of supreme wisdom? And even apart from this,
the puzzle caused by the discovery of "rudimentary" organs seems to resemble much the amaze-
ment naturally arising from the sight of any complicated arrangements of which we only know
the final outcome. For instance, a man of common
sense who knows no more about the mechanism of
a watch than that by turning the key properly, it
can be made to measure time, enters the shop of a
watchmaker well furnished with all sorts of instruments and materials. What the particular purpose
may be which each of them answers in the construction of watches, his ignorance prevents his knowing;
but it does not hinder him from the exercise of a
reasonable belief that there is none among them all
that is useless for the work of the watchmaker. Thus
he knows the *common remote* end of all the things he
sees, without understanding anything about the
particular proximate end through which each must
pass in order to reach the common remote end.

What such a man knows about the instruments he is looking at and what he does not know, seems to illustrate well both the knowledge we are able to attain about natural events and the ignorance in which we must remain. By logical reasoning based upon undeniable premisses, the certain conclusion can be arrived at that the whole universe is under the sway of one supreme infinitely wise Lord, that He penetrates with one act of His infinite Mind the essences and actions and mutual relations of all things, that He intends them all for a final end worthy of His Infinite Wisdom, and that He cannot fail to direct them rightly to this end. On the other hand, comparatively little can be known by man about the proximate object of particular things and events, although he may be sure that in some way or other they must lead up to the attainment of the final end. Even when he does catch a glimpse of the usefulness of things in particular, he never can grasp it fully, because he never *comprehends* the nature of any natural being, nor does he *comprehend* its relations to other beings, although he may *know* a great deal about both. Consequently, no solid doubt as to the wise guidance of nature can be based upon our not seeing the "why and wherefore" of things in particular. It is abundantly sufficient that the "why and wherefore" in general can be proved evidently.

Moreover, in the particular case of rudimentary structures, is it so certain that we can form to ourselves no conception at all of some possibilities of their utility? Mr. Mivart suggests that they may perhaps be useful in aiding the physiological balance of the organism. His whole passage may be appropriately quoted.

" As to rudimentary structures we may content ourselves with asking, in the words of Buffon, ' Why is it to be considered so necessary that every part in an individual should be useful to the other parts and to the whole animal ? Should it not be enough that they do not injure each other, nor stand in the way of each other's fair development ? Moreover, such rudimentary structures may have a certain utility, may aid the physiological balance of the organism after all ! It cannot yet be shown to be so, but neither can it be shown that it is not so. They are parts of a great whole, which to be adequately understood must be surveyed in its entirety. But any one of us can as little judge the scope of the whole universe, as a fly perched on a pinnacle of York Minster, can perceive the plan, pressures, and bearings of the stones of that glorious pile." [36]

Buffon's suggestion that it is sufficient if a rudimentary structure is not harmful to the individual, might perhaps seem open to the reply that if the world were designed by God, we ought to find not mere harmlessness but positive utility in each one, even the minutest of its parts. We are of the same opinion. But from that alone it does not follow that Mr. Mivart was wrong in supporting to a certain extent Buffon's view. To say that a part of an animal is not positively useful to that individual animal, to its vegetative and sensitive operations, is assuredly not the same as to say that it is of no use. The whole animal with all its parts is to be considered not only as an individual being, but also in relation to the·whole species; and the usefulness of each part is not only to be estimated from its appropriateness to physiological functions, but also from its value as contributing to the external expression of that idea of the Creator of which each organic type is a realization. It is from this standpoint that the celebrated physiologist Carpenter quotes with approval the following words of Mr. Paget: "These rudimental organs certainly do not serve, in a lower degree, the same purposes as are served by the homologous parts which are completely developed in other species or in the other sex. To say they are useless is contrary to all we know of the absolute perfection and all-pervading purposes of creation; to say they exist merely for the sake of conformity to a general type of structure is surely unphilosophical, for the law of Unity of organic types is, in larger instances, not observed, except when its observance contributes to the advantage of the individual. No: all these rudimental organs must, as they grow, be as excretions, serving a definite purpose in the economy by removing their appropriate materials from the blood, thus leaving it fitter for the nutrition of other parts, or adjusting the balance which might otherwise be disturbed by the formation of some other part. Thus they minister to the self-interest of the individual; while, as if for the sake of wonder,

beauty, and perfect order, they are conformed with
the great law of Unity of organic types, and concur
with the universal plan observed in the construction
of organic beings." [37]

121. (c) A third difficulty of Darwin against the
Argument from Design arose from the consideration
of the vast amount of suffering in sentient beings.
It seemed to him that a benevolent Creator could
hardly have predestined His creatures to so much
misery, whereas Natural Selection might sufficiently
account for it. He says: [38] " That there is much
suffering in the world no one disputes. Some have
attempted to explain this with reference to man by
imagining that it serves for his moral improvement.
But the number of men in this world is as nothing
compared with that of all other sentient beings, and
they often suffer greatly without any moral improvement. This very old argument from the existence
of suffering against the existence of an intelligent
First Cause seems to me a strong one, whereas . . .
the presence of much suffering agrees well with the
view that all organic beings have been developed
through variation and Natural Selection." The way
in which he thinks to explain the sufferings of men
and animals by Natural Selection he thus sums
up: " Such suffering is quite compatible with
Natural Selection, which is not perfect in its
action, but tends only to render each species as
successful as possible in the battle for life with

[37] Paget, *Lectures on Surgical Pathology*, p. 31 ; quoted by Carpenter,
Human Physiology, p. 281.
[38] *Life and Letters*, Vol. II. p. 311.

other species in wonderfully complex and changing circumstances."

A particular sort of suffering which caused Darwin to have misgivings in regard of design is mentioned by him in a letter to Asa Gray.[39] "I cannot persuade myself," he says, "that a beneficent and omnipotent God would have designedly created the ichneumonidæ with the express intention of their feeding within the living bodies of caterpillars, or that a cat should play with mice. Not believing this, I see no necessity in the belief that the eye was expressly designed." In the same letter, however, he admits that such suffering proves nothing *conclusively* against an omniscient Creator.

We answer to all this: An omnipotent and benevolent Creator cannot design sufferings *merely for suffering's sake;* He cannot find His delight in the sufferings of His creatures. But there is no argument to prove that He cannot will physical sufferings as a means for the bringing about of a real good connected with the final end of creation. It is not necessary that each suffering of a sentient being should have been proximately designed with a view to man's moral improvement. It may immediately have regard to something else, and may mediately serve the bringing about of a state of things of which man finally can make use for his moral improvement. In any case it will serve to reveal either to man or to other intellectual creatures higher than man the wonderful ways of God's wisdom. That there is no Divine attribute with

[39] *Life and Letters*, Vol. I. p. 311.

N

which the sufferings and moral disorders of this world can rightly be said to clash, we shall prove conclusively in the treatise on Divine Providence. "But," a Darwinian may object here, "after all it has not been shown that Darwin was wrong, when he thought that the sufferings which make life so bitter, are far more satisfactorily explained by the hypothesis of Natural Selection than by that of design." A sufficient answer to this objection is obvious enough. Whatever truth there may be in the theory of Natural Selection, certainly such process of selection could not begin before the existence of living organisms capable of struggling for the maintenance of their lives. But it has already (§§ 45, 46) been demonstrated that Natural Selection, even if it be a true cause of the habits and interests of living beings, cannot be their ultimate cause. Intelligence must even then be inferred to lie behind and to have established the evolutionary system in which Natural Selection plays so prominent a part. Granting then, for argument's sake, that Natural Selection can account for the prevalence of happiness with the addition of an un-avoidable measure of suffering, as Darwin believed,[40] it certainly is not the chief cause either of happiness or of suffering, but is only instrumental in working out the plan conceived by the First Intelligent Cause, as Darwin himself once rightly conjectured, when he wrote to Dr. Asa Gray as follows: "I can see no reason why a man or other animal, may not have been aboriginally produced by other laws, and

[40] *Life and Letters*, Vol. I. p. 310.

that all these laws may have been expressly designed by an omniscient Creator, who foresaw every future event and consequence." [41]

122. Against the proof of theism drawn from the common belief of mankind, Darwin makes this remark: "This argument would be a valid one if all men of all races had the same inward conviction of the existence of God; but we know that this is very far from being the case." [42]

There is no point in this objection unless the argument, which it attacks, takes this form: "All men have always believed in one God. But this belief would never have spread so universally if there were not really one God. Consequently we must be certain about the existence of God."

Of course such an argument is open to the objection made by Darwin. But this is not the argument we have given above. (Cf. c. ii. § 49.) We argue thus: There has always existed in the majority of men a persistent belief in a Nature of some kind or other, superior to the material world and to man; a belief against the reasonableness of which, considered in its *universal* character, nothing can be said; a belief, moreover, the origin whereof can only be satisfactorily explained by taking the belief to be well-grounded and true. Consequently, it must be admitted that there exists a Nature, superior to the material world and to man.

Any doubts that might arise against the sound-

[41] Darwin to Asa Gray, May 22, 1862. *Life and Letters,* Vol. II. p. 312.
[42] *Life and Letters,* Vol. I. p. 312.

ness of this argument have already been solved in the passage quoted above. (C. ii. § 49.) In that place attention was also called to the inability of the moral proof to stand by itself alone as an unassailable foundation of monotheism. Nevertheless, its value must not be under-rated. Although, without support from the argument of a First Cause it cannot convince us of the existence of One, Infinite God ; yet it is strong enough to satisfy every reasonable thinker that atheism and agnosticism are not congenial to human reason, and must, therefore, be abandoned by every one who would not come into the predicament in which Darwin confessed himself to be[43] in "a hopeless muddle."

123. We come next to Darwin's difficulty against the argument of a First Cause. He thus expresses it in his autobiography :[44] "Another source of conviction in the existence of God, connected with the reason and not with the feelings, impresses me as having much more weight. This follows from the extreme difficulty or rather impossibility of conceiving this immense and wonderful universe, including man, with his capacity of looking far forwards and far into futurity, as the result of blind chance or necessity. When thus reflecting I feel impelled to look to a First Cause having an

[43] Darwin wrote to Asa Gray, Nov. 26, 1860 : "I grieve to say that I cannot honestly go as far as you do about design. I am conscious that I am in an utterly hopeless muddle. . . . Again I say I am and shall ever remain in a hopeless muddle." (*Life and Letters*, Vol. II. p. 353.)

[44] *Life and Letters*, Vol. I. pp. 311, 312.

intelligent mind in some degree analogous to that of man, and I deserve to be called a theist. This conclusion was strong in my mind about the time, as far as I can remember, when I wrote the *Origin of Species*, and it is since that time that it has very gradually, with many fluctuations, become weaker. But then arises the doubt, Can the mind of man, which has, as I fully believe, been developed from a mind as low as that possessed by the lowest animals, be trusted when it draws such grand conclusions? I cannot pretend to throw the least light on such abstruse problems. The mystery of the beginning of all things is insoluble by us, and I for one must be content to remain an agnostic." In this passage Darwin confesses that the premisses which lead to the conclusion of a first Intelligent Cause are undeniable, and that the connection of that conclusion with its premisses is so close that the human mind cannot help seeing it. Such a conclusion is, according to all sound logicians, the enunciation of an objective truth. And yet Darwin stops short of being satisfied. And why? Have his careful biological observations led to the discovery of any fact incompatible with the existence of God? Assuredly not.[45] The only reason alleged by Darwin for the abandonment of his previous con-

---

[45] Even Professor Huxley acknowledges this: "The doctrine of Evolution is neither anti-theistic nor theistic. It simply has no more to do with theism than the first book of Euclid has. . . . There is a great deal of talk and not a little lamentation about the so-called religious difficulties which physical science has created. In theological science, as a matter of fact, it has created none. Not a solitary problem presents itself to the philosophical theist at the

victions is that a mind developed from that of the mind of the lowest animals is not competent to form an opinion on so grand a problem. This kind of false humility which refuses to accept the conclusions of logic and the evidence of reason because, forsooth, we are developed as Darwin imagines from the amœba, does not need refuting. Even if our minds had the origin which he ascribes to them, it would be worth nothing as an argument. A mind derived through generation from brutes would be utterly unable to draw any conclusion at all. The soul of a brute is a substantial principle "entirely immersed in matter," altogether without power of reasoning.[46] Between an imaginary soul developed from the soul of an amœba and the real soul of man there is an infinite difference. Man's soul, as we have seen, is a spiritual being, the origin of which is due to immediate Divine creation. (Th. XVII.) Considering this truth, Darwin's objection simply disappears.

As we have already shown, no natural law can be reasonably explained without reference to a first Intelligent Cause. If, therefore, progressive development and Natural Selection are laws of nature, they must, like other laws, imply belief in an "all originating, all fore-ordaining, all regulative intelligence to determine the rise and the course and the

present day which has not existed from the time that philosophers began to think out the logical grounds and the logical consequences of theism." (*Life and Letters,* Vol. II. pp. 202, 203, in c. v. written by Huxley.)

[46] Mivart, *Nature and Thought,* p. 226; Maher, *Psychology,* pp. 550--554.

goal of life as of all finite things."[47] It is, therefore, quite natural that men who are both acquainted with the results of scientific inquiry and grounded in solid philosophical principles prove to be among the first champions of monotheism. And why is Darwin not among them? Because he believes fully in the development of the human mind from what he calls the "mind of the lowest animals." Is, then, this belief grounded on fact? Not at all. A consideration of the facts to which our own consciousness continually bears witness has led us to the evident conclusion that the mind of man is a spiritual substance. (§§ 31—37, incl.) In this conclusion we are supported not only by the most subtle philosophers of all ages, but also by one of the most prominent and thoughtful biologists of our own time. "The soul," writes Professor St. George Mivart, "though existing amongst a constant succession of changing conditions, can think of an eternal unchanging absolute. The soul knows itself as looking before and after, and as that which both thinks and endures—persisting thus for years, or, in other words, as a spiritual substance. Above all, the soul can appreciate right and wrong, and now and then freely choose its motive, and so dominate and control the chain of physical causation by its free-will. All these considerations show that its nature is far more widely removed from that of the active principle of the ape than is the latter from a magnet. And as the soul or active principle of an ape differs from the activity of a magnet by a

[47] Flint, *Theism*, p. 209.

difference of kind, so the soul of a man differs yet more in kind from that of an ape." [48] Dr. Carpenter, also another distinguished biologist, tells us that the enunciations, " I am," " I ought," " I can," " I will," are " firm foundation-stones on which we can base our attempt to climb into a higher sphere of existence." [49]   He considers the human will as " something essentially different from the general resultant of an automatic activity of the mind " as " a self-determining power ; " [50] and consequently that " the death of the body is but the commencement of a new life of the soul." [51]

Darwin's doubts prove nothing more clearly than that the entertainer of them had a right appreciation of his capacity for philosophy when he wrote, " I have had no practice in abstract reasoning, and I may be all astray." [52] Our attention will now be occupied with the arguments of men who pushed their power of abstract reasoning to such lengths as to construct the whole universe *a priori*. These are our modern pantheists, leader and chief of whom is Spinoza.

SECTION 6.—*Spinoza's proof that God is the only substance, and that everything else is a mode of God.*

124. According to the pantheistic theory, expounded in Spinoza's *Ethics*, there is only one

[48] *Nature and Thought*, p. 266.
[49] *Mental Physiology*, p. 376.   [50] *Ibid*. p. 392.
[51] *Human Physiology*, p. 1120, § 888.
[52] Letter to Asa Gray in *Life and Letters*, Vol. I. p. 315.

substance, unproduced and infinite—God.[53] Besides God, no substance can exist or be conceived to exist: consequently, whatever is, is in God; it is a mode or affection of the Divine Nature.[54] God is not the transient or external cause of all things, but their immanent cause;[55] they are all determined by the necessity of the Divine Nature to exist and to act in a certain definite manner.[56] Hence it follows that so-called freedom of will is a chimera,[57] and that things could have been produced by God in no other way or order than as they have been produced.[58]

These are the leading tenets of the thirty-six propositions, in which Spinoza, in the first part of his *Ethics*, explains his views about the primary cause of all things. From the general refutation of pantheism given above (Th. X. § 78), it is evident that these propositions contradict external and internal experience, and contain a virtual denial of the first principles both of speculative and of practical reason. Yet they are worked out with a show of exactness which has captivated while it has imposed upon many minds. It becomes, therefore, worth while to deal with them in some measure. We shall, however, confine ourselves to the one underlying fallacy on which the entire system is based. This is his misuse of his ambiguous definition of substance, which we shall examine briefly, and then pass on to the principles by which the German pantheists Fichte and Hegel, in spite of the un-

---

[53] *Ethics*, Part I. Prop. vi. vii. viii. xi. [54] *Ibid.* Prop. xiv. xv.
[55] Prop. xviii. [56] Prop. xxix.
[57] Prop. xxxii. [58] Prop. xxxiii.

popularity of their systems, have led the way to more modern forms of monism.

Spinoza rests his proof that God is the only possible substance on the proposition that one substance cannot be produced by another substance,[59] which is a virtual assertion of pantheism. This proposition is proved by a series of previous propositions,[60] all of which are based on the definition of substance with which he starts. Substance is defined by Spinoza as "that which is in itself and is conceived by itself alone, that is to say, that of which the concept can be formed without involving any other concept."[61]

This definition is patently ambiguous, and in order to make sure whether Spinoza's sixth proposition is really implicitly contained in it, we must inquire into the different ways in which the definition may be understood. Its meaning depends upon the interpretation of the phrase, "that which is in itself and is conceived by itself." This may signify (1) a complete individual, physical being, as distinguished from its natural properties and accidental modifications; it may also signify (2) a self-existing being, a being under all aspects independent of any other being, whether as an underlying subject in which it inheres, or as a cause from which it proceeds. On the first interpretation, Spinoza's definition of substance is almost identical with the scholastic definition; on the

---

[59] Prop. vi.   [60] Prop. i.—v. incl.

[61] "Per substantiam intelligo id quod in se est et per se concipitur, h.e. id cujus conceptus non indiget conceptu alterius rei, a quo formari debeat."

second, his definition is not applicable to any but the first Being, the Divine Essence, and as this Essence cannot be multiplied, Spinoza's Prop. vi., "One substance cannot produce another substance," follows from it, and this involves Pantheism. Yet the absurdity of pantheistic monism (Th. X.) proves fully that nobody can interpret *substance* in the second meaning of Spinoza's definition without committing himself to sheer nonsense. Now as to the steps of reasoning by which Spinoza reaches his famous Prop. vi., it will be enough to remark on the first. His Prop. i. runs thus: "Substance is prior in nature to its affections."[62] In proof of it he says nothing but that it follows from his definitions of *substance* and of *mode*. We have said enough about the former. The latter is as follows: "By mode I understand an affection of substance or that which is in something else by which also it is apprehended."[63] This may signify a substantial principle imparting to the whole its specific character, or a natural property really distinct from the being of which it is predicated, or an accidental modification of a being. Thus the soul of a dog is in the matter of its body as a specifying principle (*forma substantialis*): the faculty of understanding, considered in its operations, is in the human soul as a natural property really distinct from the soul; and the derangement of mind is in the lunatic as an accidental modification.

If, then, we take Spinoza's definition of *substance*

---

[62] "Substantia prior est natura suis affectibus."
[63] "Per modum intelligo substantiæ affectiones sive id quod in alio est, per quod etiam concipitur."

in the first of the two senses given above, and his
definition of *mode* in the first of the three senses
just explained, his first proposition is false. It is not
true, for instance, that a dog is prior in nature to
the specifying principle called his soul. Taking the
same interpretation of the definition of *substance*
along with the second and third interpretations of
the definition of *mode*, we find the first proposition
to be evidently true; for it is undeniable that
natural properties and accidental modifications of
a particular being cannot be conceived, except as
following the existence of that being. In so far as
they do not follow its existence *in the order of time*,
they at least follow it in the order of nature, that is
to say, their existence cannot be conceived but on
the supposition that the being exists of which they
are predicated. Finally, if we take Spinoza's definition of substance in the second sense given above,
and his definition of mode in any of the three senses
explained by us, it appears at once that his first
proposition is altogether false. We have proved
that God is physically and metaphysically simple.
He is therefore not a substance like matter, which
can be raised to diverse substantial degrees by the
reception of diverse specifying principles. Nor are
there in Him natural properties to be conceived as
something under certain aspects really distinct from
His essence, and following that essence, in the
way that an act of our understanding is really
distinct from and follows the essence of the soul.
Much less can God be the subject of merely
accidental modifications.

But in what sense does Spinoza take his two definitions? *Explicitly* he does not tell us. Yet in the arguments by which he supports his following propositions[64] there is not any force, unless *substance* be taken in the second sense; and, as he declares creatures to be affections or modes of the One infinite substance,[65] *mode* is taken in the third sense explained by us. Hence it is evident that in Spinoza's very first proposition there are hidden two false suppositions, the one that *substance* is synonymous with *self-existence*, the other that self-existence is changeable. The first of these two assumptions we have refuted in Th. X., the other will explicitly be refuted in Th. XXII.

SECTION 7.—*Remarks on the theories of Fichte and Hegel and others.*

125. According to Fichte the *Ego* is the embodiment of all reality. All individual things, to the existence of which consciousness and experience testify, are nothing but different aspects of the infinite reality of the *Ego*, bound by fatal necessity to oppose itself to itself. Whatever therefore man perceives is properly speaking in himself, inasmuch as his own being is one reality with the many-sided infinite *Ego*.

The foundation upon which this pantheistic idealism rests is the belief that knowledge of existences separate from that of the person knowing transcends the bounds of possibility.

---

[64] Prop. ii.—vi.   [65] Prop. xiv. xv.

"Whatever you are looking at as outside your-self," says Fichte, "is always your own self; whatever you are conscious of in it, you are really contemplating yourself." [66]   This opinion grew upon him by reading the first edition of Kant's *Criticism of Pure Reason.* Following out logically what Kant had said about the impossibility of giving a satis-factory account of the objectivity of our knowledge by speculative reason, Fichte did away with the *object*, and thus converted the world into a necessary illusion of the *One Infinite Subject.* The general refutation of pantheism given by us above (§§ 78—81, inclus.) suffices abundantly to show how utterly Fichte's system is opposed to sound reason. And we may add that those who like Fichte consider the entire world to be but a series of interesting games played by consciousness with its subjective phenomena, are quite unreasonable in challenging their opponents to point out a bridge by which they may pass from real subject to real object. Either they believe that they have opponents or they do not. If they do not, why ask the question? If they do, therein is the acknowledgment that in their own cognitive faculties they possess a bridge which is sufficiently safe.[67]

126. In a quarrel between the followers of Fichte and those of Hegel, the latter may claim for their master the distinction of greater dialectical skill, but it will be impossible to show that the Hegelian

---

[66] Fichte, *Die Bestimmung des Menschen*, p. 228.
[67] The idealism contained in Fichte's system has found a fuller refutation in the treatise of this series entitled *First Principles.*

system *considered in its essence* is more in harmony with reason than that of Fichte.

Hegel calls the Divine Essence the *Idea*, and explains it so as in reality to signify by the term the abstract concept of being. ,Thought and Being are one in his system. If he had said this of the Divine Nature distinct from and above the world, he would have been perfectly right. God is at once Infinite Being and Infinite Thought. What is thus true of God, Hegel affirms of the *Idea of Being*, under which our mind conceives whatever is and can be. This Idea of Being, as Hegel regards it, is something infinite, something generating within itself by natural evolution all finite things, opposed as they are to one another, and persevering in its own reality as the unity of these opposites.[68]

The basis of this theory is the fiction, that not the *singular*, but the *universal* is properly real. Hence it follows that as there is one concept which expresses the most universal object, *i.e., Being as such*, that concept must be the foundation of all reality, so much so, that all existing things are but determinations of abstract Being, evolving itself into finite beings opposed to one another. This fiction has its origin in the confusion of the real order of things with the ideal order ; in other words, in the confusion of the beings conceived by us with our way of conceiving them. Though our external and internal experience bears witness that there are many finite beings altogether distinct from one

[68] Cf. *Encyclopädie*, Band. i. §§ 79—82.

another, and though by reasoning we arrive at the knowledge of one Infinite Being, really existing apart from all finite beings, yet with our intellect we can abstract from all the differences between Finite and Infinite, and from all the differences between various finite beings, and come to consider whatever is, simply in so far as it is not nothing.

Thus we form one indeterminate concept of Being, applicable to all beings, however vast the difference between them. But from this abstraction producing the concept of universal Being, it does not follow that there is in reality one universal Being, of which all particular beings are modes or determinations. On the grounds which moved Hegel to maintain that all being is properly one being, we should have just as much right to say that all Englishmen are properly one Englishman, and that the English race dies out as often as an Englishman breathes his last, and nevertheless lives on as precisely the same Englishman in another shape.

127. The system of Schopenhauer, who takes the world to be the evolution of an underlying "will," and that of Hartmann, who makes the "unconscious" answerable for the multitude of creatures, exhibit the self-evolution of the First Cause in a form more offensive not only to Christian but also to human sentiment.

Another form of monistic error is the materialistic evolutionism according to which "material and mental groupings have gradually advanced from the simple to the complex, until the extraordinary complexity of the human brain and human thought processes have been reached."[69] Such hypotheses spring from erroneous opinions on the nature of intellect and causality, and they suppose the possibility of eternal succession. These subjects have been sufficiently dealt with, partly in the present volume and partly in other of the series.

The adherents of these various systems like to be called "monists," and they are wont to apply the name of God to their One Reality, into which they profess to resolve all existence. But the true name for them is "atheists," and we must protest against the practice of giving to the name of God a meaning distinct from that which it has hitherto borne, and even opposite to it in all that gives to the idea of God its special value as the basis of moral conduct and obligation.

SECTION 8.—*Aristotle's reasons for the necessity of eternal motion. Similar modern arguments from the writings of Kant and Cousin.*

128. Aristotle was a monotheist, but he did not understand the dependence of the universe upon the free-will of its Creator, and therefore fell into the error of advocating the necessity of eternal motion. By motion he means not only local change, but every change in bodies, and it is his opinion that God, the self-existent immoveable mover of all things, if He caused the existence of a universe in motion, must have caused it from eternity. In support of

[69] *Nature*, October 28, 1886. In a review of Sidgwick's *Outlines of Ethics*, by C. LL. M.

O

this position, Aristotle brings forward three arguments, of which the second and third are repeated in another form by Kant and Cousin.

129. His first argument is this :[70] Before a body can be changed, it must exist. But it cannot come into existence except in virtue of a change, and this change supposes another change, and so on to infinity in the past. Consequently matter has been changing from eternity.

Answer. Granting the major of the argument, we deny the minor. A changeable body can originate by creation out of nothing, a mode of origin which does not contain a process of *change*, as proved above. (Cf. Th. XIV. § 84.)

130. *Second Argument of Aristotle.*—Where time is, motion is. But time had no beginning; for every moment of time is the end of past and the beginning of future time. Consequently there was no first moment.

Answer. Again we have no objection to the major, but we must deny the minor. The truth underlying the statement made in the minor is this, that there must always have been *duration.* But there is a great difference between duration in general, and that special form of duration called *time.* Duration is a general term simply denoting persistency of existence. Time is a particular kind of duration of which the characteristic is *succession ;*

---

[70] We give here Aristotle's reasons in a compendious form. See the text in Aristotle's *Physics,* Lib. VIII. cc. i. vi. and St. Thomas in his commentary in Lib. VIII. *Physicorum,* Lect. 2, especially from n. 16 to the end, and Lect. 13, n. 8 towards the end.

a new phase of being ever succeeding in the place of another which ceases to be. Time, therefore, supposes things liable to change. So far as it signifies the common measure of the durations of transitory existences and actions in our globe, it is in reality nothing else but the continual rotation of the earth round its axis, which by the observing mind of mankind has been divided into its natural parts, each consisting of one day and one night, of which all our artificial divisions of time are either parts or multiples. From this it is evident that time must have had a beginning no less than succession, as we have shown above. (p. 146.) The only duration which must have been without beginning is the unceasing existence of the one infinite Godhead.

Bearing this in mind, we can meet the turn by which Aristotle tries to strengthen his second argument. He says: If there was a beginning of time, then there was no time before the first moment of time. But this cannot be allowed; for he who says "before" indicates time past. It is therefore impossible that time had a beginning.

The answer is this: You can only say "*before* the first moment of time," if you mean to use the phrase in reference to an *imaginary* backward prolongation of it, devised by the mind as an aid to language: or else it denotes only the eternal duration, the unchangeable persistency in existence of the Divine Being. Ordinarily speaking, the first of these alternatives is that which is actually present to the mind of the speaker who uses the expression "*before* the first moment of time," or "before the first moment of the existence of created things liable to changes."

Similar to that of Aristotle is the following reasoning of Kant: "Let us assume that it (the world) had a beginning. Then as beginning is an existence which is preceded by a time in which the thing is not, it would follow that antecedently there was a time in which the world was not, that is, an empty time. In an empty time, however, it is impossible that anything should have its beginning, because of such a time no part possesses any condition of existence or non-existence to distinguish it from another."[71] We answer, that empty time is no time. There was no real time before the beginning of the world. God alone existed, and made the beginning of time by creating the world. But God's duration is unchangeable eternity. Therefore the beginning of the world was preceded by eternity, not by time.

131. *Third Argument of Aristotle.*—The origin of all motion is ultimately due to God, the first absolutely unchangeable cause. But the first absolutely unchangeable cause cannot produce motion except from eternity to eternity: for otherwise He would undergo change Himself. It is therefore impossible that motion if existent should ever have had a commencement.

Answer. The proposition that a cause which continues unchanged cannot have an effect *now*, unless it has had the same effect *before* and will

[71] Cf. Kant's *Critique of Pure Reason*, by M. Müller, Vol. II. p. 369.

have it *afterwards*, holds good only on the supposition that the cause produces its effect by natural necessity. It is in no way applicable to God, who calls His creatures into existence by an eternal free decree of His will, and by the same decree determines the limits of their existence and motion, both in time and manner. We have already suggested as a help to realize this compatibility of the creative exercise of Divine free-will with the non-eternity of the effects, the analogy of the relation of the exercise of the human free-will to its effects in the moral order. The decrees of the sovereign, though all made together, come into effect at various times, some sooner, others later. There is no need of any contemporaneousness between the commencement of the effects and the determinations of sovereign will by which they are caused. We do not propose this illustration as an argument, but rather as an analogy which enables the mind to conceive to itself under some concrete form the mode of action which we are led by due course of reasoning to attribute to the Divine exercise of free-will. From this illustration we are entitled to gather at least this much, that, if the Divine will is able to produce physical realities of itself, by its sheer exercise, and if the decree of that will persists unchangeable, as it was conceived from eternity, then no further difficulty arises from the non-contemporaneousness of the commencement of the effect with a corresponding commencement of the Divine decree which is its cause.[72]

[72] Cf. pp. 138, seq.

That the Divine will is thus effective, we prove from the infinity of the Divine Nature.

With the argument of Aristotle may be compared the assertion of Victor Cousin, that God is the one absolute and infinite substance, and as such is essentially a cause. Consequently, argues this author, He cannot abstain from producing effects.[73]

To this our reply is, that God is essentially a cause only inasmuch as by virtue of His essence He *can* cause, but not as though His essence determined Him *irresistibly* to create finite things. As we have proved in the fourth chapter, God chose freely from eternity the act of creation, being able not to choose it. And as He has chosen the act itself, so He has freely fixed the moment of the beginning of His creatures.

SECTION 9.—*Mansel's arguments for the doctrine that all our attempts to form to ourselves the idea of God involve us in contradiction.*

132. Among the defenders of the groundwork of Christian faith against atheism in England some twenty or thirty years ago, not the least conspicuous was Dean Mansel. His *Limits of Religious Thought* went though several editions. There is a great deal of valuable matter in the work, entitling the author to be regarded as one who has in some respects done good service. Yet it is to be regretted that some passages betray a want of sound principles, and contain statements

[73] Cf. Cousin, *Cours de 1828*, Leçon v. p. 26.

which in the hands of an acute adversary can serve as weapons for attacking the very cause they are meant to uphold. They have been taken advantage of by Mr. Herbert Spencer in his advocacy of agnosticism.

Mansel's work consists of eight lectures. In the second of these he tries to prove that when we compare the attributes of God one with another, though each of them seems to be brought home to us by lawful reasoning, yet our intellect cannot help seeing contradictions between them. At the same time he is of opinion that man has sufficient grounds for ignoring these contradictions, and for supposing that they are not *objective* but only *subjective*, owing to the weakness and ineptitude of our minds for dealing with a Being so immense as God. This is the escape by which he saves his religious convictions, as he declares in the third lecture.

His final conclusion he states as follows: "It is our duty, then, to think of God as personal; and it is our duty to believe that He is infinite. It is true that we cannot reconcile these two representations with each other; as our conception of personality involves attributes apparently contradictory to the notion of infinity. But it does not follow that this contradiction exists anywhere but in our own minds; it does not follow that it implies any impossibility in the absolute nature of God. The apparent contradiction, in this case, as in those previously noticed, is the necessary consequence of an attempt on the part of the human thinker to transcend the boundaries of his own consciousness." [74] Mr. Herbert Spencer, after giving in his second and fourth chapters on the Unknowable long extracts from Mansel's argument, refers in his fifth chapter to Mansel's conclusion in the following terms: "That this is not the conclusion here adopted, needs hardly be said. If there be any meaning in the foregoing arguments, duty requires us neither to affirm nor deny personality. Our duty is to submit ourselves with all humility to the established limits of our intelligence, and not perversely to rebel against them. Let those, who can, believe that there is eternal war set between our intellectual faculties and our moral obligations. I, for one, admit no such radical vice in the constitution of things." [75]

The "eternal war" and the "radical vice," of which Mr. Spencer speaks here, are certainly to be deprecated by any reasonable man. But is either the one or the other a necessary consequence of true monotheism? Let us judge for ourselves by examination of the extracts from Mansel to which Mr. Spencer appeals.

133. Mansel thus reasons about the metaphysical idea of the Infinite: "The metaphysical representations of the Deity, as absolute and infinite, must necessarily, as the profoundest metaphysicians have acknowledged, amount to nothing less than the sum of all reality. 'What kind of an absolute Being is that,' says Hegel, 'which does not contain in itself all that is actual, even evil included?' We

---

[74] *Limits of Religious Thought* (Third Edition), p. 89.
[75] *First Principles*, p. 108.

may repudiate the conclusion with indignation; but the reasoning is unassailable. If the Absolute and Infinite is an object of human conception at all, this, and none other, is the conception required. That which is conceived as absolute and infinite must be conceived as containing within itself the sum, not only of all actual, but of all possible modes of being. For if any actual mode can be denied of it, it is related to that mode, and limited by it; and if any possible mode can be denied of it, it is capable of becoming more than it now is, and such a capability is a limitation."[76] Mr. Spencer seems to suppose that against this explanation of the notion of the Infinite nothing can be said; yet there is everything to be said against it. It is not true that the Absolute and Infinite Being must contain whatever is actual, and whatever mode of being is possible. In so far as that which is actual contains an imperfection, and *a fortiori* in so far as it contains a privation, it cannot possibly be conceived as belonging to the Infinite: for the Infinite is an embodiment of all perfections without admixture of imperfection. Created perfections exist in God, as we have explained, not *formally* with their limitations, but *eminently* as in one undivided unchangeable Essence. If the perfections of creatures are in God without limit, they are in Him certainly without the presence of any evil whatsoever, for evil is more opposed to perfection than mere limitation; it is a privation of the perfection that is *due* to a being. To say with Mansel that the exclusion

[76] *Limits of Religious Thought* (Third Edition), p. 46.

of any possible mode of existence from the Infinite would be to put a limit to its nature, is against reason. There is no possible mode of created existence without limit, because, as we have proved, only one Being unlimited in perfection is possible. Consequently, not merely one or another possible modes of created existence, but all possible modes of created existence, must, *as such*, be alien to the Divine Being. Nevertheless, as we have shown in treating of the Infinity of God, whilst the modes with which created perfections exist cannot be in God, the reality expressed by the abstract concept of each perfection is in the most proper sense of the word included in His simple and infinite Essence. Creatures are distinct from this Essence, but put no limit to it, because their nature is infinitely below the Divine Nature. Created beauty does not suffer in any way from its being represented by artists, now in stone, now in metal, now on canvas; because all these representations are only imperfect imitations of the original. How, then, should God cease to be infinite by being distinguished from a multitude of creatures, each of which is only a very imperfect copy of His simple Being, though it may excel among its fellow-creatures?

134. Another argument of Mansel against the intelligibility of the First Cause is based upon a comparison of the idea of Cause with that of the Absolute. Both must be predicated of God, and yet they seem to exclude one another. "A Cause," says he, "cannot, as such, be absolute: the Absolute cannot, as such, be a cause. The cause, as such, exists only in

relation to its effect : the cause is a cause of the effect ; the effect is an effect of the cause. On the other hand, the conception of the Absolute implies a possible existence out of all relation. We attempt to escape from this apparent contradiction, by introducing the idea of succession in time. The Absolute exists first by itself, and afterwards becomes a Cause. But here we are checked by the third conception, that of the Infinite. How can the Infinite become that which it was not from the first ? If causation is a possible mode of existence, that which exists without causing is not infinite ; that which becomes a cause has passed beyond its former limits." [77]

To the first part of this argument, we concede that a cause cannot be absolute, if it causes under the pressure of necessity; for in this case the existence of the cause is dependent on the existence of its effect, inasmuch as it requires it as its essential complement. Nor can it be absolute and infinite, if it does not produce an effect without undergoing internal change. But there is no reason for saying that the nature of a Being cannot be an absolute and infinite cause, if its causation is both free and conducted without any internal change. The possibility of such a way of causation is, as we have already urged, not only not opposed to the Divine attributes of Absoluteness and Infinity, but is a necessary consequence of them. God being absolute and infinite, must be infinitely powerful, infinitely free in His volition regarding the existence of

[77] *Limits of Religious Thought* (Third Edition), p. 47.

creatures, and at the same time immutable. His causation is consequently a free act of His will, which, on account of its infinity, is capable of such an act without being changed. Such causation is *incomprehensible*, but it is not *inconceivable*. We know perfectly what we mean by asserting it, and we see clear reasons for asserting it, though on account of our finite nature we cannot fathom the manner in which it exists.

135. The proposition, that our mind sees contradiction between God as a Cause and God as Absolute, is argued by Mansel also in another way. Supposing rightly that creation must be thought of as an effect of God's free volition, he says: "Volition is only possible in a conscious being. But consciousness again is only conceivable as a relation. There must be a conscious subject and an object of which he is conscious. The subject is a subject to the object; the object is an object to the subject; and neither can exist by itself as the absolute. This difficulty, again, may be for the moment evaded, by distinguishing between the Absolute as related to another and the Absolute as related to itself. The Absolute, it may be said, may possibly be conscious, provided it is only conscious of itself. But this alternative is, in ultimate analysis, no less self-destructive than the other. For the object of consciousness, whether a mode of the subject's existence or not, is either created in and by the act of consciousness, or has an existence independent of it. In the former case, the object depends upon the subject, and the subject alone is the true

absolute. In the latter case, the subject depends upon the object, and the object alone is the true absolute. Or if we attempt a third hypothesis, and maintain that each exists independently of the other, we have no absolute at all, but only a pair of relatives; for co-existence, whether in conscious-ness or not, is itself a relation."[78]

This whole argument is based upon a wrong hypothesis regarding the nature of knowledge. Mansel, like many modern authors, labours under the false impression that knowledge essentially supposes a plurality of terms; and that consequently no knowledge is possible, unless there exist a subject knowing and an object known, really distinct from one another. This is true of sense perception only; it cannot be applied to intellectual self-consciousness. If you apply it to the latter, you never can explain how a man knows that he exists and thinks and wills. An intellectual being is spiritual, and of such a nature that it cannot know anything different from itself without knowing itself as the knowing principle. In so far, therefore, as we apprehend ourselves as thinking principles in all acts of our intelligence, we are at the same time subject and object of our knowledge. Now God, the Absolute, Infinite, unchangeable Being, does not only know that He knows, but He is *essentially* a Being knowing Himself. There is no real difference between His Essence and the act of His self-consciousness.

In answer, therefore, to Mansel's difficulty, we deny that his three hypotheses to explain the

[78] *Limits of Religious Thought* (Third Edition), pp. 48, 49.

self-corsciousness of the Absolute exhaust the possibilities of the case. He has left out precisely
that alternative against which no solid reason 'can
be brought forward, and which is an evident consequence of the infinity of God. God does not
know Himself by creating a mode of existence in
His Essence, or by having such a mode really
distinct from His Essence in Himself. He knows
Himself in virtue of His Essence alone, which is
both infinite Being and infinite Thought, the one
not really distinct from the other.

136. In the simplicity of God, Mansel finds
another source of apparent contradiction in the
Divine attributes. "The almost unanimous voice
of Philosophy," he says, "in pronouncing that the
Absolute is both one and simple, must be accepted
as the voice of reason also, so far as reason has any
voice in the matter. But this absolute unity, as
indifferent and containing no attributes, can neither
be distinguished from the multiplicity of finite
beings by any characteristic feature, nor be identified
with them in their multiplicity." [79]

This argument proceeds from a wrong conception of God's simplicity. God is not one and
simple in this sense, that He is an indeterminate
substratum underlying all existences; but He is
one and simple inasmuch as His Essence in virtue
of its self-existence contains without division and
composition, equivalently and supereminently, all
conceivable perfections.

137. Not less unsound than the preceding argu-

[79] *Limits of Religious Thought* (Third Edition), p. 50.

ments are those by which Mansel labours to show a contradiction between other Divine attributes. " How," says he, " can Infinite Power be able to do all things, and yet Infinite Goodness be unable to do evil ? " This difficulty falls to the ground when we consider that omnipotence does not mean infinite liability to defects, but infinite power of calling into being any conceivable reality, not in the omnipotent Being itself, but distinct from and dependent upon it. He who commits sin allows himself to be over-come by wrong motives of action. The malice of sin does not consist in the production of a physical effect, but in the voluntary neglect of a rule of conduct which reason prescribes as inviolable. The question, therefore, " How can God be omnipotent if He cannot sin ? " betrays either a wrong notion of omnipotence or a wrong notion of sin.

Mansel's next question is: " How can Infinite Justice exact the utmost penalty for every sin, and yet Infinite Mercy pardon the sinner ? " We may allow this question to stand over till we come to treat of the Divine will. A right conception of justice and mercy in God will put an end to the difficulty.

Our author proceeds: " How can Infinite Wisdom know all that is to come, and yet Infinite Freedom be at liberty to do and to forbear ? "

To this we reply: God's free decrees are as eternal as His knowledge of the future. Whatever He freely does or forbears to do in time, that He does or forbears to do, not in consequence of a new decree, but in harmony with His eternal decrees.

The rest of Mansel's reasonings are virtually

solved by the preceding answers. The most important among them is the old difficulty against
God's perfection drawn from the existence of evil.
This difficulty deserves a special treatment, which
it will receive in our disquisition on Divine Providence.

138. After having dwelt in his second lecture on
the contradictions contained in the idea of God,
Mansel in the third tries to explain their origin.
As a believer in Christian revelation, he endeavours
to show that they are a necessary consequence of
the limitations of our human understanding, and
ought not, therefore, to be assumed to have objective
validity. If, however, it is possible that the contradictions may not really exist, it is worth inquiring
whether we can find any grounds for believing that
they do or do not. From the position thus taken
up he passes afterwards to the conclusion that the
belief in God, as He is revealed to us by Christ and
His Apostles, may, in spite of all contradictions
enumerated before, find a reasonable foundation
in the positive evidences by which it recommends
itself to the needs of our nature. Following this
line of argument, he has drawn down on himself
a storm of agnostic criticism, against which his
idealistic theory of knowledge leaves him no defence.

The argument by which this theory is supported,
and which consequently is the second chief proof
of the impossibility of conceiving the Infinite and
Absolute, rests upon the relativity of human knowledge. "To have consciousness of the Absolute as
such," says Mansel, "we must know that an object,

which is given in relation to our consciousness, is identical with one which exists in its own nature, out of all relation to consciousness. But to know this identity we must be able to compare the two together; and such a comparison is itself a contradiction. We are, in fact, required to compare that of which we are conscious with that of which we are not conscious; the comparison itself being an act of consciousness, and only possible through the consciousness of both its objects. It is thus manifest that, even if we could be conscious of the absolute, we could not possibly know that it *is* the absolute; and, as we can be conscious of an object as such only by knowing it to be what it is, this is equivalent to an admission that we cannot be conscious of the absolute at all. As an object of consciousness, everything is necessarily relative; and what a thing may be out of consciousness no mode of consciousness can tell us." [80]

This argument proves too much. We might conclude from it that Mansel could not be conscious of the paper on which he was writing his lectures, of the audience before whom he delivered them, and of the existence of atheists, of whose impiety he complains. All these things were known to him only as related to his consciousness; and his consciousness being in its real existence limited to his individual soul, he could not possibly know whether beyond his consciousness there was any paper to write on, or any persons to talk to, or any adversaries to fight against. All may have

[80] *Limits of Religious Thought* (Third Edition), pp. 74, 75.

P

been a part-creation of consciousness deceiving itself with idle phantoms. But this conclusion is revolting to common sense, and leads to universal scepticism.

139. A third reason why Mansel thinks it impossible for man to form a positive idea of God is expressed thus : " It is impossible that man, so long as he exists in time, should contemplate an object in whose existence there is no time. For the thought by which he contemplates it must be one of his mental states; it must have a beginning and an end : it must occupy a certain portion of duration as a fact of human consciousness. There is, therefore, no manner of resemblance or community of nature between the representative thought and that which it is supposed to represent ; for the one cannot exist out of time, and the other cannot exist in it." [81] If Mansel merely meant to say that a temporal being could not have a *comprehensive* knowledge of an eternal being, this is manifest from the diversity of nature between the two.[82] But he means more than this ; he means that a temporal being can form no distinct trustworthy notion whatever of an eternal being. We can reply that our proofs do not lead up to a *comprehension* of the eternity of God, but they make us sure of the existence of God as an eternal Being, inasmuch as we have a clear and distinct, though inadequate, concept of this Being as an Infinite Substance, existing without beginning

[81] *Limits of Religious Thought* (Third Edition), p. 81.
[82] St. Thomas, *Sum. Theol.* i. 12. 4.

and without end, and without any change in the way of its existence.

140. A similar answer must be given to the last reason by which Mansel endeavours to prove the purely negative character of our idea of God. He says rightly that we can conceive the various mental attributes of God only as existing in a personal being. "But," he continues, "personality, as we conceive it, is essentially a limitation and relation. Our own personality is presented to us as relative and limited, and it is from that presentation that all our representative notions of personality are derived. Personality is presented to us as a relation between the conscious self and the various modes of his consciousness. There is no personality in abstract thought without a thinker; there is no thinker, unless he exercises some mode of thought. Personality is also a limitation; for the thought and the thinker are distinguished from and limit each other; and the several modes of thought are distinguished each from each by limitation likewise. If I am any one of my own thoughts, I live and die with each successive moment of my consciousness. If I am not any one of my own thoughts, I am limited by that very difference, and each thought as different from another is limited also. This too has been clearly seen by philosophical theologians; and accordingly, they have maintained that in God there is no distinction between the subject of con-sciousness and its modes, nor between one mode and another. 'God,' says St. Augustine, 'is not a Spirit as regards substance, and good as regards

quality; but both as regards substance. The justice
of God is one with His goodness and with His
blessedness; and all are one with His spirituality.'
But this assertion, if it be literally true (and we have
no means of judging), annihilates personality itself
in the only form in which we can conceive it. We
cannot transcend our own personality, as we cannot
transcend our own relation to time; and to speak of
an Absolute and Infinite Person, is simply to use
language which, however true it may be in a superhuman sense, denotes an object inconceivable under
the conditions of human thought."[83]

In this passage Mansel himself carries us so far
on the way as this, that if there be no distinction in
God between the conscious self and the modes of
consciousness, as again between the modes of consciousness among themselves, there is no foundation
for conceiving of His Nature as in this particular
respect implicated in relations and limitations.
And although he says here that we have no means
of judging whether this absence of internal distinctions really exists in God, he has previously
remarked with much justice, in words already
quoted, that "the unanimous voice of Philosophy,
in pronouncing that the absolute is both one and
simple, must be accepted as the voice of reason
also, so far as reason has any voice in the matter."
Nor can the qualification in the last clause be
allowed to explain away the force of this admission.
If reason is to have a voice in creating the contradictions, she has certainly a claim to be heard when

[83] Mansel's *Limits of Religious Thought,* pp. 84, 85.

she represents that the contradictions are not really of her creating, but arise from a misconception of the true nature of her utterances.

There remains then but one outstanding point in Mr. Mansel's passage to be considered. Do we by identifying in God the conscious self and the modes of consciousness, "annihilate personality in the only sense in which we can conceive it"? This depends on the sense in which we do conceive it. Speaking in the name of Catholic Philosophy and repeating the utterance of all true thought and self-introspection, we understand by personality the "subsistence of a rational nature." Let us explain this technical term. Subsistence is what characterizes the existence of a natural whole as distinguished from the existence characteristic of the component parts of a natural whole. The arm of a man exists not in itself, but in the man, as a part in the whole; so also does the body, and so again does the soul, though here one has to speak more carefully, the soul being able to exist apart and exercise by itself the principal functions of the whole. On the other hand, the man exists in himself and in nothing else as in a containing whole that is, in a containing *natural* whole, for of course things can be taken together as component parts of a system of aggregates like the universe. For anything to subsist then is to exist in itself and not as a natural part of something else. Personality we have defined to be subsistence of a rational nature. That is to say, when the being which subsists has a rational nature and therewith consciousness, we call it a

person, and its subsistence personality. Accordingly,
when we say that God is a personal God, we mean
that He exists in Himself and not as a part of some
whole, and that He possesses Mind and Consciousness. This is the only concept of Personality we
can consent to deal with, when we claim it for
God. We cannot accept the description given by
Dr. Mansel, that personality is merely a "relation
between the conscious self and the modes of his
consciousness."

Do we, then, virtually deny the personality of
God in the only form in which we can conceive it,
when we deny of Him relation and limitation by
asserting that the perfections which we represent
to ourselves by distinct concepts as His attributes
and modes are objectively in Him as a single and
absolutely simple reality? Clearly not. It is true,
we do not attribute to Him the perfections which
we find in ourselves as existing in Him in the
same "formal" manner as they are in us, just
because in us they are characterized by attendant
imperfections and limitations. We take the perfections found in ourselves as a nucleus; we divest
it of its accompanying imperfections and limitations
by an act of negation; we then enlarge the measure
of the perfection to infinity by affirming that not
only those limits are excluded from it which are
inseparable from human perfection, but all limits
whatsoever. In this way out of the original nucleus
furnished by direct observation we form to ourselves
by affirmation and negation a composite concept,
and then led by just inference we proceed to take

this as a valid and valuable though inadequate representation of the Divine Nature under some one or other of its aspects. This doctrine has already been propounded. But no apology is needed for the repetition, since the failure to bear it in mind lies at the root of the imagined contradictions which form the unsolved problem of Dr. Mansel's philosophy.

Let us now apply the doctrine explained to the point immediately under consideration. Although personality is not consciousness, yet, as we have stated, it implies consciousness as an attribute of the person, and it is the nature of consciousness which Mansel considers to involve an essential relation and limitation. That there is any real relation and consequent mutual limitation between the subject and object of consciousness—inasmuch as intellectual consciousness comes under consideration—we have denied even in regard to our own created consciousness, maintaining on the contrary that in consciousness the subject and object are essentially one. But there is in man the distinction, with its admitted consequences of relation and mutual limitation, between the self-conscious subject and the modes of his consciousness, and again between the latter among themselves. This distinction appears, therefore, in the original concept which we form to ourselves of consciousness. It appears then, however, only as incidental, not as the central and direct element in the concept. This central element, therefore, we can take as a nucleus, since· *in itself* it is pure perfection. We then by negation and affirmation represent to ourselves a consciousness which is realized not by the passage of the subject from the potential into the actual state, but is ever actual: a consciousness which embraces in its vision the entire being of the subject; a consciousness which is not realized by even an abiding act distinct from the conscious subject itself, but is realized inasmuch as the subject is in virtue of its infinity Infinite Consciousness as well as Infinite Being.

Thus, then, we arrive at an inadequate indeed, but nevertheless a distinct and true, idea of God, an idea not purely negative, but *negativo-positive.* And thus, for all the apparent contradictions in the monotheistic idea of God, which Mr. Spencer has drawn from Mansel's famous work, it remains true that " we adore that which we know."[84]

[84] St. John iv. 22.

NATURAL THEOLOGY.

Book II.
The Divine Attributes.

PROLEGOMENA.

141. The origin of the universe, though neither an object of immediate intuition nor of pure *a priori* demonstration, is nevertheless knowable ; and that, not on authority only, but also by reason.

From the causality of things surrounding us, from the thoughts and volitions of our own mind, from the orderly arrangements visible everywhere in Nature, from the universal belief of mankind in some sort of Deity, and finally from the logical consequences of atheism and agnosticism, we arrive by lawful reasoning at the conclusion that the universe is not an effect of the forces of matter, nor of the evolution of some Unknowable being, but has started into existence at the will of a self-existing Mind, through the power of a personal God, whose Essence is one, simple, infinite, and who is the cause of all finite things, not by self-evolution, as pantheists would have it, but by creation out of nothing. His decree to create was a free act, and had no beginning; but there is nothing to prove that the effect of that decree must have been without beginning. On the contrary, creation from eternity is hardly admissible, even if its absolute impossibility is not demonstrable. Moreover, as regards the existence of the universe known to us, we have in its changes and generations an evident proof of its limited duration, and in this its limited duration an additional argument for its dependence upon the good pleasure of the one, infinite, personal God.

These are, in short, the conclusions proved and defended in the previous book. We now pass on to the further and fuller investigation of the nature of the attributes of God. The basis on which throughout we shall have to build is the doctrine of the Divine Infinity, which itself rests on the doctrine of the Divine Unity and Simplicity. In carrying it out we shall be guided by the three canons of Divine attributes laid down already. (§§ 70—72 inclus.)

According to these canons those names of created perfections must be predicated of God, the meaning of which by abstraction and total denial of limits can be conceived without their implying any imperfection. They cannot indeed be predicated of God and of creatures univocally, but they can analogically, as we have explained in the place just referred to. We have also seen that names of created perfections which necessarily connote imperfection, cannot be predicated of God save in a metaphorical sense.

142. It may be interesting to note how these canons were expressed by the ancient writer who

goes under the name of St. Dionysius the Areopagite.
Among his works there is one, *De Divinis Nomi-*
nibus, held in high esteem during the middle ages,
and explained by St. Thomas.

In this book the attributes of God are said to be
established in three ways, which are named, the way
of *removal*, the way of *affirmation*, the way of *eminence*.

(1) *The way of removal we may call also the way*
of negation.—By this way what are termed the
negative Divine attributes are found. We "remove"
from God in thought any name of created perfection,
the meaning of which cannot be conceived in the
abstract without connoting a defect. Thus we say,
by the way of removal, that God is *incorporeal, i.e.*,
cannot be formally extended according to three
dimensions; that He is *simple, i.e.*, not composed of
parts; that He is *immutable, i.e.*, cannot pass from
one state of existence to another. These negative
attributes, whilst explicitly denying certain imperfections of created beings to exist in God, affirm
thereby implicitly the opposite perfections to be in
Him.

(2) *The way of affirmation.*—By this is predicated
of God whatever created perfection can be conceived
in the abstract without connotation of imperfection.
Thus we state that God is *powerful, wise, truthful,*
benevolent, &c. Power, wisdom, veracity, benevolence, are perfections conceivable without necessarily connoting a defect. In affirming them of
God we must however be on our guard not to apply
to Him the limitations encompassing their abstract
meaning, in so far as the latter is verified in

creatures. The expedient open to us in order to guard ourselves against this error is called,

(3) *The way of eminence.*—We have recourse to this way when we affirm positive attributes of God in such sort as to deny at the same time that the perfection affirmed is limited in Him. Thus we say by way of eminence that God's wisdom, power, goodness, benevolence, are boundless or infinite.

143. We have also to bear in mind the mutual relations of the attributes among themselves before we can thoroughly grasp the explanation to be given of them. In treating of the Divine simplicity (§§ 61—64 inclus.) we have seen that God is not only physically simple but also metaphysically, which means that no two concepts can be formed of His Essence without the one overlapping the other. Consequently, as the physical simplicity of God forbids us to admit accidental perfections in Him (§ 61), the significations of any two Divine attributes must implicitly cover one another. From this it does not, however, follow that the names of different attributes of God convey the same knowledge to our mind. The term, "Divine Mercy," differs explicitly in its meaning from that of "Divine Justice." We say, therefore, that both attributes (and the same holds good of any two Divine attributes taken together), are distinct from one another *metaphysically*, though they do not combine in *metaphysical composition*. They express the idea of One Incomprehensible God inadequately under different aspects. For this reason St. Thomas well says that the names of God are not "synonymous." "Though the names given

to God signify the same thing, yet they signify it under many different mental aspects, and consequently are not synonymous," for "those words are said to be synonymous which signify one and the same thing from the same point of view."[1]

144. We now proceed to treat of the Divine attributes in particular, developing more fully what has been established in the first book.

In the second chapter of that book we proved that there exists a self-existent, intelligent Being, righty called a personal God; and in the third chapter we demonstrated that unity, simplicity, and infinity are proper to Him. These fundamental truths are the basis upon which our further speculations on the Divine attributes must rest. Having established that God is infinitely perfect, we see at once that we are to deny of Him whatever attribute necessarily involves an imperfection, and to affirm whatever attribute can be conceived without connotation of a defect. Consequently, the Divine attributes are partly negative, partly positive. We shall treat in the three first chapters respectively of God's immutability, eternity, immensity; in the next three, of His infinite knowledge, His infinitely perfect will, and His infinite power. After this we shall add a special chapter on the metaphysical essence of God. Since the chapters on the knowledge and will of God are of higher importance than the rest, we shall treat of them at greater length.

---

[1] St. Thomas, *Sum. Theol.* i. 13, 4. "Nomina Deo attributa, licet significent unam rem, tamen quia significant eam sub rationibus multis et diversis non sunt synonyma." . . . "Nomina synonyma dicuntur quæ significant unum secundum unam rationum."

CHAPTER I.

Thesis XXII.—*The Divine Being is absolutely immutable.*

145. Change is a passing from one state of being to another. If a thing passes from one species to another, it is said to be *substantially* changed. Thus, according to the scholastic view, oxygen and hydrogen change substantially when transformed into water. Food is changed substantially by assimilation into a living body. If the specific being of the thing is not affected, the change is called *accidental*. Instances of accidental change are mechanical motion in a body; in a living being, growth and sensation; in a human mind, a new set of thoughts and volitions.

God is not liable to any of these changes. This truth some scholastic authors express by saying that God is *physically immutable*. They distinguish between *physical* and *moral* mutability, understanding by the former a liability to change of physical *being*, by the latter a liability to change of *will*. Thus men are morally mutable, because they can form new resolutions, and abandon those previously adopted. In human beings such a moral change cannot go on without a physical change accompanying it; but it is not *immediately* evident that every moral change of God would also be a physical change. The infinite Being is adequately sufficient to choose and not to choose from eternity, as we have explained in the chapter on creation. Why, then, should He not be able to choose at one time one thing, at another another, without change in His Being? Why must He be not only physically, but also morally unchangeable? This question we shall treat of in the chapter on the perfection of God's will. For the present we are only concerned about proving that the *Being* of God cannot be changed in any way.

146. In proof of this we appeal first to God's *simplicity*.

By every change a thing must either lose or acquire some quality or affection of its being. On the former supposition, it must consist of at least two really distinct realities before it changes; otherwise it would lose nothing. On the latter, it is composed of at least two distinct realities after the change. In neither case can it be a necessarily simple Being. But, as we have shown (Th. VIII. §§ 61, seq.), God is necessarily simple to the exclusion of all real and even of all virtual composition. Consequently He must be absolutely unchangeable.

The same conclusion may be drawn from the *infinite perfection* of God. As has been proved above (Th. IX. §§ 65, seq.), God is infinitely perfect. But evidently He could not be so if He were liable to any change; for by this He must either become more or less good. If we take the first alternative, and suppose Him to be bettered by the change, He could not have been infinite before it. The other alternative is still more obviously untenable. If He became less good by the change, His infinity would evidently cease to be.

147. It is, indeed, very difficult to see how the immutability of God thus proved can be consistent with His supreme freedom of choice, but we shall treat of this subject in the chapter on the Divine will. Here we shall merely call attention to the difficulties which arise from the fact of creation and the revealed mystery of the Incarnation.

(1) *Difficulty.*—God of His own free choice created the world out of nothing. He was not necessitated to create it, and if He had not done so, He would not be the Creator. Consequently the attribute *Creator* has been added to His Being. But it could not be added without causing a change. Therefore God has undergone a change.

Answer. To solve this difficulty, we are to explain what is meant by the statement, *God created the world.* It means that God by an eternal free decree resolved to produce the world out of nothing, and fixed the moments of its commencement and the term of its duration. He then in harmony with that decree originated it by His infinite power. Both the decree of creation and the power by which it was executed are truly in God, but not as entities really distinct from His Essence. His Essence is infinite, and in virtue of its infinity is sufficient for forming and executing any decree without internal change. From this it follows that the attribute *Creator* is not an intrinsic denomination signifying some intrinsic affection or state accruing .to the Essence of God, but an extrinsic denomination, signifying the dependence of the world on God as regards its origin.

The same must be said of the attributes, *Preserver of all things, Ruler of the universe*, and the like. They are extrinsic denominations signifying different respects under which creatures depend upon God's will and power.

The difficulty, then, is solved by denying the statement that the attribute of *Creator* has been *added* to the Being of God. The truth is, that by creation God has produced things outside Himself, and from this production, by which in Himself He is in nothing changed, God is extrinsically denominated *the Creator*.

(2) *Difficulty.*—Any difficulty drawn from the mystery of the Incarnation, strictly speaking, has no place in a philosophical treatise. Still it is convenient to give it a place, as it is one likely to occur to the minds of readers. The Son of God, who is really one Being with the Divine Essence, became Man at a definite moment of time. Since that moment He has had not only a Divine Nature, but also a Human one. But it would seem that the union of a Human Nature with a Divine Person could not be accomplished without a change in the latter.

The answer to the difficulty is that the infinite.

Q

God does not need any self-adaptation for any work which He pleases to perform. Consequently the Son of God needed not to adapt Himself for the assumption of a human nature. Without change of Himself, He was able to assume humanity at any moment, on the supposition that a human nature existed in such a state as to be fit for assumption by the Divine Person. Consequently the mystery of the Incarnation neither denotes nor connotes any change in the Son of God; but it denotes the creation of a particular human nature supernaturally raised to union with the Second Person of the Blessed Trinity, and it connotes the absence of human personality in that nature, on account of its being taken up into the personality of the Son. It was not, so to speak, the Divinity moving towards the Humanity, but the Humanity moving towards the Divinity.

CHAPTER II.

Thesis XXIII.—*God is eternal in the strict sense of the word.*

148. The word "eternal" taken in a wider sense signifies endless existence, though that existence may have a beginning, and may run through various successive phases. Thus, the life of men after the day of the general resurrection will be eternal, though not without successive mental acts and bodily movements. It is called eternal simply because it will never cease.

In its strict sense the word *eternity* implies an existence which is *essentially* without beginning and without end, and without any successive phases of being. We beg the reader not to overlook in this definition the word *essentially*. If we imagine a spirit created by God from eternity, and preserved by His infinite power for ever without any internal change, the existence of such a spirit would be indeed without beginning and end, and without successive phases of being, but it would not be eternal in the strict sense of the word. And why not? Because the essence of that spirit would have no existence of itself, but would be indebted for its existence and its boundless duration to the free choice of the omnipotent God.

From the definition of eternity just given it is evident that the term, if predicable at all in its strict sense, is predicable of God alone. No creature can be *essentially* without beginning and end and internal succession. Not essentially without beginning, for there is no reason why any creature must be created from eternity. Not essentially without end, for God may withdraw from the creature His preserving power. Not essentially without internal succession, for at least the infinite power of God can cause in it a new phase of existence.

149. Is then God Himself eternal in the strict sense of the word ? Yes ; because as the First Cause, and the only source of all possible being, He must exist with absolute necessity, and therefore can have no beginning. Absolute necessity of existence must be identical with His essence, on account of His simplicity, which we have proved to be not only physical but metaphysical (Th. VIII. § 61, seq.); and therefore it is impossible that He should cease to be. His existence is unchangeable (Th. XXII.); therefore it cannot contain any different successive phases or modes of being.

Boëthius, who flourished about A.D. 500, in his work, *De Consolatione Philosophiæ*, thus defines eternity:[1] "Eternity is a simultaneously full and perfect possession of interminable life." What in

---

[1] "Æternitas est interminabilis vitæ tota simul et perfecta possessio." (V. Prosa vi.)

our definition was implied by the terms "existence essentially without beginning and without end," is expressed by Boëthius more explicitly in the phrase, "possession of interminable life." Indeed, as eternity proper belongs to God alone, it is identified with the highest life conceivable, the self-activity of infinite Intellectual Will. This life is "interminable," or boundless, because it endures of absolute necessity. It is "simultaneously possessed" in its fulness and perfection, because, being infinite, it is neither capable of development nor liable to defect. As it is now, so it has been always in the past, and will be always in the future. Coexisting with all assignable moments of time, the eternal God is above any of our measures of the contingent duration of created being. In Him, therefore, is neither present, nor past, nor future. As Boëthius expresses it, *Nunc fluens facit tempus, nunc stans facit æternitatem*—" The *passing now* makes time, the *standing now* makes eternity."[2] In other words, the duration proper to the eternal Being must be conceived as one everlasting state, whereas the duration of temporal being is liable to a succession of states really distinct from one another.

150. Between temporal and eternal duration there is a duration intermediate, which, for the sake of distinction, is called by the scholastics, *æviternal* duration, or *ævum*. It is the duration of created spirits. Both *time* and *ævum* are contingent durations, dependent upon the free-will of the one eternal Being. But while *time* is

[2] *De Trin.* c. iv.

made up of successive states or phases of being, *ævum* does not imply any succession. A created spirit may be annihilated, but the specific spiritual being proper to it cannot be changed; consequently there is no succession in it, as regards its substantial perfection. Nevertheless, spirits are not quite above time, or succession of states in their existence; for, though the specific perfection of their substantial being is unalterable, they can still pass from one thought and volition to another, and the Creator may cause in them now one, now another accidental perfection. Their essential being is above time, but they are liable to accidental modification of temporary duration. The duration, called *time*, belongs most properly to matter, which changes as well in its substantial as its accidental perfection.

St. Thomas expresses the difference between time, *ævum*, and eternity briefly in this way : "*Time* has an 'earlier' and a 'later'; *ævum* has no 'earlier' and 'later' in itself, but both can be connected with it; *eternity* has neither an 'earlier' nor a 'later,' nor can they be connected with it."[3]

In other words : *Time* is made up of a series of changes in a substantial stratum, or in the accidental state of a complete substance; *Ævum* is not itself a series of either substantial or accidental changes, but in the finite incorruptible substance, of which it is the duration, there may be accidental changes;

---

[3] "Tempus habet prius et posterius; ævum autem non habet in se prius et posterius, sed ei conjungi possunt; æternitas autem non habet prius neque posterius, neque ea compatitur." (St. Thomas, *Sum. Theol.* 1a. q. 10. art. 5. in corp.)

Eternity is the duration of a Being above all change, whether substantial or accidental. As the duration called eternity is nothing really distinct from the Eternal God Himself, we are right in saying that all and each of the successive events which happen in this world are coexistent with the whole of eternity *considered in itself.* But none of them is coexistent with the whole of eternity *in so far as eternity is considered in its relation of coexistence with preceding or following events,* for the simple reason that each temporary event is a passing reality, whilst eternity is, so to speak, a standing reality, the everlasting Being whose Essence is Existence, abiding always the same with absolute necessity. The works of His hands are the heavens. They shall perish, but He shall continue; and they shall all grow old as a garment, and as a vesture shall He change them, and they shall be changed ; but He is the self-same.[4]

151. Hence we gather the solution of difficulties against the eternity of God, such as the following :

Two things, the duration of which *wholly* coincides with the *whole* duration of a third thing, must coexist with one another. But the Deluge and the Franco-German War are two things, the duration of which according to the exposition given, wholly coincide with the *whole* duration of God. Consequently, whilst the Germans were fighting against the French, the earth was covered with the waters of the Deluge.

This difficulty, though commonly urged, need not detain us long, after the explanations given of the

[4] Cf. Heb. i. 10—12.

strict contents of the meaning of time as distinguished from duration. Both in God and in created things there is duration, for duration in itself is pure perfection. But the Divine duration, since it is a changeless persistency in existence, does not in itself offer any means of distinguishing *before* and *after*. When, however, substances are created whose being is liable to successive phases of existence, they, at each period of their existence, coexist with God, they last, whilst the entire being of God is persisting. But this clearly does not cause them all to be contemporaneous with one another, since although coexisting with the entire being of God, they are not coexisting with the entire duration of God.

The same difficulty and the same solution will present themselves when we correlate the Divine immensity with the localization of bodies. Since God is everywhere, and everywhere whole and entire, wheresoever any extended substance is placed it is in the same place with the whole of God: but it would be absurd to conclude therefore that all bodies are coincident in point of place. But the Divine immensity is the subject to which we must now pass.

CHAPTER III.

Thesis XXIV.—*God is immense.*

152. The word "immense," explained according to its etymology, signifies a state of things not capable of measurement, or of reference to another thing taken as a rule or standard. Things of this world are measured chiefly under one of three aspects, either according to their extension in space, called simply *extension;* or according to their extension in time, called *duration;* or according to their extension in being, called *perfection.* Under none of these aspects is God measurable. In so far as no created perfection can be applied as a measure to His infinite perfection, we call Him *infinite;* in so far as His duration is beyond the measure of any created duration, we call Him *eternal;* and in so far as He is so present to all things in space, that His presence cannot be measured either by parts of space or by the whole of it, we assign to Him the attribute of *immensity.*

In virtue then of this perfection God exists everywhere in space, without consisting of parts corresponding to parts of space, and without being limited to any extension of space. To understand more fully what this means, the reader must bear in mind what space properly is, and in what different ways things can be conceived to exist in space.

As time is not a particular enduring reality existing in itself, but an object of thought, which is formed by collecting mentally and reckoning together the successive states of changeable things; so space is not a thing having its own individual being different from the corporeal beings which are said to exist in it, but it is an object of thought, formed by thinking about the extension of bodies under a peculiar aspect, namely, by thinking of the relation of distance between their surfaces, which distance involves three dimensions, and may therefore be called *volume*. Representing to ourselves the volume between the surfaces of one or several particular bodies, we form the idea of a space, or place within the world ; and thinking of the volume between the extreme surfaces of the whole material world, we conceive the whole of actual space. Space, therefore, is only actual in so far as extended bodies exist.

Beyond the corporeal world there is, however, infinite possible space, inasmuch as by the power of God the extension of the world can become larger, and exceed any assignable limit.

The whole of actual space coincides with the whole of the corporeal world, considered as included within the extreme surfaces of the extreme bodies. Each particular body has its own particular space, which means that it is extended according to three dimensions between the surfaces surrounding it. In so far as it is included in its own surfaces it is sometimes said to have an *internal* space or place; whilst the surfaces of other bodies surrounding it are called its *external* space or place.

153. We have next to consider and discriminate the way in which things can exist in space. A thing is said by the scholastics to exist *circumscriptively* in space, if it be divisible into parts corresponding to the parts of the surfaces surrounding it. As only bodies are thus divisible, they alone can exist in space circumscriptively.[1]

A thing is said to exist in space *definitely*, if its presence be limited to a certain part of space, and its whole substance be everywhere within the bounds of that part of space. Thus the human soul is said to exist *definitely* in the body, because its existence is conterminous with the body in such a way, that its whole substance exists whole in the whole body and whole in every part of it,[2] and on the other hand is found nowhere outside of the body. A thing which exists in space circumscriptively is said to be *formally* extended. The definite existence of an indivisible substance in space is called *virtual* extension.

By the immensity of God we understand a mode of existence in corporeal things or space, which is neither circumscriptive nor definite. It is not circumscriptive, because in God there are no parts

---

[1] St. Thomas is wont to speak of this circumscriptive existence in space as *esse in loco.*

[2] St. Thomas, *Sum. Theol.* 1a. q. 76. art. 8.

assignable corresponding to the parts of space. And it is not definite, because there is no space real or possible where He does not exist in His entirety, or in other words, because no limit of possible space can be given beyond which He would not be present to created things, if the world were extended thus far by His power.

154. Is then the way of existence we are speaking of really proper to God? That He must exist without having parts corresponding to the parts of space, is evident from His simplicity. But how shall we prove that His essence must extend its presence to every possible space that may be created, and is not confined to any fixed limits of corporeal magnitude?

For our first argument again as ever we may appeal to the infinity of God. On account of this attribute we have to predicate of Him whatever perfection can be conceived without connotation of defect. But the perfection of being indivisibly and unlimitedly present to any possible created being, and of surpassing by an extension which we may call *infinitely virtual,* the formal extension of every conceivable corporeal magnitude is evidently a perfection without defect. Consequently it is in God, that is to say, He is immense.

A slightly different way of arriving at the same conclusion is opened by the consideration that the *creative power* of God is infinite. God can create any number of worlds outside the present, and God alone can do it. If, therefore, He will create them, He must create them by the immediate application of His own power.[3] Now it is inconceivable that any efficient cause should immediately apply its power there, where it is not by its substance. Consequently the Divine substance is such that it would be present to any possible world supposing that world to start into existence. This presence would not be anything new in God : or He would not be immutable. Therefore we must say that the Divine substance has an existence eminently equivalent to any possible extension whatever of corporeal worlds, *i.e.*, that God is really immense.[4]

It is gratifying to see this great truth accurately stated by Newton in *Scholion Generale*, added to the third book of his *Principia*, where he says : " God is present everywhere, not only by His power, but also by His substance ; for power cannot subsist without substance."[5]

155. To express more fully how God is in all His creatures, scholastic philosophers are wont to say that He is in each of them " by essence, presence, and power." St. Thomas[6] illustrates the meaning of this phrase by some instances taken from human life. "A king is said to be in his whole kingdom by his *power*, though he is not present everywhere. A thing is said to be by its *presence* in all things which are in view of it, as all things that are exposed in a room are present to a visitor, who nevertheless is not in substance in every part of

---

[3] Cf. Bk. I. c. iv. Th. XVI. § 90.

[4] St. Thomas, *Sum. Theol.* 1a. q. 8. art. 1.

[5] " Deus omnipræsens est non per virtutem solam sed etiam per substantiam ; nam virtus sine substantia subsistere nequit."

[6] St. Thomas, *Sum. Theol.* 1a. q. 8. art. 3. in corp.

the room.   Finally, a thing is said to be according
to its substance or *essence* in that place in which its
substance actually is to be found."

St. Thomas proceeds to apply this doctrine to
three forms of error not at all too antiquated to
deserve mention in our day.   The first found an
eloquent advocate in John Stuart Mill,[7] the second
was partly at least adopted by some of the deists
of last century;[8] and the third is, to say the least,
not opposed with enough decision by some Christian
authors who have written on the subject.[9]

These are St. Thomas's explanations: " There
have been some, to wit, the Manicheans, who
have said that spiritual and incorporeal things
were subject to the Divine power, but visible and
corporeal things to the power of a contrary principle.
Against these then we must say that God is in all
things by His power.

" There were others who believed indeed that all
things were subject to the Divine power; yet did
not extend Divine Providence to the things here
below.   Their mind is well expressed in the words
of Scripture: ' He walks about the poles of heaven
and does not consider our things.'[10]   Against these
we are to say that God is in all things by His
presence.   Again, there were others who granted

---

[7] *Essays on Religion,* p. 116.

[8] Thomas Chubb (1679—1747) taught that since creation God
has never acted immediately upon His creatures, and does not
care whether man lives well or badly.   Viscount Bolingbroke
(1672—1751) held that God did not care for men as individuals.

[9] Crombie, *Natural Theology,* i. p. 64, disapproves of Newton's
saying that God is everywhere by His substance.

[10] Job xxii. 14.

that in some way all things are under the sway of Divine Providence, but at the same time made the assertion that not all things were immediately created by God.   According to them He created immediately only the first creatures, and these created the rest.   Against them we must maintain that God is everywhere by His essence.

"Thus then He is in all things by His power, in that all depend upon Him, and by His presence, inasmuch as all things are 'naked and open to His eyes;'[11] He is in all by His essence, because He is with all as the cause of their existence."

In order to prevent any misunderstanding of the phrase, "God is in creatures by His essence," St. Thomas presently remarks that it does not mean that His essence is an ingredient of created essences, but only that His substance is with them all as the cause of their existence.

And, in the same place, he tells us that the being of God in creatures by His *essence* signifies a closer proximity than His being in them by His *presence*.   It signifies His being, not at a distance from His creatures, as one who sees them from afar, but at their side, sustaining them by His power. Or, to quote the words of the Saint : " God is in all things so as to surround them on all sides with His Being ;"[12] and, " Nothing is distant from God, as though He had it not in Himself." [13]

[11] Cf. Hebrews iv. 13.

[12] "Deus est in rebus sicut continens res." (St. Thomas, *Sum. Theol.* 1a. q. 8. art. 1. ad 2.)

[13] "Nihil est distans ab eo quasi in se illud Deus non habeat." (*Ibid.* ad 3.)

CHAPTER IV.

THE DIVINE INTELLECT.

156. THE Divine attributes of which we have thus far treated do not explicitly suggest to us anything about the action of God. We come now to others which represent Him in His Divine activity.

The first of them is the Wisdom of God, which we shall consider under five sections.

(1) The perfection of the Divine Intellect contrasted with the defects of the human.

(2) The knowledge of God completely determined by His Essence.

(3) The objects of Divine Thought.

(4) The way in which God knows the free acts of rational creatures.

(5) The knowledge of God distinguished according to the diversity of its objects.

SECTION I.—*The perfection of the Divine Intellect contrasted with the defects of the human.*

Thesis XXV.—*The knowledge of God is not capable of progressive improvement; but whatever a human intellect can understand by compounding together different ideas in affirmative and negative judgments and by the*

processes of inductive or deductive reasoning, is grasped
" eminently " and with absolute perfection by one simple
unchangeable act of the Divine Intellect.

157. This proposition, being intimately connected
with the doctrine of the intellectual nature and
infinite perfection of God as proved in the First
Book, needs rather explanation than demonstration.

We say, then, first that there is no progressive
development about the Divine knowledge, no gradual
growth of information. The various things of this
world which fall under the experience of a child,
are in the beginning represented by his mind under
very general and confused ideas. Only in the course
of time does he become aware of their particular
properties, and is able to form judgments affirmative
or negative concerning them. Years pass by before
he properly begins to reason, whether by the ascent
of induction from particular facts to general principles, or by the descent of deduction applying
universal truths to individual cases. What the
reader has here to notice is that this method of
procedure involves the multiplication of ideas in
the human mind. Ideas are formed in vast numbers
of the various objects of consideration. Judgments,
another kind of idea, and reasonings, which are
still another kind, have to be formed in vast numbers
so as to arrange and classify these innumerable
ideas according to the exigencies of the objective
order. Yet to the end man remains ignorant of the
greater portion even of those truths which are
accessible to human understanding. The more facts

R

he tries to master, the less attention can he devote to each. If we consider even the whole treasure of human knowledge, stored up through countless generations, by multitudinous mental acts of innumerable men, how imperfect is it all! How are the greatest geniuses baffled by unsolved problems! How many centuries shall mankind still wait for philosophy and science to be complete? But in vain do we wait for such a consummation. The human mind is unable to acquire a *comprehensive* knowledge of even one of the innumerable species of creatures that surround us. And as regards spiritual things, man left to his natural faculties will never proceed beyond an analogous conception of their nature.[1]

With the Divine mind there is none of all these shortcomings. The Divine knowledge is infinitely perfect in its embrace of every conceivable object of thought, and it is infinitely perfect from the first, or rather from eternity. And this infinite perfection of knowledge is attained not by any succession of ideas, not by any compounding of predicates with subjects, nor again by any passage from premisses to conclusions. It is attained by one all-embracing act of intuition. And this one act what else can it be but the Divine Essence itself? If it were anything really distinct from it, God's essence would neither be simple, nor infinite, nor immutable nor eternal, as we have proved it to be. We must then conclude with St. Thomas, " It must be affirmed that God's knowledge is His sub-

[1] St. Thomas, *Sum Theol.* 1a. q. 88. art. 1. 2. 3.

stance."[2] He, the infinite Being, is unchangeable, infinite, actual Thought.

SECTION 2.—*God's Knowledge completely determined by His Essence.*

Thesis XXVI.—*The Divine Mind does not need any determination from without to enable it to know all truth. God's mere Essence is determination sufficient for Him to comprehend whatever there is to know. Hence His Essence is the " species intelligibilis " by which He understands all things different from Himself as well in general as in particular.*

158. The mind of man is in communication with that which it knows; nay, it possesses it in a certain way within itself. This truth is implied by the terminology of common language, as when people say: "I have grasped it; I comprehend it," in order to signify that they have understood something. As often as the object understood is not one and the same with the mind by which it is understood, the union between the two cannot be such that the actual reality of the thing known shall be in the knowing mind, but a representation only will be present there. This representation is a certain property or quality in the mind, in virtue of which it is determined to know a certain object.

Intelligible species is the name by which scholastic philosophers call this mental representation, whereby the human mind is determined to grasp and under-

---

[2] " Est necesse dicere quod intelligere Dei est ejus substantia." (St. Thomas, *Sum. Theol.* 1a. 14. 4. c.)

stand the object. As is explained in the *Psychology*
of this series, there is a special spiritual power of
the human soul called by scholastics *intellectus agens*.
By this are formed the intelligible species that afford
a direct mental intuition of material things, after
they have been perceived by sense. Before sense-
perception and the action of the *intellectus agens*
following it, the human understanding is *quasi tabula
rasa*, a blank tablet on which nothing has as yet
been written. Stimulated by sensitive representations, the soul may form intelligible species of
countless material objects, and ascend by steps from
the cognition of things sensible to that of things
spiritual; but considered *in its essence alone*, the
soul is not determined and adapted to the knowledge of anything whatsoever. It needs intelligible
species.

159. Now the question arises, Is there in God
anything corresponding to the "intelligible species"
determining the Divine mind to the possession of
an intellectual representation of the object : and if
so, how are we to explain it ? Some among the
scholastic philosophers were inclined to believe that
the term in question is not predicable of God in
its proper sense. St. Thomas, however, and others
are of a contrary opinion; and we go with them.
It is true that in the concrete an intelligible species
of the human mind is not a pure perfection, but has
a very limited and imperfect being. Yet this does
not prevent us from affirming it of God, if only in
the abstract it can be conceived without connotation
of defect. And it can be so conceived by fixing our

attention on this feature alone, that an intelligible
species is a perfection by which the mind is adapted
to know something different from its own being.
Doing so, we conceive neither beginning nor multiplicity, nor change, nor limitation, and thus do not
connote any defect mixed up with its perfection. At
the same time the perfection thus conceived is not
denoted by any other term accurately except "intelligible species" or its synonyms. Consequently we
must predicate this term in its proper meaning
of God. Let us now hear what St. Thomas
has to say on this subject.[3] "As God can have
no potentiality for further perfection, but is pure
actuality, there cannot be in Him any difference
between intellect and intellectual representation.
Consequently He is neither without an intelligible
species, as our intellect, before it understands
something actually; nor is His intelligible species
different from the substance of the Divine Intellect,
as is the case with our intellect when it has actual
understanding. On the contrary, the intelligible
species (of God) is the Divine Intellect itself."
This comes to the same thing as saying that the
Essence of God is the intelligible species of His
Intellect; for we have seen in the preceding thesis

---

[3] "Cum igitur Deus nihil potentialitatis habeat, sed sit actus
purus, oportet quod in eo intellectus et intellectum sint idem
omnibus modis; ita scilicet ut neque careat specie intelligibili,
sicut intellectus noster cum intelligit in potentia; neque species
intelligibilis sit aliud a substantia intellectus divini, sicut accidit in
intellectu nostro, cum est actu intelligens; sed ipsa species intelligibilis est ipse intellectus divinus." (St. Thomas, *Sum. Theol.* 1a. q. 14.
art. 2. in corp.)

that His Essence is His Intellect. Let us set forth the same truth in other words, so far forth as it applies to the knowledge God has of the actual world. Since all things else save God are so many adumbrations of Himself which He has called into existence, His Essence bears to each and all of them the character of a pattern in which whatever perfection they have has its archetype and its perfect representation. He needs, therefore, no other determination by which to know them adequately. To compare great things with small, He beholds them all adequately in His Essence as the architect beholds the building he has set up in the plan which he has in his own mind and which he has faithfully copied. The Divine Essence exceeds indeed all creatures infinitely by its own Infinite Being; nevertheless, it expresses all and each of them distinctly, in so far as its Infinite Being is identical with Infinite Thought, and God's creative power realizes accurately His conceptions of creatures chosen for creation.

SECTION 3.—*The objects of Divine Thought.*

Thesis XXVII.—*God has not only a comprehensive knowledge of Himself and of the essence of each possible thing and each possible event; but He sees also from eternity all His creatures, before they exist, knowing adequately whatever is knowable about their existence and activity, so much so that He foreknows distinctly all future free acts of His rational creatures, even those which are only conditionally future.*

160. The general reason why God must know all things knowable is again the truth repeatedly mentioned in the two preceding sections, that His Intellect is infinitely perfect. This reason alone suffices to convince us that He knows with absolute perfection all those things which are at least imperfectly knowable to us. But in order to show how it follows that He knows things of which we know nothing, some further explanations are wanting; for it must be shown that *there do exist objective truths perfectly hidden from created intellect*, which are evident to the uncreated mind. Thus it appears that the proof of the subjective infinity of the Divine Intellect given above, does not supersede a detailed exposition of the objects of His knowledge. Even as regards those truths, the Divine knowledge of which can be inferred from human knowledge, it is not superfluous to explain carefully their relation to the mind of God. The effect of this explanation will be that we shall be struck more forcibly by the infinite wisdom of our Creator, and filled with deeper admiration of His Majesty. At the same time it will enable us to solve more clearly the difficulties raised against the knowledge of God.

161. First, then, we affirm that God knows Himself by a comprehensive knowledge, that is to say, by a knowledge which comprises absolutely every point knowable about Him, whether as He is in Himself or as He is in relation to other things. This much will hardly be disputed. The Divine intellect must evidently know with comprehensive knowledge what-

ever object of knowledge is intimately present to it. But the Divine Essence is intimately present to the Divine intellect so much so that it is even identical with it.

Now every finite perfection possible and actual pre-exists eminently in God; so that when anything comes to be created, its actually existing essence is necessarily an imperfect imitation of the infinite Essence of God. Consequently the Essence of God is necessarily *imitable* by creatures, though *its actual imitations* are due to the free act of Divine creation. This being so, God in comprehending Himself must know all the different ways in which His Being is susceptible of imperfect imitation by finite beings. Such a knowledge involves an actual comprehension of the essences of all possible creatures, with all the perfections they may acquire, and all the defects and privations conceivable in them. Consequently it implies a knowledge of their faculties, their possible acts, their relations to one another and to their Creator, and all manner of combinations, states, and alterations incident to them. Briefly, God seeing Himself has an adequate knowledge of all possible creatures and of all possible events. With one act of comprehensive intelligence He so represents the whole of them that each is known to Him fully and distinctly. Consequently, whatever God now knows as actual for any given period of time, He would know it as distinctly as He knows it now, even if He had never created. The difference would be that then He would judge the same things to be not actual which now He judges to be actual, and thus distinguishes from the indefinite multitude of purely possible things and events. Indeed that He cannot fail to make this distinction is readily understood, if we consider the dependence of all creatures and all the incidents of created existence upon the decrees and power of the Creator. Whatever exists and whatever happens cannot exist or happen, unless God has decreed that it should exist or happen, or, as regards moral evil, that He would not prevent its existing or happening.

As we shall prove later on, God does not form new decrees in the course of time, but His decrees are eternal, and are now what they were from eternity. Consequently from eternity He foresaw whatever actually exists or happens in the course of time. Otherwise how could He have decreed it? Therefore all actual creatures past, present, and future, all their actions and all circumstances of their existence, were present to the mind of God from eternity. He foreknew them all without any exception, even the free actions of His rational creatures.

162. To prove this still better we will abstract here from the immutability of the Divine decrees. We will also distinguish the existence of creatures and events, according as they are independent of or in any way dependent upon free choice on the part of men.

As regards the former, the perfect knowledge of them is included in the comprehensive cognition which God has of Himself and all possible things. Knowing Himself and all possible things, He knows

which of these according to His will must become
actual, and what facts will be necessarily connected
with their creation.   Thus He knows the history
of His creatures, so far as it depends upon His
decrees and His creative power alone.

Of His knowledge of the rest of their history,
there can be no doubt, if only we are able to
demonstrate that He foresees the free volitions of
His rational creatures.   Everything except free
volitions runs its course according to certain laws
pre-established by God.   The efficacy of created
freedom with regard to these laws does not extend
beyond initiating by free choice either of two alternatives. The natural consequences of the alternative
thus initiated are to be set down to the freedom of
the creature only inasmuch as they were implicitly
contained in the act of choice.   If a man yields to
a propensity for liquor and becomes a drunkard, the
consequences which drunkenness carries with it for
his health, his mental faculties, his fortune, his good
name, and the future of his offspring, &c., are not
controllable by his free-will. He is, however, answerable for them, not because they are wished by him,
but because he did not prevent the cause by which
they are produced, when he was free and obliged
to prevent it. Let us take another instance. A
sinner who feels moved by the inspiration of Divine
grace to blot out his sins by due penance, is free
to follow the lead of grace or to neglect it.   On
the supposition that he follows it, he will receive
a full pardon for his sins, according to a law of the
supernatural order pre-established by God; if he

resists grace up to his death, he will die in his sin, and according to another supernatural law never reach his last end.

These explanations presupposed, it is evident that an eternal knowledge of all free volitions of rational creatures would enable God to foresee everything from eternity. No one can deny that God has a knowledge of free volitions, at least at the time when they are actually elicited. Such a denial would be an impugning of the Divine intellect, representing it as falling short of understanding all objective truth, that is to say, as being limited. God therefore, whose intellect has no limits, comprehends all volitions elicited by His creatures at the moment when they are elicited. But if He knows them, each in its turn, when they become actual, He must have known them from all eternity; otherwise His knowledge would have grown, He would have learned something which He did not know before, an hypothesis manifestly incompatible with His infinite intellect. It follows, then, that He foreknows from eternity whatever happens in the course of time, even the free actions of His rational creatures.

163. But how shall we prove that God must know from eternity what a free creature would do, if it were placed in this or that situation, in which it really never will be placed? How could He foreknow from eternity that the inhabitants of Tyre and Sidon would have done penance, if amongst them Christ had wrought those miracles against which the citizens of Capharnaum, of Corozain, and Beth-

saida hardened their hearts?[4] How could He foreknow the detailed course of action which Napoleon
III. would have taken, if he had conquered the
Germans at Sedan, and made the German monarch
his prisoner?

Without entering upon the " How " which in this
as in many other cases is an insoluble mystery to us,
we can prove evidently that the knowledge of God
must extend even to those hypothetical cases.

God certainly knows the possible lines of action
open to a free creature, who finds himself with the
full use of his freedom in a certain situation, in
which he is able to attend to and consequently to
choose, among a limited number of possible alternatives. Of each of these possible ways of action open
to the person so circumstanced, two propositions
can be formed, contradictorily opposed to each
other. A type of the one is this : *Put in the situation
C, Peter will choose the alternative* A. A type of the
other is this : *Put in the situation* C, *Peter will not
choose the alternative* A. Every one knows from his
own experience how limited is the number of alternatives to which he really can attend under given
circumstances, and which really move him, although
they do not force him. We grant much, if we say
that sometimes ten alternatives together may be
open to a man. But whether it be ten or any other
number n, of each there can be formed two propositions of the type given above. If we have, then,
n alternatives, we get n pairs of propositions contradictorily opposed to each other. In every pair there

4 Cf. St. Matt. xi. 20—23.

must be a true and a false proposition ; for we know from Logic that two propositions contradictorily opposed to each other, never can be both true or both false, but one must be true, the other false. But God, from whom no .objective truth can be hidden, must know which is the true one and which the false one. Knowing this, He knows thereby the course which any free creature really would take under any given condition.

The belief in this truth is beautifully expressed in the Collect which the Catholic Church makes use of on the Seventh Sunday after Pentecost : "O God, whose Providence in its arrangements is never deceived, we humbly ask of Thee to take away all hurtful things, and to grant whatever will be useful for us."[5] Every Christian knows that "hurtful" and "useful" in the language of the Church, are spoken of with reference to our last end, our future beatitude. Now, whether in view of this any set of circumstances, in which we may be put, will prove hurtful or useful, depends, under Divine grace, upon the use of our own freedom. If, then, the Church beseeches God to take away all hurtful things and to grant whatever will be useful to us, she evidently supposes that He knows under what conditions we shall make a good or excellent use of our freedom, and under what others we shall use it less well, or even abuse the same to our ruin. We must now answer one or two objections.

[5] "Deus, cujus providentia in sui dispositione non fallitur : te supplices exoramus, ut noxia cuncta submoveas et omnia nobis profutura concedas."

164. (1) Mr. Herbert Spencer says in his *Principles of Psychology* :[6] "A thing cannot at the same time be both subject and object of thought." But evidently on the supposition that God comprehends Himself, He is at the same time both subject and object of thought. Consequently, in attributing to God a comprehensive self-consciousness, we have put ourselves in opposition to the conclusions of psychological science.

Answer. We have had already occasion to make some reference to this author. That the subject and object of thought cannot be identical, is a proposition which Mr. Spencer does not support by any argument, nor can any be given unless we admit the materialistic hypothesis and reduce all activity to the pulling and pushing of material particles. On the other hand, Mr. Spencer's assertion is in glaring contradiction to the evidence of consciousness, and incompatible with moral freedom. Who doubts that at the moment when he has knowledge of anything he knows himself to be knowing? Were it otherwise, how could he know afterwards that he knew the thing before, though meanwhile he may have forgotten it? Again, how can I be morally free and answerable for my actions, unless at the moment when an eligible object is presented to my intellect, my conscience tells me whether I am right or wrong in choosing it? Yet if my conscience tells me this at the moment, it follows that I myself am at the same time subject and object of my thought.

[6] *Principles of Psychology,* i. p. 148.

We must then dismiss as false this piece of Spencerian psychology even in its application to the human soul. Much less can it be admitted in regard to God, who comprises eminently in the simplicity of His Essence whatever is conceivable as an intellectual perfection, not however possessing it by any act really distinct from His Essence.

165. (2) We have stated that God sees all possible things by comprehending His Essence as imitable. But among other possible things· evils are to be found, and accordingly we are compelled in consistency to affirm that God knows evil as well as good, inasmuch as He comprehends the imitability of His Essence. This, however, seems to involve us in the Hegelian absurdity of supposing the Infinite to contain in itself everything, evil not excepted.

Answer. This objection rests upon the wrong supposition that evil is a thing existing in itself, and consequently knowable in itself. The truth is that evil consists in the absence of some perfection due to a substance. The want of a physical perfection which the nature of the substance concerned requires is a physical evil; and the want of moral rectitude in the will of a rational creature is a moral evil. Neither physical nor moral evil can be in God. Nevertheless God knows all possible physical and moral evils by knowing, in virtue of the comprehension of His own Essence, all possible finite essences. For the perfect knowledge of these involves a knowledge of all their natural requirements, and so far as rational creatures are concerned, their moral obligations.   It involves also an adequate knowledge of all possible actions of free creatures, and of the relation of those actions to the requirements of their nature, physical and moral.   Consequently it carries with it a comprehensive understanding of all the ways in which the activity of creatures can come into collision either with the integrity of their own natural being or that of their fellow-creatures.   Thus all possible physical evils are known.   And inasmuch as an adequate knowledge of all possible rational creatures, of their faculties and of the relation of those faculties to their last end, is inconceivable without an insight into all the possible abuses of their free-will, by which they can miss the narrow path of duty, God cannot fail to know all those possible abuses : which is equivalent to His knowing all possible moral evils.

166. (3) Against the foreknowledge which God has of our free actions, there is the obvious difficulty which has been raised repeatedly in various forms.   If God foreknows from eternity what men deliberately are doing now and will do in future, their actions must necessarily be in harmony with the cognition that God has of them.   If men could act otherwise than as God foresees, they would be able to make the infallible knowledge of God fallible, which is absurd.   They act therefore of necessity as God has foreseen that they will act.   But actions which of necessity agree with the judgment God has formed of them from eternity, cannot be free actions.   Consequently, admitting Divine prescience of free human

actions, we must deny the freedom of the human will.

Answer. The apparent strength of this difficulty gives way as soon as a distinction is made between the necessity of affirming an action as future, and the necessity of affirming the same action, not only as future, but also as necessary. He who admits that God foreknows the future actions of men is logically compelled to allow that these actions will certainly take place, but Logic by no means constrains him to affirm that they will be performed as *necessary* and not as *free* actions. The foreknowledge of God is a truth from which we must logically infer that the event foreseen by Him will happen precisely as He has foreseen it. But does it follow that He cannot foresee events, unless they are the outcome of natural necessity and not of free choice? True, if God's foresight did not reach farther than to the *causes* of free actions, and consequently could foresee them only by comprehending the nature of His free creatures and all the impelling motives which precede their resolutions, He never could be absolutely and adequately certain about their particular free acts. Whatever object may be put before a rational creature that enjoys the full use of its faculties, it remains at liberty to choose or not to choose until the choice is made. However, the knowledge of the Infinite Mind extends beyond causes; it has a direct vision also of actions and effects; it expresses all objective truth to whatever time it may belong. Of the two propositions, "The free creature A under the circumstance B, in which the

S

action C will be possible to it, will, by the exercise of its freedom, perform this action," and again, " The free creature A under the circumstance B, in which the action C will be possible to it, will, by the exercise of its freedom, not perform this action," the one must be necessarily true, the other necessarily false. That which expresses really what A, under the circumstance B, will do as regards the action C, is formally true, because it is really the expression of an objective future fact. Consequently the Infinite Intellect of God must represent it as future. Moreover, that proposition, inasmuch as *ex hypothesi* it is the enunciation of a choice both really future and really free, expresses a fact which is out of all necessary connection with any preceding fact. Therefore God knows it as it is, out of any such necessary connection. His knowing it as it will happen before it actually happens does not change the nature of the fact itself.

God necessarily foresees from eternity what men will do in the course of time, but His foresight does not force them to act the one way or the other. If the drunkard had chosen otherwise, God, without any change in Himself, would have seen a free act of abstinence where He now sees a free act of intemperance. Nevertheless, if the creature chooses now, for instance, to write rather than to read, God has foreseen this choice from eternity, because He represents objective truth as it is or will be under any given circumstance.

Tourists who are walking through an Alpine valley may be seen easily by one who is at the top of a mountain bordering on it. Whilst they are walking there, it cannot be true that they are not doing so, though it depends upon their free choice to walk or not to walk. Consequently their passing by cannot be hidden from the spectator within the range of whose eyesight they are coming. And if he were able to see with his eyes future events as clearly as he can see those that happen at a short distance, he would see the excursionists coming before they were actually on the way. Yet his foresight would not be the reason of their coming; it would be nothing but an anticipated announcement of a future event.

In a similar way God looks, as it were, from the summit of His Eternity down upon the course of future times, and sees the free actions of His rational creatures. Their future resolutions are expressed by His infinite mind exactly as they will come about; consequently, not as natural consequences of habitual or actual impulses, but as self-determinations, as events which will come to pass at the bidding of rational creatures, making use of that power of accepting or rejecting any particular good which He Himself will grant them. This is well expressed by St. Thomas: "God is altogether outside the order of time. He is standing, as it were, upon the high citadel of unalterable eternity. Before Him is spread out the whole course of time, which He takes in by one simple intuition. Consequently, by one act of vision, He sees everything that happens in the course of time ; and each fact He sees as it is in itself, not as something that is to be present to His gaze in the future, and is for the present involved in the sequence of causes on which it depends; at the same time He does also see that sequence of causes. He sees every event in a manner altogether proper to an eternal being. Each fact, to whatever period of time it belongs, He sees even as the human eye sees Socrates seated. The sitting itself, not its cause, is seen by the eye. But from the fact of a man seeing Socrates seated, it must not be inferred that the sitting is an effect flowing from its cause necessarily. On the other hand, the human eye sees most truly and infallibly Socrates seated whilst he really is seated, because everything, as it is in itself, is a fixed and determined fact. Thus, then, we must admit that God knows with absolute certainty and infallibility whatever happens at any time. Nevertheless temporary events do not happen of necessity, but are the effects of causes that might have acted otherwise."[7]

[7] " Deus est omnino extra ordinem temporis, quasi in arce æternitatis constitutus, quæ est tota simul, cui subjacet totus temporis decursus secundum unum et simplicem ejus intuitum. Et ideo uno intuitu videt omnia, quæ aguntur secundum temporis decursum et unumquodque secundum quod est in seipso existens non quasi sibi futurum quantum ad ejus intuitum, prout est in solo ordine suarum causarum, quamvis et ipsum ordinem causarum videat ; sed omnino æternaliter sic videt unumquodque eorum quæ sunt in unoquoque tempore, sicut oculus humanus videt Socratem sedere in seipso, non in causa sua. Ex hoc autem quod homo videt Socratem sedere non tollitur ejus contingentia quæ respicit ordinem causæ ad effectum ; tamen verissime et infallibiliter videt oculus hominis Socratem sedere dum sedet, quia unumquodque prout est in seipso, jam determinatum est. Sic igitur relinquitur, quod Deus certissime

We may now state the difficulties in their usual form with compendious answers, applying the doctrine just expounded.

(*a*) An act which God foresees will necessarily take place. But an act which necessarily takes place cannot be a free act.

Answer. There is a fallacy in the use of the word "necessarily." In the minor it denotes the physical necessity under which a certain class of causes produce their effects. When there is this necessity, of course, by force of terms, freedom is excluded. In the major the necessity denoted is logical necessity; the Divine mind being infinitely perfect, necessarily sees the truth wherever and however it is, past, present, or future. It is impossible for the thing to be without God foreseeing it, and by necessary consequence the Divine foreknowledge is an infallible evidence of what it will be.

(*b*) An act the omission of which is impossible cannot be a free act. But the omission of an act which God foresees is impossible. Thus such an act cannot be free.

Answer. Again the same fallacy. The omission of such an act is logically impossible, but not on this account physically impossible. The act and its omission cannot both exist. The one is necessarily exclusive of the other. And in that sense, if the act is really future, its omission is impossible, but in no other sense is it impossible; and in no

et infallibiliter cognoscat omnia quæ fiunt in tempore, et tamen ea quæ in tempore eveniunt non sunt vel fiunt ex necessitate, sed contingenter." (In *Perihermeneias Aristotelis*, Lib. I. Lect. 14.)

other sense is any necessity on the part of the event
the basis of the infallibility of the Divine foreknowledge.

(c) That act is necessary and not free which
necessarily follows upon something else that does
not rest with the free choice of the agent. But an
act foreseen by God follows necessarily upon the
Divine foreknowledge, which foreknowledge does
not rest with the free choice of the agent.

Answer. The major is correct, if the necessary
following upon "something else" is because that
something is a necessarily acting cause, but not if
the "something else" is only a necessarily truthful
spectator or seer.

(d) If God were to foresee the free actions of
creatures His foreknowledge would be dependent
on their choice, for it would depend upon their
choice whether it should be framed in this way
rather than in that. But it is absurd to make an
attribute of the Infinite God dependent on the
action of His creatures.

Answer. The alleged dependence can only be
called dependence in a broad and mitigated sense.
True dependence is the relation by which the effect
is bound to its physical cause, not that by which
truthful knowledge is necessitated to conform itself
to its object. The former, so far forth as it is
dependence, is an imperfection. It is a perfection
indeed to possess being, but an imperfection to have
it in dependence on the causality of an external
agent, and the greater the dependence the greater
the imperfection. The latter is pure perfection, and

the fuller the conformity with the object, the greater the perfection.

SECTION 4.—*The manner in which God knows the free acts of His rational creatures.*

Thesis XXVIII.—1. *Whereas God infallibly knows what any given rational creature would do if left to exercise its freedom under given circumstances and in regard of a given object, this infallible knowledge must not be traced to any Divine decree predetermining the creature to act in that way.*

2. *Nor must it be traced to the adequate comprehension which God has of the nature of the creature, and of all the influences which under the circumstances would bear upon its free-will previously to its actual choice.*

3. *The true reason why God has a distinct intuition of conditionally future free actions is because His infinite intellect must represent those truths which pre-exist in their causes contingently only, no less than other truths which follow from their causes by natural necessity.*

4. *Hence the infallibility of the Divine foreknowledge of free acts, as not merely conditionally future, but really future, is to be explained thus : Knowing what use the creature would make of its freedom under certain circumstances, God has decreed to allow those circumstances to come about. Thus He knows the free act as absolutely future, because knowing it as conditionally future, He further knows that He has decreed to realize the condition.*

167. In the preceding section we have proved that God knows not only all that is possible, but also whatever either *is* actually existing, or *will be* actually existing, or *would be* actually existing under certain circumstances. We have seen that even the future free acts of rational creatures, whether they be absolutely or only conditionally future, are objects of the Divine Intellect.

Now the question arises: In what relation do the objects known by God as distinct from Himself stand to the knowledge He has of His essence and His free-will? The answer to this question is easy enough, so long as we confine our consideration to things and events purely possible, and to those actual things and events which depend upon His will alone, so that the free-will of rational creatures does not interfere with them. If God did not know whatever is possible, He could not have a comprehensive knowledge of His essence; and again, if He were unable to discern the natural effects of the causality of creatures who owe their existence to His decrees alone, He would have an imperfect knowledge of what He decreed. So far there is no special difficulty about the explanation of the Divine knowledge. The difficulty begins with the free volitions of rational creatures. Much labour has been spent upon this question by Catholic philosophers, especially since the latter half of the sixteenth century. In the three first parts of the thesis we are concerned about the explanation of the knowledge which God has of free actions as conditionally future, and in the fourth about the explanation of

His knowledge, inasmuch as it represents free actions as really or absolutely future.

168. We say then in the first place that the knowledge God has of the conditionally future existence of free actions cannot be explained by saying that He knows them by reason of His decree to pre-determine creatures under certain circumstances to the performance of them. By this assertion, we express our disagreement from an opinion which has every claim to our respect on account of the renown of its author and of the many illustrious and learned theologians who have adopted it. Bannez, who was the first who taught explicitly the opinion we reject, was the founder of a distinguished school of theology. The predetermination which they allege is called *physical premotion*. According to the explanation given of this premotion by those who follow Bannez, it influences the free-will previously to the self-determination of the latter, and in such a way that *by the very nature of its influence* the free-will is infallibly drawn to the predetermined choice, which, nevertheless, is genuinely free. This explanation supposes God's knowledge of the conditionally future free act to be contained in the comprehensive knowledge which He has of His decree of physical premotion.

The defence of free-will in this hypothesis becomes extremely difficult. " Predetermination," writes Cardinal Pecci, " includes a determination which precedes human deliberation. But a determination made by the Divine will must be fulfilled. Consequently necessity precedes human deliberation.   Such deliberation can no longer be free."[8] The solutions that are offered of this difficulty seem to us by no means clear.[9]   And we shall argue later (in Bk. III.), that the reasonings upon which the assertion of a physical predetermination of free acts is based are not more convincing.

169. The earliest opponent of Bannez was Molina. The explanation of the way in which free acts are knowable to God, is found by Molina in what he calls the *supercomprehension* which the Divine intellect has of the free creature.[10]   By this *supercomprehension* he understands the adequate knowledge of the nature and faculties of the free created being, and of all the attracting and repelling impulses to which it will be subjected previously to its choice. That there is a knowledge of all this cannot be denied ; but it does not appear how we can thereby explain the knowledge God has of the free choice itself. As it seems repugnant to the nature of free acts that they should be foreseen in the comprehension of predetermining decrees, so neither does it harmonize with their nature that God should know them from eternity by supercomprehending the created beings from whom the free acts proceed. Nothing that is seen by God as preceding the free act, can imply an infallible knowledge of the free act itself. Neither the nature of the creature nor

---

[8] *Lehre des heiligen Thomas über den Einfluss Gottes auf die Handlungen der vernünftigen Geschöpfe*, &c. (Translated from the Italian by G. Triller, D.D.), Part II. § 16, pp. 39, 40.

[9] Cf. Zigliara, *Summa Phil.* ii. p. 391, at the bottom of the page.

[10] Molina in Part I. *Divi Thomæ*, q. 14. a. 13. d. 15. p. 217.

its faculties, nor any attractive or repellent motives brought to bear upon its free-will, can prevent this will from choosing or refusing a given object. Consequently an infallible cognition of its choice is in no way implied in the cognition of anything preceding it. But the knowledge God has of the conditionally future choice must be infallible. Therefore it cannot be based upon a supercomprehension of the creature in the sense of Molina. Molina had the merit of pointing out that a Divine knowledge of free acts must be admitted independently of predetermining decrees. But the positive explanation he gives of this knowledge only takes us from Scylla into Charybdis. On these grounds those who are called Molinists, as following Molina in the rejection of predetermining decrees, commonly do not follow him in admitting what he substitutes in their stead. They might, in fact, more properly be called Suarezians, for Suarez is the great representative of the teaching they defend, and which we shall advocate in the third and fourth part of our thesis.

170. We maintain in the third place that God sees the conditionally future free actions of creatures, because they are objective truths and His infinite intellect sees all objective truth. If a truth is predetermined in its cause, God sees it by comprehending that cause. But if it has no predetermining cause, as a free act really has not, God sees it nevertheless. But He sees it as something which *is*, or *will be*, or *would be*, caused *in fact*, though it is in no *necessary* connection, but only in a *contingent* connection with its causes. Saying this we do not commit ourselves

to the statement that God foresees a conditionally future free action as an event out of all connection with His decrees. On the contrary, we hold most firmly with Suarez that a conditionally future use of freedom supposes a Divine decree to grant the use of freedom, which decree by the scholastics of the three last centuries is commonly called "the decree of immediate Divine concurrence." But this decree is a decree not to predetermine the creature to the acceptance or rejection of a certain object, but simply to render it perfectly able as well to reject as to accept. Thus the free choice of the creature, inasmuch as it is the act of choosing between two alternatives, depends upon God; but inasmuch as this act of choosing is a self-determination of the creature to accept rather than to reject, it depends upon the creature. We shall say more on this subject in the Third Book.

171.   Hence it is readily inferred that God foreknows those free actions that will in fact be future, in that He comprehends His actual decrees. These decrees are formed in the light of the knowledge which He has of the conditionally future. For instance, God knows that a man, whom we will call Peter, under such and such circumstances would give an alms to a poor man, if He granted him the actual use of his freedom of will as regards this object. In the light of this knowledge He decrees either not to grant Peter the requisite use of his freedom or to grant it. If the decree is not to grant it, He will see the omission of the free act of almsgiving as really future and its performance only as

conditionally future. But if He decrees to grant it, He will see the omission as conditionally future and the performance as really future. In other words: The free act, which will be really future, God knows as really future, because He knows it as conditionally future, and He further knows that He has decreed to realize the circumstances under which it will be really future. This is just what we have stated in the fourth part of our thesis.

SECTION 5.—*The Divisions of the Divine Knowledge.*

172. Though the Divine knowledge is one undivided act, not really distinct from the Divine Essence, we may nevertheless divide it according to the diversity of the objects to which it extends. Such a division is useful, inasmuch as it is based upon the different relations of the objects of Divine knowledge to God Himself, and thus recalls to us in few words what we have explained fully in the preceding section.

First, then, if we take the whole body of truths which God knows concerning Himself and concerning finite things, His knowledge may be said to be partly *necessary*, partly *free*. It is necessary, inasmuch as on no supposition could it have been in any other relation to its objects than it is now; it is free, inasmuch as things are now known as actual, which might not have been known as actual under a different use of the freedom of the Creator and of His creatures. Therefore God has a *necessary* knowledge of Himself, and of all finite things and actions *in so far as they are purely possible.* And by a *free* knowledge He knows His own decrees, and whatever in consequence of the exercise of His own freedom or that of His rational creatures has been actual, is actual, will be actual, or would be actual under certain circumstances, *considered precisely in its past, present, future, absolute, or conditional actuality.*

At first sight it might seem that such a division is inconsistent with God's immutability. Yet it is not so. In saying that the knowledge which God has of His own decrees and of existences outside Himself might have stood otherwise towards its objects than it does stand, we do not say that His act of knowledge could have changed internally, or that the range of His knowledge could have extended further or less far: we state only that He now sees things as actual which He might have seen as merely possible. If God had created neither matter nor spirit, He would nevertheless have distinctly seen material bodies with all their vicissitudes and all finite spiritual beings with all their actions and states; yet all these things He would have seen as purely possible, whereas He sees now as actual at one time or another the things which He has decreed from eternity to bring into existence, together with their necessary and free actions and the results of both. Yet in no case is His knowledge determined from without: He has it in virtue of His unchangeable essence. Nor would His knowledge of the exercise of created freedom be less, strictly speaking, than it now is, even though He

had created no rational creature. The only difference would be that the actions, which now His
Intellect represents as *really* future free actions,
would in that case have been represented as *conditionally* future. And the reason of this difference
would be the absence of the free decree to create
rational creatures and to provide the circumstances
under which they use their freedom as they use it
in the present order of things.

173. There is another division of Divine knowledge
which has regard only to things distinct from God.
These are said to be known by God partly through the
scientia visionis (knowledge of vision), partly through
the *scientia simplicis intelligentiæ* (knowledge of simple
intelligence). The nature of this distinction is clearly
explained in the following words of St. Thomas:
" A difference must be marked as regards things
which are not now actually existing. Some of
them, although they are not existing now, yet have
existed or will exist, and all these are said to be
known by God through the *knowledge of vision*. For
since God's understanding which is His being, is
measured by eternity, and eternity is something
which, unchangeable in itself, embraces all time,
it follows that the intuitive vision of God, as it is
at the present moment, takes in all time and all
things that are at any time whatever, and He
sees all this as distinctly as if it were really
present. But there are other things which are in
the power of God or of creatures, but which
never exist, nor will exist, nor have existed, and of
these we do not say that God has a knowledge of

vision, but only that He knows them through the *knowledge of simple intelligence.*" [11]

From this passage of the Angelic Doctor it appears that, according to his terminology, the *knowledge of vision* comprises whatever is actual outside God at whatever time, whereas to the *knowledge of simple intelligence* everything is relegated which, though never actual, is in the power either of God alone or of creatures under God. Of conditionally future free actions, St. Thomas did not treat *ex professo.* These actions cannot be said to be merely possible, and yet they are never actual, if the circumstances under which they will happen are never realized. Hence the question arises: Are they seen by the *knowledge of vision* or by the *knowledge of simple intelligence?* We might refer them to the *knowledge of simple intelligence,* by saying that to it belongs whatever is seen as possible, and yet not actual, whether not actual simply (purely possible), or not actual except under certain conditions (conditionally future). We might also refer conditionally future free actions to the *knowledge of vision* by saying that to it belongs whatever is at any time either really or conditionally actual.

[11] " Horum quæ actu non sunt est attendenda quædam diversitas. Quædam enim licet non sint nunc in actu, tamen vel fuerunt, vel erunt, et omnia ista dicitur Deus scire *scientia visionis.* Quia cum intelligere Dei, quod est ejus esse, æternitate mensuretur, quæ sine successione existens totum tempus comprehendit, præsens intuitus Dei fertur in totum tempus, et in omnia quæ sunt in quocumque tempore, sicut in subjecta sibi præsentialiter. Quædam vero sunt, quæ sunt in potentia Dei vel creaturæ, quæ tamen nec sunt, nec erunt, neque fuerunt, et respectu horum non dicitur habere scientiam visionis, sed *simplicis intelligentiæ.*" (St. Thomas, *Sum. Theol.* i. 14.)

Those Catholic philosophers who reject the notion of physical predetermination, say commonly that conditionally future free actions are seen by what they call *scientia media* (middle knowledge), as having for its object something neither purely possible nor really actual, but between the two. We ourselves hold strongly to what is meant by the term *scientia media*, without insisting upon the necessity of retaining this term as such. We conclude then by defining the *scientia media* as the *knowledge that God has of the conditionally future existence of the free actions of His rational creatures, without having decreed physically to predetermine the said creatures to the said actions.*

CHAPTER V.

Introductory.

174. IN every being on this earth we find a natural tendency to follow a certain way of action that suits its nature, and to avoid other ways out of harmony with or altogether repugnant to its nature. Thus every element of matter has a certain chemical affinity and atomicity, which it satisfies in all combinations as well as circumstances will allow. Every plant works upon the nourishment which it takes up from the soil in such a way as serves its specific evolution. The instinct of animals leads them with astonishing accuracy to the food they stand in need of, to arrangements for their future offspring, and to avoidance of danger.

In man, the head of the visible creation, there is not only a longing for things that suit the physical organism, as in brute animals, but an insatiable appetite for truth.

That which in one way or another is in harmony with the nature of a thing is called its *good*. The tendency of a thing to obtain what suits its nature is in scholastic language called its natural appetite (*appetitus naturalis*), although this appetite is not always a desire or craving in the strict sense of the word, but often only a natural tendency in some sense analogical to a desire or craving. Where this natural appetite is directed by knowledge, its scholastic name is elicited appetite (*appetitus elicitus*), because it is roused to action (elicited) by the knowledge of good. Of elicited appetite there are two varieties which essentially differ from one another—organic or sensitive appetite (*appetitus organicus vel sensitivus*), which is an inclination to good as apprehended by mere sense-perception, and spiritual or rational appetite (*appetitus spiritualis vel rationalis*), which tends towards good as presented by intellectual knowledge. This rational appetite is what is commonly called *will*.

175. It is evident that in God there can be no *merely* natural appetite or appetite without knowledge, nor any sensitive appetite or appetite following organic perception; for He is essentially Intellect, and therefore cannot be without knowledge; He is also essentially simple, and therefore without the composition of material parts involved in sense-perception. He is the most pure Spirit in which being and knowledge are really one. The question then arises, Shall we predicate "will" of Him? The answer to this depends upon whether "will" denotes a pure perfection or not. If it does, God must be infinite Will. But there can be no doubt that "will" *in its abstract meaning* signifies nothing but perfection. It is love for good consequent upon knowledge of it. We cannot conceive that intellectual being as other than imperfect which

should know good and yet not approve it as good.
Some love of good is inherent in every intellectual
nature. Intellect is by its very nature directed
towards truth. Truth, therefore, is the good of
intellect, being in harmony with its essence. From
this it follows that there is no act of intellect which
does not carry with it an act of will. And as God
is infinite Intellect, so also He must be infinite
Will.[1]

The truth that God is endowed with will, not
merely metaphorically, but in the strict sense of the
word, may also be indirectly shown from the fact
of creation. Creation is production out of nothing,
and such production is inconceivable, unless it be
conceived as the effect of infinitely powerful volition.
Thus the Psalmist expresses it, comprising the
whole history of the origin of the universe within
the compass of these few words: *Ipse dixit et facta
sunt: ipse mandavit et creata sunt*—"He spoke, and
they were made; He commanded, and they were
created."[2]

It will now be our duty to explain the truths
which by the light of natural reason can be ascertained concerning the Divine will.

Our investigation will fall into three branches;
we shall have to consider the necessity and freedom
of the Divine will, its holiness and other moral
attributes, and, lastly, its quality as supreme life
and beatitude.

[1] Cf. St. Thomas, *Contra Gentes*, i. c. 72, § "Ex hoc enim quod
Deus est intelligens, sequitur quod est volens," &c.

[2] Psalm cxlviii. 4.

SECTION I.—*Necessity and freedom of the Will of God.*

Thesis XXIX.—*God loves Himself with absolute necessity, infinitely, and for the sake of His own goodness. His love towards creatures is an outcome (or outpouring) of the love which He bears to His own Being. He loves them with a love not absolutely necessary, but generous and free; and His decrees about them are at once free and irrevocable.*

176. Self-respect is not self-conceit, and there is a well-ordered love of self, quite a distinct thing from selfishness. The self-conceited man, over-estimating his own importance, assumes a position of superiority or authority not due to him. The selfish man cares for nothing but his own satisfaction and enjoyment. But the man who is possessed by a noble self-respect will not stoop to anything incompatible either with his dignity as a man or with the post assigned to him by Providence. A well-ordered love of self leads a man to utilize all his faculties and all his surroundings for the perfection of that in himself which is noblest in human nature.

177. Now ascending from the image of God to its original, we see at once that in Him there can be no self-conceit nor selfishness. It is impossible that He should over-esteem His own being or His authority, for He is infinitely perfect and the only Lord of all. Neither can there be in Him an inordinate and exaggerated seeking after His own advantage. In His essence He finds the source and fulness of everything grand and excellent, loveable and enjoyable. He finds it there estab-

lished on the immoveable rock of His eternity, not liable to decay from within nor open to aggression from without. Consequently, care for Himself in the proper sense of the word, care for His own aggrandisement or for the increase of His own happiness, is as inconceivable in God as the loss of His existence. And as all selfishness is the outcome of such care, nothing is more remote from the Creator of all things than selfishness. Yet well-ordered esteem and love of self belong to Him in an infinite degree. If He did not value His nature in proportion to its goodness, if He did not esteem and love Himself in proportion as He is worthy of esteem and love, He would be wanting in knowledge of or due affection for good. His nature is infinitely good, and therefore infinitely worthy of esteem and love. Hence God has necessarily an infinite esteem and love of Himself for His own goodness.

178. From this it follows that His love for creatures is an outcome (or outpouring) of His love for Himself. It is necessarily so, for no creature is loveable of itself. All its goodness is based upon the being that it has, and that being is a free creation of God. The creature, then, is indebted to the Creator for whatever it possesses worthy of esteem and love. Again, the grounds on which rests the creature's claim for love consist either in its natural perfection or (in the case of a rational creature) in its moral goodness. Its natural perfection is the handiwork of the Creator; and its moral goodness, though in a certain sense due to

the exercise of the creature's own freedom, is worked out after the ideal set before the creature's mind by the natural or supernatural law of God, manifested in the voice of conscience or through the teaching of revelation. In any case, God sees no perfection in any creature which is not derived from Himself, the source of all good. Now a created rational being, however enlightened about this dependence of creatures upon their Creator, may wilfully withdraw its understanding from paying attention to the fact. Hence men who have learned much about God sometimes do not rise to His love, but make a creature the centre of their affections. No such inordination can possibly exist in God, whose intellect and will are infinitely perfect. Hence all the love He bears to creatures must be based upon His love towards Himself. This truth is compatible with another, of which we shall say more in the Third Book, that He loves His rational creatures in a certain sense for their own sake, inasmuch as He wills their happiness on condition that they co-operate with His benevolent intentions.

179. As the Divine mind cannot abstract from the natural relation in which each finite nature stands to its infinite prototype, and as the Divine will can never be displeased with His own production, God necessarily loves everything He has created, and is pleased with its natural goodness. How far this love must lead Him to take care of the well-being of His creatures, we shall see later on. For the present we wish to show that the love of God for

creatures, though necessary in a certain sense on the supposition of their existence, nevertheless is to be called a free and not a necessary love. God being infinite has no need of any creature, nor would He be less good if He had created none. He has given existence to finite beings because He freely willed so to do. He willed to give them a share in His goodness, though He knew that He might be infinitely happy by Himself alone. This has been proved in Book I. Thesis XVIII. § 97. Hence it follows that the love God bears to creatures does not suppose any attraction or loveableness belonging to them independently of the exercise of Divine freedom. On the contrary, if they possess anything to attract God to love them, it is due to His free decree of creation. But for this decree all creatures would have been eternal nothingness, unworthy of being loved. In the free volition by which God chose to produce beings different from Himself, there is included the free decree of all the natural and supernatural good that creatures ever enjoy. Consequently, all and each of them are indebted to their Creator for everything good they are and have. We may justly put to every creature St. Paul's question: "What hast thou that thou hast not received?"[3]

180. Having thus proved that the love God bears to His handiwork is an overflow of pure generosity, and not a constraining natural affection, we are still to show that His decrees regarding creatures are at once free and irrevocable. In saying that the

[3] 1 Cor. iv. 7.

decrees by which God rules the fate of His creatures are *free*, we by no means wish to imply that they are *not referred to any standard whatsoever*. Certainly they are. The standard to which they are necessarily referred is the infinite wisdom and righteousness of the Creator. It is impossible that He should decree anything about His handiwork that would appear unwise or unjust in the light of the eternal truth of His understanding. But of the many ways by which He may lead the creature without acting against wisdom or justice or any other of His Divine perfections, He chooses one way or another according to His good pleasure without any necessity from within or without. Such necessity would betoken either dependence upon the good of creatures or want of supreme power over them, defects inconceivable in the infinite and absolute Lord of all things.

181. The exercise of Divine freedom we are speaking of, is necessarily an eternal act. God could not delay any decree without a wise reason. But no such reason could exist for Him. A resolution cannot be reasonably put off to a later date, if he who is to approve or reject it, knows already beforehand which side he will take. God knows this of necessity. Consequently He cannot delay His resolve: such delay in Him would be setting Himself against His own wisdom. Nor can He retract the course once settled by His eternal decrees. They are irrevocable. A decree cannot be repealed without a motive, nor *wisely* repealed without a *reasonable* motive. But for God there

can be no reasonable motive ever to recall what He has once decreed. A reasonable revocation of a decree is always based upon a better knowledge or a fuller consideration of the matter and circumstances. Neither the one nor the other is conceivable in God, whose essence is identical with infinitely perfect intuition of all truth. Hence in God there is properly speaking but one free decree abiding for ever. This one decree, however, is equivalent to an innumerable multitude of decrees, which according to our way of thinking are contained in it. It is formed in the light of infinitely perfect knowledge of all possible contingencies. Consequently in it God has also regard to the free volitions of His rational creatures. It abides in the Divine will, not only in this sense that it never is retracted; but it is an eternally-lasting, never-changing, actual determination of that will. In other words, what God has decreed from eternity, that He approves now and wills now actually, and that He will approve actually throughout the future.

182. Against this doctrine the following objection is often made.

If my fate has been settled once for all, why should I trouble myself about the performance of religious and moral duties, since no performance of mine can move God to arrange anything for me better than that which He has already decreed?

Those who raise this difficulty forget that the decrees of God are not formed without regard for human freedom. God does not settle the fate of a reasonable creature without paying attention to the way in which that creature will use the freedom of its will. As His decrees cannot violate justice, He certainly has not decreed that the faithful observance of the moral law which He has stamped upon your heart, should lead you to final misery. On the other hand, if you reason rightly, you must conclude from the common consent of mankind; from the desire of happiness craving for fulfilment in the breast of every man, and never perfectly satisfied in this life; and finally, from the necessity of a sufficient sanction of the moral law, that there is another life to follow beyond the grave. As your soul is spiritual and incorruptible, you have reason to believe that this future life will last for ever. A little reflection shows you, moreover, that it would be absurd for an infinitely just and holy God to have decreed that it should not make any difference throughout all eternity, whether a man had finished his time of probation here on earth in a state of rebellion against his Creator, or in humble submission to His will. Consequently, even if you were not favoured with the light of Christian revelation, under the guidance of reason alone you might know enough about the nature of the eternal decrees of God to become convinced that the only safe course a man can take is to comply as accurately as possible with the law of God, manifested by the voice of his conscience, and to bear in his heart and to express by his whole external behaviour those feelings of reverence, of trust and love, which it behoves a reasonable creature to entertain with regard to a Creator of infinite power, wisdom, and goodness. As God from eternity would not but decree to lead every rational creature who freely and perseveringly obeys the voice of conscience, to final happiness, so *He decrees it now at this very moment*, whilst you are anxious about your final fate; for His decrees are now, as they were from eternity. From this undeniable truth it follows evidently that *it depends upon your free co-operation with the benevolent intentions of your Creator, whether eternal happiness or final misery will be your lot.* If against this conclusion the objection suggests itself: How can I be free, if God foreknows my future actions, we beg the reader to ponder again what was said in answer to this objection, § 166. Although Philosophy, as such, does not rest on the teaching of revelation, it is as well here to remember that Christians have that other source of knowledge to confirm them in their philosophical belief that they possess a true liberty, upon the right exercise of which their future depends. According to the Christian doctrine, it is an eternal decree of God that every one shall receive his reward according to his works, that God will render "to them indeed who, according to patience in good works, seek glory and honour and incorruption, eternal life:" but also that there shall come "tribulation and anguish upon every man that worketh evil."[4] According to the same doctrine, it has been decreed by God that every prayer made with confidence for really "good gifts" shall be heard, that Heaven shall rejoice over the con-

---

[4] Romans ii. 7, 9.

version of a sinner, that the ministers of Christ shall have power to forgive all sins, however grievous and numerous: that after death judgment shall follow, and the wicked shall be condemned to everlasting punishment and .the just be rewarded with never-ceasing glory.[5]

Whether, then, we consider the eternal decrees of God from the standpoint of reason or from the standpoint of Christian faith, they in no way favour indolence and indifference. To him who does not allow himself to hold as true every vagary of thought that can suggest itself, but takes suggestions for what they really are, the very irrevocability of these decrees, far from offering an excuse for idleness or bad morals, will rather be the strongest stimulus to guard against sin and to practise diligently prayer and good works. Such a one knows that, according to the unchangeable will of God, it depends upon the use of his moral freedom during life, whether after death that misery is to befall him which is the unavoidable doom of those who end their days in obstinate wickedness, or whether he shall have a share in the happiness held out by unfailing promises to those who die in loving submission to the laws of their Creator.

183. Still another difficulty concerning the eternal decrees of God is to be discussed here. How can God, being immutable, have any free volition at all? If He cannot change, His will remains always in the same state in which it is by virtue of His

[5] Cf. St. Luke xi. 5—13, xv. 10; St. John xx. 23; Heb. ix. 27; St. Matt. xxv. 46.

essence. How then can He will anything but with absolute necessity ?

To this difficulty we may answer in the first place that a puzzling *how* is never a solid reason for doubting an evident *that*. We have proved that God is both immutable in Himself and free in His decrees. Nay, a denial of Divine freedom would lead us logically to a denial of our own moral liberty, indeed to a denial of virtue and truth itself.

However, we further submit the following considerations.

Volition is an *immanent* action in the strictest sense of the word. What we express when we say, " I will this or that," is not a change either in ourselves or outside ourselves, but an actual state of our mind bearing a definite relation to a certain object, a relation the nature of which can only be understood by him who knows from self-consciousness what it is *to will*. Thus the most competent philosophers, from St. Thomas down to those of our own age,[6] are of opinion that the action of volition *considered in its essence* does not imply any change added to the actuality prerequired in the subject in order that volition may become possible. This holds good of all volitions of all rational beings whatsoever. It is true that in us men there is no volition without change going before and coming after. We cannot will anything without actual knowledge of the object willed. This actual knowledge is not included in

---

[6] Cf. St. Thomas, disp. *D* *Veritate*, q. 8. a. 6. ; Suarez, *Metaph.* disp. 48, sect. 2. n. 2. et sect. 4. n. 14. "Dico quarto ; " Kleutgen, *Phil. Schol.* n. 21 ; Lahousse, *Theol. Nat.* n, 209, p. 173.

our essence, but is acquired through a series of changes. Again, in consequence of our volition of any object, our mind is necessarily modified by being, as it were, *bent* upon that object—to say nothing of the accompanying changes in the nervous system. However, these changes do nôt touch the essence of volition. They do not prove that volition precisely *as volition* adds anything to the internal state in which a reasonable being exists when it is perfectly able to decide whether it wills `or refuses a certain object. If I am now *perfectly* able to accept or to reject the object *A* with my free-will, the act of self-determination proceeds in one direction or the other without any further physical change. If it did not, there would be no truth in the saying that I am now *perfectly* able to embrace either of the two alternatives. Nevertheless, my self-determination, as it proceeds, does carry a physical change with it; yet not because it is self-determination or free volition, but because it is free volition having a place in a being essentially changeable, and unable to persevere in its self-determination without undergoing some modification of its being.

Let us now apply these observations to the solution of our difficulty. God is infinite. By virtue of His essence He possesses whatever actuality is required for any volition compatible with His perfection. As we have explained, volition does not imply change *essentially*. Consequently, God can will any object without any real modification of His being.

Does it follow from this that whatever He wills

He wills with absolute necessity? By no means. It follows only that the internal act of His will, which is really identical with His essence, can without change either involve, or not involve, that relation to an object which we call *choosing* and *willing*. Whether God wills the object with absolute necessity or not, depends therefore only upon this, whether He understands it to be on every supposition loveable for its own sake. But apart from His decree to create, no finite being is loveable in itself. The conclusion is that without any internal change, God can will or not will any finite existence : consequently all finite beings are indebted for their existence to *the free choice* of His eternal unchangeable will. To express this shortly in scholastic terminology :

The will of God in its relation to creatures is absolutely necessary in its *entity* (*i.e.*, in its internal actual state), but not in its *term* (*i.e.*, it does not necessarily bear to creatures that relation which we call volition).

SECTION 2.—*Holiness and other moral attributes of the Divine Will.*

Thesis XXX.—*On account of the infinite rectitude of His will, God is to be called perfectly and absolutely holy, benevolent, and merciful, just, faithful, and true in His threats and promises.*

184. The word "holy," as used of creatures, has a wider and a more restricted sense. In the wider signification it means "being removed and distin-

guished from other things, or persons, by a sort of special dedication to the Divinity." In this sense we speak of churches as holy places; we call altar-plate and priestly vestments holy things; we say that bishops, priests, and others specially conse-crated to God, are to be revered as holy persons: and we give the visible Head of the Church the title of " Holy Father," and " Your Holiness."

The word " holy " predicated thus does not denote any distinction in the line of morality. Pope Alexander VI., in that he was the representative of the Divine Founder of the Church, had so far forth as much right to the title of Holy Father as St. Peter himself; although in point of moral excel-lence Peter as far surpassed the common standard of human virtue as Alexander fell short of it.

In a more restricted sense, holiness is predi-cated of men alone, to signify perfection of moral character ; in other words, perfect agreement of the free volitions and actions of a man with the moral law. The moral law itself is the eternal law of God, prescribing the line of action to be followed by rational creatures in the pursuit of their last end. The moral character of a man is perfect, if he does his duty with unfailing integrity. His duty as a reasonable being is to use his freedom reasonably. One of the first demands of reason in him is that he should submit freely to the will of his Creator as soon as he knows it. Doing so, he renders his actions in complete accordance with the dictates of infinite wisdom ; for as God's will is really one with His infinite intellect, it is impossible that God

U

should impose any duty upon us otherwise than in absolute harmony with His supreme reason. Hence we may define a holy man to be *a man who uses his free-will constantly in such a way as to comply with the rule of action that infinite wisdom has laid down for him from eternity.*

185. This definition, derived as it is from the common acceptation of the word, enables us to see that the attribute " holy," taken in its stricter sense, may be predicated of God. His free-will is not only united with His infinite wisdom, but *in its subjective aspect* is identical with it. It is, therefore, absolutely impossible that any free volition of God, any decree of His, any Divine action, or ordination, regarding creatures, should be different from what it ought to be according to the judgment of infinite wisdom. Independently of any other being, in virtue of His essence, God has an infinitely perfect knowledge of the way in which it behoves Him to use His freedom of will. Out of the purest love to His own infinite goodness (which is the spring and source of whatever is good), He wills and works according to that knowledge. Hence He is perfectly and absolutely holy, Holiness itself.

186. This holiness is the standard by which we must judge of the rest of God's moral attributes. The first of these attributes is the *love and benevolence* God bears towards His creatures. He loves all inasmuch as He wills they should all have some natural good. But in a stricter sense of the word God is said to love His rational creatures. Towards them He has a *love of benevolence or friendship.* On

the other hand, strictly speaking, we cannot say that He is *benevolent* to irrational creatures; the reason whereof is simply this, that benevolence is either joy over, or a wish for, another's happiness; and only rational beings are.capable of happiness. Love of friendship towards irrational creatures can only be based upon a misapprehension of their true nature. In view of the traces of the Divine goodness which they exhibit, and the generic similarity which they bear to the inferior part of our nature, we may call them our friends, or even, with the pious exaggeration of St. Francis, our brothers and sisters; we may be much opposed to reckless hurting of their sentient organism. All this accords perfectly with reason. But as soon as we begin to represent them to ourselves as self-conscious, as reflecting upon their state, and consequently, as capable of happiness and misery in the proper sense of the words—as *persons*, and not as *things only*— our behaviour becomes unreasonable, and borders on morbid sentimentality. It would be blasphemy to suppose such a violation of reason in God. In conclusion, as regards the benevolence of God towards His rational creatures, we know from reason alone that that benevolence is ample enough perfectly to satisfy the demands of infinite wisdom. From Revelation we are certain that God *on His part* is ready to make each of His rational creatures in a certain sense infinitely happy in a future life, and that only abuse of freedom *on their own part* can thwart and frustrate the benevolent intention of their Creator.

187. Light is thrown upon the benevolence of God by another of His moral attributes closely connected with it—*Divine mercy.* Mercy, as it is a virtue, and not blind feeling, consists in *the efficacious will to remove the misery of others to the extent approved of by rightly enlightened reason.* In men the practice of this virtue is frequently attended with a sort of tender emotion caused in our sensitive organism by the sight or imagination of misery. And just as benevolence is not seldom misapplied by us, so we may also err in the exercise of mercy. In those who are called to govern others, for instance, mercy may degenerate into a vice, if they allow themselves to be drawn away from preventing public danger by compassion for individual criminals, who experience pain and hardship if laws against crime are laid down and enforced.

Not a shadow of these and similar defects, which disfigure human mercy, can exist in the absolutely perfect mercy of God. In it there is nothing of blind emotion. It is purely spiritual, and the rule of its application is benevolent wisdom. For this reason the mercy of God must manifest itself here on earth in nothing so much as *providing means by which men may deliver themselves from moral misery.* In fact, as men alone of all visible creatures are able to attain happiness, so men alone can fall into that state which is properly termed misery. It is shown in Ethics that the final happiness of man must consist in union with God by perfect knowledge and love, a union to be expected in a future life. According to Christian revelation, this happy possession of God will be a supernatural one, an immediate intuition and fruition of the infinite beauty and goodness of our Creator, carrying with it a complete and never failing satisfaction of all our longings and desires without the least admixture of satiety or disgust.

From this it must be inferred that man is to be called substantially happy, in this mortal life, so long as he is on the right path to his future union with God, and really miserable, so soon as he goes astray from it. Here, then, there arises the question : Which is the true way to that union ? Reason answers clearly : *Compliance with the law of God in the use of moral freedom.* Christianity stamps this judgment of human reason with the seal of Divine authority; and assures us, moreover, that nothing is able to endanger man's final happiness but a deliberate breach of the law of God.

This being so, God cannot show His mercy in this world more splendidly than by leading men to the knowledge of Himself and to the observance of His law, and offering to those who transgress it a remedy against the evil consequences of their transgression.

188. Different from but not opposed to the effects of Divine mercy are the manifestations of another moral attribute of God—His justice. By this term we do not signify *commutative justice,* or that moral disposition which inclines us to render to others what they have a right to ask. This virtue cannot belong to God, who is the First Cause of all rightful claims, and against whom, strictly speaking, no one can

have a right, as He is the only Lord of all. However, besides that kind of justice there is another kind, called by writers on Ethics *distributive justice.* This term denotes a virtue proper to rulers of a community, a virtue which consists in *a constant will to treat every subject according to his dignity and merits.* Such a will is a moral excellence which does not connote any imperfection, and therefore cannot be wanting in God, whose absolute dominion extends over the whole of creation. Being possessed of infinite knowledge, He thoroughly comprehends the natural and supernatural dignity of each of His rational creatures, and estimates exactly its merits or demerits. Knowing, moreover, how many ways of treatment there are applicable to a concrete case without violation of wisdom, He is free to choose between those; but He cannot choose any way forbidden by His wisdom.

These few statements embrace almost everything that can be said on the subject of Divine justice *a priori.* To determine accurately the way in which creatures are to be dealt with in harmony with their natural dignity and merit, is the work of God alone, whose judgments man has not to criticize, but in all humility to accept. Created reason rightly used cannot be opposed to the reason that is uncreated.

189. From the identity of this uncreated reason with the will of God we argue that He possesses two other moral attributes, *veracity* and *fidelity.* God is truthful, that is to say, He never can utter falsehood, nor approve of any such utterance on the

part of His creatures. The reason is obvious. He is essentially infinite Intellect and infinitely righteous Will. Under the former aspect His essence is the expression of all objective truths in such a perfect way that He is constantly conscious of each of them; under the latter aspect He loves Himself necessarily as an infinitely complete representation of truth. His dealing with creatures must be in conformity with this love which is essential to Him. But an utterance made with the intention of leading into error would evidently be opposed to this essential love of truth. Such an intention would necessarily be involved in any false utterance coming from God: for Infinite Wisdom cannot tell an untruth by mistake. It follows then from God's very nature that His every utterance must be true.

But can God ever approve of a lie told by one of His rational creatures? To solve the question, we have only to weigh the fact that lying is directly in conflict with the natural desire for truth proper to rational beings. The good of a creature endowed with intellect is truth. Its final happiness is in the possession of God, the Infinite Truth. The preparation to be made for this happiness must be the direction of the creature's free-will towards God by the way of true knowledge and true love. For these reasons man feels himself instinctively repelled by the suggestion of deliberate insincerity. The child's first lie is told with remorse and confusion and sense of moral disorder. How could it be otherwise? The intention to tell a falsehood is a stain on the natural image of Eternal Truth

stamped upon the human heart. God Himself has
an infinite detestation of uttering what is false, and
necessarily wills that His rational creatures should
in all free acts conform their will to His will, and
consequently to the exigencies of their nature. It is
therefore altogether inconceivable that God should
ever approve of the deliberate spreading of falsehood.
Every deliberate lie must be condemned by Him
as something intrinsically bad : and all the more
condemned, the more it tends to draw men away
from God the Truth. Before all others therefore
those liars must be held in special abhorrence by
God who under the false pretence of Divine authori-
zation try to lead others into error as regards
religion and morals. Their endeavours cannot
possibly be favoured by evident marks of Divine
approval, as are true prophecies and true miracles.
No false religion can be supported by such marks.

God's veracity is the light which guides the
Christian safely along the narrow paths of faith.
Another moral attribute of God, His fidelity,
guarantees the attainment of the goal of happiness
to which living faith leads.

"God is faithful," writes St. Paul.[7] To prove
this, we need but to consider the veracity along
with the physical and moral immutability of God.
Being truthful, He does not reveal that He will
punish or bless, without at the time of the revelation intending to award punishment or blessing,
either absolutely or under certain conditions. This
intention, in virtue of His physical and moral

[7] 1 Cor. i. 9, and x. 13.

immutability, remains unchangeable. Consequently, when the time arrives to which the threat or promise is attached, and the condition fulfilled under which it was uttered, He is as determined to keep His word as He was when He first uttered it. As we shall see in the next chapter, He is also omnipotent. Therefore nothing can prevent Him from doing what He wills. Consequently, *He is faithful.* He will never be mocked by the sinner who despises His warnings, nor will He ever disappoint the just man who relies upon His promises.

Note.—Difficulties against the moral attributes of God will be solved in the chapter on Providence.

SECTION 3.—*The Will of God as supreme Life and Beatitude.*

Thesis XXXI.—*God lives an infinitely perfect intellectual life, and enjoys an infinite beatitude; consequently sadness, anger, and repentance are not to be predicated of Him except in a metaphorical sense.*

190. There are three principal kinds of life in this world: vegetative, sensitive, and intellectual. Vegetative life is carried on by the processes of nutrition, growth, and reproduction.

Sensitive life manifests itself in organic perception, imagination, organic instinct and craving, and in locomotion.

Intellectual life consists in acts of understanding and will.

As is proved in *Psychology*, plants have only vegetative life, brutes vegetative and sensitive but not intellectual life, whilst man unites in himself all three lives. God cannot have vegetative and sensitive life, for these involve a material organism, and God is a pure Spirit. But He must have intellectual life, which does not involve any *essential* dependence on matter, and is a pure perfection. His life is therefore essentially intellectual; and as His intellect and volition are infinitely perfect, He must be said to live an infinitely perfect life.

191. Even without the light of Revelation we can understand that the life of God must be infinitely blissful, a state of supreme beatitude. Beatitude is defined in scholastic language as the *bonum perfectum intellectualis naturæ, i.e.*, the fulness of everything really desirable to a rational being. Such a being has a natural longing for truth. Consequently, beatitude must attend the full possession of truth. This full possession is to be found in God, and in God alone. From this it follows that beatitude is greater in proportion as the union with God through knowledge and love increases. But God comprehends Himself with absolutely perfect knowledge, and has an infinite love for His own infinite goodness. He is therefore infinitely happy in virtue of His infinitely perfect life.

As He is unchangeable, so His beatitude can undergo no change. Neither the material universe, with its countless beauties and wonders showing forth everywhere traces of God's power, wisdom, and bounty, nor the world of created spirits, reflecting in legions of incorruptible beings the image of the Divine Majesty, nor the blessed in Heaven, praising their

Creator day and night, nor the just on earth serving Him under trials and temptations, can augment His beatitude in the least. Nor does the rebellion of Lucifer and his wicked band, the indifference and ingratitude of mortals, the never-ceasing obstinacy of the damned in Hell, mar in any way the happiness of Him whose essence is the centre and the only source of all happiness. He is the Lord who embraces His servants with a care and love infinitely more pure and generous than that of the tenderest mother, *but without anxiety and sorrow.* His Justice sentences the impenitent to everlasting misery, *but without anger and excitement*, and without wishing them evil *as evil*, out of love to the order demanded by His infinite Wisdom. " He was," to use the words of Cardinal Newman, "from eternity ever in action, though ever at rest ; ever surely in rest and peace, profound and ineffable : yet with a living present mind, self-possessed, and all-conscious, comprehending Himself and sustaining the comprehension. He rested ever, but He rested in Himself ; His own resource, His own end, His own contemplation, His own blessedness."[8]

192. It is then evident that no affection of will implying want of perfect peace and serenity of mind is compatible with the infinitely blissful state proper to the Divine Existence. *Sadness*, therefore, especially that sort of sadness called *envy*, which finds a reason for grief in the prosperity of others, and which by the heathens of old was attributed to their false gods, is altogether alien to the Divine Nature.

---

[8] *Discourses addressed to Mixed Congregations*, p. 289. (Seventh Edit.)

It follows from this also that *anger* and *repentance,* which have their root in some sadness, cannot be predicated of God *properly.*

Notwithstanding all this, there is a deep truth in the Scriptural expressions by which on certain occasions sadness, anger, and repentance are attributed to God. But they must be explained *as metaphors,* as Catholic Doctors have always explained them.[9]

God is said to be *angry,* because He decrees to inflict penalties on sinners; and thus deals with them as a king on earth might deal with a subject who had provoked his anger. But while the earthly potentate may be really angry, and act out of passion, God is neither liable to the passion of anger, nor can He inflict punishment for the sole object of causing pain. He does not punish save for justice' sake, and that in absolute calmness. Infinite, therefore, is the difference between what is metaphorically called the *anger of God,* and what is really the *anger of man.* The one resembles the other, not in its essence, but in its effects.

The same holds good of *repentance,* attributed to God *metaphorically,* and existing in man *really.* Repentance taken in its proper meaning is essentially sorrow and dissatisfaction arising from the consciousness of having done something evil, or omitted something good which should have been done. Such sorrow cannot be genuine, unless it includes the wish and resolution to undo the past mistake as much as possible. This purpose of following another

---

[9] Cf. St. Thomas, *Contra Gentes,* i. 89, and 91. § "Sciendum tamen."

line of action for the time to come is marked by special firmness and determination in the case of true repentance. For this reason the term " repent-ance " is a very apt metaphorical expression, to signify that God in virtue of His eternal decrees will henceforth either withdraw certain blessings and inflict certain penalties on account of the sins of men, or will cease to punish and pour out favours in consideration for sinners being sincerely converted to Him. In the former sense repentance is attributed to God in the Book of Genesis:[10] " It repented Him that He had made man." This phrase means that God foreseeing the spread of vice among the contemporaries of Noe, had decreed from eternity to destroy them off the face of the earth. The same term is used also to denote God's eternal decree to stay the infliction of penalties, on condition of true conversion. Thus God orders the Prophet Jeremias to speak to the cities of Juda, all the words which He had commanded him : " If so be they will hearken and be converted every one from his evil way, that I may repent Me of the evil that I think to do unto them for the wickedness of their doings."[11]

There are in Scripture other terms applied to God which signify *disgust* and *sadness* at the doings of others. This language metaphorically denotes the extreme hatred that the Divine will bears to sin, especially to those sins which are committed after the reception of special favours, or which imply want of faith and confidence in the word of God.

[10] Genesis vi. 6.   [11] Jeremias xxvi. 3.

Thus we read in reference to the ingratitude of the chosen people: "In those days the Lord began to be weary of Israel."[12]   The want of faith in the unbelieving King Achaz, the representative of the house of David, calls down the reproach: "O house of David, is it a small thing for you to be grievous to men, that you are grievous to my God also?"[13]

So long as men remain sensitive-rational beings —they will continue thus to express spiritual truths in metaphorical language.   And the more they contemplate the infinite perfection of the Creator of matter and spirit, and the more their heart is set on fire with love for "the First Author of beauty,"[14] the more impressively will they speak of Him in language rich with imagery.   Those who at once suspect anthropomorphism when they hear the language of metaphor used of the First Cause, are as unreasonable as he would be who should accuse men of anthropomorphizing nature when they seek a shelter against the *rage* of a snowstorm, protect the *sensitiveness* of a delicate instrument, disport themselves in the *smiling* meadows, or watch the sun sinking to his *couch.*

---

[12] 4 Kings x. 32.   [13] Isaias vii. 13.
[14] Cf. Wisdom xiii. 3.

CHAPTER VI.

THE OMNIPOTENCE OF GOD.

Thesis XXXII.—*God is able by the infinite efficacy of His will to effect whatever is not intrinsically impossible; wherefore He is all-powerful or omnipotent.*

193. Power is ability to effect. In created agents there is no ability to effect anything beyond changes in things that are already existing in virtue of God's creative act, as we have proved in Book I. Even this power of producing changes in already existing things is in many ways imperfect, as creatures possess it. In inanimate matter, plants and dumb animals, the power is exercised without the agent being able to control it. The magnet has no choice, but must communicate its mysterious power to the iron that comes near it; the oak-tree of necessity pushes its roots beneath the earth to obtain nourishment; nor can the dog help running to the food that tempts his appetite, or turning against another animal which has provoked his anger. It is evident that such blind power is essentially defective, and therefore altogether inconceivable in God.

Let us now turn to the consideration of the power of man. In him, as in the lower animals, there are material forces, vital power, sensitive perception, animal instinct, and the faculty of loco-motion. But in him there is, besides all this, intellect and free-will; and in virtue of the intel-lectual life sustained by these two faculties, he has the power of producing an effect freely chosen. He alone therefore among all beings of the visible world has a power which can properly be predicated of God. No production of any effect can be a mani-festation of pure perfection, unless it be controlled by free-will. Yet not all production thus controlled, when considered in the concrete, is pure perfection. It is enough to glance at the exercise of man's power in order to see the truth of this statement. Man has the power of choice and of carrying out what he has chosen, only on certain conditions independent of his free-will. There is, moreover, in him a real distinction between the faculty of choosing and the faculty of carrying out the effect chosen. The former resides in his will, the latter in the faculties subject to the rule of his will. If he chooses something for which these faculties are unfit, his faculty of choice is not borne out by the faculty of execution, as in the case of a paralytic resolving to walk. In this case choice is not only distinct from execution, but is altogether divorced from it. Choice thus void of efficiency is not power. That power alone is absolute perfection which *essentially* involves at once the faculty of choosing and the faculty of carrying out the choice: and this is the exclusive privilege of the power of God. God is essentially Free-will in His relation to everything

distinct from His own unchangeable essence. Whatever He chooses to effect, that He carries out by
the efficacy of His will. " Power," says St. Thomas,
" is not attributed to God as something really
different from His knowledge and will, but as
something expressed by a different idea; as power
means the principle which carries out the command
of the will and the advice of the intellect. These
three (viz., intellect, will, power), coincide with one
another in God." [1]

194. The power of God, being absolutely perfect
and really one with His intellect and will, and consequently with the simple, infinite, Divine essence,
must be infinite; that is to say, it must suffice of
itself to produce whatever is not intrinsically impossible. Hence it follows that God can, by His
will alone, produce things out of nothing. This
truth we have proved in Book I., by showing that
no other hypothesis than that of creation can
account for the origin of matter and mind, in
accordance with the nature of God and of material
and spiritual things. The explanation just now
given of God's power, and of its identity with His
will, is calculated not only to bear out the fact of
creation, but also to show how the possibility of
creation is necessarily attached to the essence
of God.

---

[1] " Potentia non ponitur in Deo ut aliquid differens ab scientia
et voluntate secundum rem sed solum secundum rationem, in
quantum scilicet potentia importat rationem principii exequentis
id quod voluntas imperat et ad quod scientia dirigit ; quæ tria,
Deo secundum idem conveniunt." (St. Thomas, *Sum. Theol.* 1a. q. 25.
art. 1. ad 4.)

It further follows that the range of Divine power infinitely surpasses its actual productions. These are regulated by irrevocable eternal decrees. Once such decrees are made by Him, God can apply His power only in agreement with their import.

Therefore we have to distinguish between the *absolute* and the *regulated* power of God (*potentia Dei absoluta et ordinata*). By His absolute power He can do everything which is not intrinsically repugnant. By His power, however, as ruled by His decrees, or by His regulated power, He cannot carry out anything but that which He has decreed. Thus, for instance, God has the absolute power to preserve man altogether from death: but He cannot do so in the present order, because He has decreed otherwise. To express this technically, scholastics say: God can preserve man from death, *potentia absoluta;* He cannot do so *potentia ordinata.*

195. Against the omnipotence of God thus explained the following difficulties are often raised.

(1) God cannot commit a sin. But the commission of a sin is something intrinsically possible. Therefore God cannot do everything intrinsically possible.

Answer. In answering this difficulty we have first to remark that the essence of sin does not consist in the production of an effect, but in the opposition of free-will to the eternal law of God. If a sin carries an effect with it, as in the case of blasphemy, theft, murder, and other crimes, such an effect is sinful only inasmuch as it is brought about by the abuse of moral freedom to the neglect of the Divine law. Sin therefore is intrinsically possible only in a being whose will can neglect the law of God, and whose faculties can be used in opposition to that law.

But the will of God cannot be opposed to the law of God, because that law considered under its subjective aspect is really identical with the act of the Divine will. Nor can any Divine faculty be used in opposition to the Divine law, because none is really distinct from its source, the unchangeable Divine essence. Although, therefore, sin in a created being is intrinsically possible, yet the proposition, " God can sin," is intrinsically contradictory. Nor can it be said that this intrinsic repugnance between the nature of God and, the nature of sin implies any defect of power in God. It would do so indeed, if sin *considered precisely as sin* consisted in the production of something really distinct from the *free self-determination of the will to neglect a line of thinking, judging, desiring, acting, sufficiently manifested by the voice of conscience as prescribed by the Creator.* The perfection underlying the action of self-determination is the faculty of free-will; and this faculty, of course, is in God *formally and eminently.* The action of self-determination itself, as we have repeatedly remarked, is not a production of any reality distinct from the free choice of the will, but it is the will itself, inasmuch as it approves, or rejects, or neglects an object presented by the understanding as eligible. When a being endowed with free-will and capable of sinning, enjoys the use of its freedom, it does not want more power to commit sin than to abstain from sin, but its power in that state suffices for either of the two alternatives.   On the other hand, the ability to commit sin involves liability to be overcome by false, unreasonable motives, and this liability is rather weakness and imperfection than power and perfection.   Consequently, if God could commit sin, he would not possess more active physical power, but would be exposed to moral weakness.

(2) God can produce no other God.   But if His power were infinite, He should be able to do so; because infinite power must suffice for the production of an infinite Being.

Answer. As we have seen in Book I., it is repugnant to the nature of a self-existing being that it should exist in several separate individuals.

Hence another God is something intrinsically impossible.   Infinite power, *precisely because it is infinite*, cannot be fully manifested, whether in a particular effect or in a series of effects; it is essentially *inexhaustible power.*

For this reason it also excludes the possibility not only of another *God*, but even of an *absolutely* best *world* or best *creature*, as we have explained in Book I. chap. **iv.**

CHAPTER VII.

THE METAPHYSICAL ESSENCE OF GOD.

Thesis XXXIII.—*The metaphysical essence of God, or that Divine attribute by which the human intellect must principally distinguish Him from all created beings, is the attribute of self-existence. In other words, God is best defined by saying that He is the self-existing Being, or "He who is." Consequently, the transcendental attributes, "Truth," "Goodness," "Beauty," belong most properly to God, who is to be called the first and supreme Truth, the first and supreme Goodness, the first and supreme Beauty.*

196. The essence of a created thing is that in virtue of which it is what it is (*id quo res est id quod est*), or that which constitutes its inmost being, and without which it could not possibly be what it is said to be. Using the term in a wider sense, we apply it not only to natural substances, but also to artificial things, to accidental determinations of substances, and even to defects. Thus we speak of the essence of a machine, of the essence of colour, of the essence of a disease, of sin, &c. But primarily the word "essence" is used of natural substances.

Under this aspect of the meaning of "essence"

a distinction is to be drawn between the essence of a thing *as existing* and *as conceived by a human intellect.*

There are in the order of existence as many essences as there are different substances; for each particular substance has its peculiar being, and is in virtue thereof one particular substance and no other. As St. Thomas expresses it : *Esse proprium cujuslibet rei est tantum unum*—"The proper being of each thing is only one."[1]

If a particular individual thing could be conceived by us adequately and according to its proper being, our knowledge of its essence would be complete; in other words, we should have grasped what some among modern scholastics call *the physical essence* of the thing.[2]

But no substance is fully known by us according to the inmost constitution of its being. Consequently of none do we know exactly its physical essence. Such distinction as we are able to draw between one individual thing and another, is based upon a difference of accidental determinations, or individual marks (*notæ individuantes*). Thus we tell one man from another by his figure, gait, size, countenance, voice, &c.

The essence of created things *as conceived by us* does not contain all, but only some of the realities of which its physical essence is made up, to wit,

[1] *Contra Gentes,* i. c. 42.

[2] Cf. Grand-Claude, *Breviarium Philosophiæ,* ii. n. 355. What here is called physical essence corresponds in *natural* substances to the *esse* of St. Thomas as distinguished from *essentia.*

such as are found in other things of a similar, though not really the same, physical essence.

Conceiving for instance the essence of an individual man as a sensitive rational being, I conceive it in no way adequately as it is existing, but only inadequately according to those notes which I conceive as obtaining in all individual men. These individuals differ from one another *precisely in virtue of their different physical essences*, whilst at the same time they resemble one another on account of the *similarity* of those essences. The notes which form the basis of such a resemblance constitute the metaphysical essence of each member of the group.

The metaphysical essence is consequently an inadequate mental expression of the physical essence of a thing. That expression may be of various shades of perfection. It may express only the remote *genus* to which a thing belongs, or its proximate *genus* only, or its proximate *genus* together with the specific difference, by which the lowest species of which it is a member, differs from other species. Thus I express the metaphysical essence of my friend very inadequately by saying that he is a *substance*, more to the point by giving him the name of *living being*, still better by affirming that he is an *animal*, and best of all by declaring that he is a *rational animal*.

What we have said about physical and metaphysical essence, is based upon the doctrine laid down by logicians that the universal *as such* has no existence, but exists only inasmuch as it is realized in particular things resembling one another. Hence it is readily understood that the metaphysical essence of a created thing is a true but imperfect mental delineation of the physical essence; and that consequently the distinction between metaphysical and physical essence, *in so far as both are verified in one individual thing*, is not a distinction existing *as such* objectively, but in thought only. Yet as it is based upon the objective similarity of physical essences, it is not a mere fiction, but founded on a real fact.

The limitations of the human intellect prevent our having any more accurate conception of the essence of a created being than is obtained by putting together those notes which constitute its lowest species. We say accordingly that we know the essence of a thing, when we are able to express the realities intelligible in each member of its lowest species. For the same reason the definition of a thing is supposed sufficiently to express its essence, when it gives a good account of its specific nature, as is done by indicating the proximate *genus* and the specific difference of that nature. Here then the old principle of St. Thomas is verified, that our way of speaking imitates the inadequacy of our conceptions. Although the metaphysical essence of a thing expresses its real physical essence but very imperfectly, yet it is simply called "essence." "Essence or nature," says St. Thomas, "comprises only those notes of a thing which fall under the definition of a species, as for instance humanity comprises only those notes which are contained in the definition of man; for by these man is man."[3]

"Essence is properly that which is signified by a definition. But a definition comprises only the constituents of a species, not those of an individual."[4]

"The essence of each thing is that which is signified by its definition."[5]

197. These remarks about "essence" may suffice to explain the sense in which Catholic philosophers speak of the *Divine Essence*. Sometimes they use the term to express what would correspond to the physical essence of creatures. We meet for instance with passages like the following: "Although the existence of God and some of His attributes are knowable, yet His Essence cannot be known by us, so long as we are in this life." In such phrases "Essence" means *the Being of God as it is in itself.* Thus considered, it is hidden from our direct and immediate intuition. Our natural knowledge about it is altogether inferential, analogical, and inadequate. And, indeed, so it must be. Experience testifies that we are unable to grasp adequately the physical essence of even the meanest of creatures. How then shall we fathom that of the Creator?

---

[3] St. Thomas, *Sum. Theol.* 1a. q. 3. art. 3. in corp. "Essentia vel natura comprehendit illa tantum quæ cadunt in definitione speciei; sicut humanitas comprehendit in se ea quæ cadunt in definitione hominis; his enim homo est homo."

[4] "Essentia proprie est id quod significatur per definitionem. Definitio autem complectitur speciei principia, non autem principia individualia." (St. Thomas, *Sum. Theol.* i. 29. 2. ad 3.)

[5] "Essentia enim uniuscujusque rei est illud quod significat definitio ejus." (*Compendium Theol.* c. x.)

The question then arises: Is there among the attributes of God any one attribute that may rightly be called His metaphysical Essence? This attribute, if such there be, must distinguish God from all species of finite beings after the manner in which the metaphysical essence of creatures of a certain species distinguishes them from those of another species of the same proximate *genus.* And as the metaphysical essence of a creature is for our intellect the root of its specific properties, so the metaphysical essence of God should furnish a foundation for our mind to construct thereupon in systematic order the rest of the Divine attributes.

To this question different answers have been given by different schoolmen. Scotus thought that the attribute of infinity was aptly called the Essence of God; Billuart held that the Divine intelligence, inasmuch as it is self-existing, deserved that name.

Neither of these two opinions satisfies the explanation of metaphysical essence given above. To human reason, unaided by revelation, infinity is not the *root* of all the attributes of God.; for we cannot understand why God must be infinite, before we have understood that He is self-existent and one.[6] Nor again is the attribute of intelligence, considered as self-existent, the starting-point from which our intellect proceeds in order to establish the rest of the Divine attributes. Moreover, this attribute of intelligence contains more than is necessary to distinguish God from all creatures.

[6] Cf. Bk. I. p. 100.

For this purpose it is not requisite to affirm that He is a self-existent Intelligence; it is enough to say that He is self-existent; for a self-existent being must be infinitely intelligent, as our previous arguments have shown.

It is then in the attribute of self-existence alone that we find these properties which make a Divine attribute correspond to what we call in creatures *metaphysical essence*. In this attribute there is expressed as well that which is (analogically) common to God and to creatures, as also that by which He is distinguished from them all. God *exists really* and creatures *exist really*. God has *His proper being*, or, rather *is it*, and so has every creature *its proper being*. Inasmuch therefore as "being," conceived in the highest possible abstraction, means nothing more than opposition to nothingness, we say truly: God *is* and the creature *is*. Yet the Divine being and the created being differ infinitely from one another in that *the former is independent*, the latter *dependent;* the former *uncaused*, the latter *caused;* the former has *all things of itself*, the latter has *absolutely nothing of itself*, but is itself an effect produced out of nothing according to a preconceived idea derived from the Divine essence. This infinite difference is indicated by saying, that God not only *is*, but *is of Himself*, in virtue of His own essence; in a word, He is self-existent. From this concept of self-existence we have unfolded the unity and infinity of God and established rules for determining whether any given created perfection is to be affirmed or denied of the Creator and in what

sense.[7]   Following these rules we found the chief
negative and positive attributes of God, as expounded in the six previous chapters of this Book.

Self-existence is consequently, for a logically
reasoning human intellect, not merely a distinctive
excellence of the Divinity, it is the one fundamental
excellence from which all others are to be explained.
Therefore it deserves the name of *Divine Essence.*

198. The only objection worthy of consideration
against this view is this, that self-existence does
not sufficiently mark off the one true God from the
fictitious deity of pantheists and the uncreated
atoms of materialists. It would seem that monotheists, pantheists, and materialists agree with one
another perfectly in that they suppose a self-existent
source of all being. *Monotheists* believe in a *self-
existent* personal and infinite God, who created all
things other than Himself out of nothing by His
omnipotent will. *Pantheists,* at least our modern
Spinozists and Hegelians, assume *a self-existent
substance or idea* developing into various spiritual
and material things as so many modes or determinations of its proper being. *Materialists* imagine
self-existent atoms driven by inexplicable laws to
evolve out of their innermost potentiality life and
sense and reason.

If then self-existence is predicated both of
fictitious first causes and of the one true First
Cause, how can we say that it expresses the essence
of God?

To understand fully the answer to this question,

7 See the rules laid down in Bk. I. pp. 101, seq.

the reader must bear in mind what has been proved in Book I. chap. iv. against the pantheistic and materialistic hypothesis. It has been shown there[8] that both the self-existent and self-evolving deity of pantheists, and the self-existent atoms assumed by materialists, are intrinsically absurd. Now definitions are not made to distinguish the thing defined from intrinsic absurdities, but to point out its difference from realities. The definition of God must therefore contain that by which God is clearly and primarily distinguished from all *real things* that are not God. And from all these He is clearly and primarily distinguished by the definition : *God is the self-existent being*. If, therefore, according to the common way of speaking, the essence of a thing is the import of its definition, self-existence must be the essence of God.

The truth underlying the difficulty which we have solved amounts to this, that the phrase, *God is the self-existing being*, is not a definition, which in an age like our own should be put forward without proper explanation. Yet this does not prevent it from being a good definition in itself. All definitions need explaining according to the circumstances of those to whom they are propounded.

199. Comparing the definition given with the name under which God revealed Himself to Moses: "*I am who am. . . .* Thus shalt thou say to the children of Israel: *He who is* hath sent me to you ; "[9] we see that the phrase, *He who is*, is identical in meaning with *the self-existent being*. The term, "self-existent

8 Bk. I. c. iv. § 78, seq. and §§ 93, seq.   9 Exodus iii. 14.

being," denotes that actual essence which alone is incapable of being rightly conceived otherwise than as existing in itself. Every other actual essence can be conceived as not existing in itself, as a mere term of the Divine intellect, a purely possible imitation of the Divine essence. But this is exactly what is meant by the Scriptural phrase, " He who is." God is accurately defined to be *the self-existent being, ipsum esse in se subsistens,*[10] and He is equally well defined, *He who is, Qui est.*

For the appropriateness of this name revealed by God Himself, St. Thomas [11] gives three reasons.

(1) This name suggests to us that God is not a being made according to a preconceived eternal idea, but a *necessarily existing essence.*[12]

(2) This name, as it is of the widest universality, does not, like other names, such as *Mighty, Wise, Just,* connote a certain class or classes of beings. Consequently, when used with emphasis as the proper name of the Divine Being, it suggests to us that that Being is not limited in His perfection to the reality conceivable in one or more genera of finite things, but unites in Himself *eminently* whatever outside Himself can be conceived as *being,* in opposition to *privation* or *defect.*[13]

---

[10] St. Thomas, *Sum. Theol.* 1a. q. 4. art. ii. in corp.

[11] St. Thomas, *Sum. Theol.* 1a. q. 13. art. xi. in corp.

[12] " Primum quidem propter sui significationem. Non enim significat formam aliquam sed ipsum esse," &c.

[13] "Secundo propter ejus universalitatem. . . . Quolibet enim alio nomine determinatur aliquis modus substantiæ rei ; sed hoc nomen *Qui est* nullum modum essendi determinat, sed se habet indeterminate ad omnes, et ideo nominat ipsum pelagus substantiæ infinitum."

(3) The name *He who is*, as it contains the substantive verb *to be* in the present tense, connotes the essence of God to be unalterable eternity, an unchangeable standing "now" in the midst of transitory created existences.[14]

200. The metaphysical essence of God naturally suggests His three transcendental attributes : Truth, Goodness, Beauty. We call them transcendental, because they transcend all the genera and classification of substances inasmuch as they are not properties of a certain class or classes of substances, but are, to a certain extent, verified in every creature. They express the perfection of all being whatsoever, as bearing certain relations to intellect and will.[15]

Every being, in so far as it is conceivable as a positive reality, is *true;* in so far as its perfection is matter of approval or desire to a rational will, it is *good;* and in so far as its perfection involves an excellence which the intellect cannot contemplate without the will, if duly disposed, being moved to a certain complacency and delight, it is *beautiful.*[16]

As then God unites in His self-existent essence all conceivable perfections, He must stand in such a relation to every intellect and will as to deserve in a

---

[14] "Tertio vero ex ejus consignificatione. . . . Significat enim esse in præsenti ; et hoc maxime proprie de Deo dicitur, cujus esse non novit præteritum vel futurum."

[15] This is the original meaning of the word "transcendental," as it was employed for centuries by scholastic philosophers. Since Kant it has been employed with another meaning in quite a different connection. According to Kant, the transcendental is what surpasses our experience.

[16] St. Thomas, *Sum. Theol.* 1a. q. 5. art. 4. ad 1.

most proper sense the denominations of Truth, Goodness, Beauty. A short explanation and proof of this will aptly conclude this chapter.

201. (1) *Truth.* We must distinguish objective truth, intellectual truth, moral truth. A thing is *objectively* or *essentially* true, in so far as it deserves the name of *thing*, and is not a mere chimera. Every conceivable possible or actual substance is consequently *objectively true.* Besides this properly transcendental meaning of truth, there are two other senses in which truth is found only in rational beings. A rational being apprehending and judging a thing in harmony with its possible or actual existence, and not confounding the one with the other, has *formal* or *intellectual* truth; *its intellect is formally or intellectually true.* Intellectual or formal truth is the conformity of the knowing intellect with the object known (*adaequatio intellectus cum re*).

A rational being when it addresses itself to other minds by speech or equivalent modes of expression, is said to be truthful or not according as it manifests or not what it takes to be objective truth. This sort of truth or truthfulness is generally called *moral* truth. The speaker is under a moral obligation to be truthful in this manner.

In each of these three meanings *truth* is proper to God without limit. He is *infinitely perfect objective Truth;* for He is not only a really conceivable Being, but He is the only Being the acknowledgment of whom explains all realities, as He is the principle of all possible being and the First Cause of all actual being outside Himself. Being possessed of an infinite intellect, which is really identical with His essence, He is the first *intellectual Truth*, not liable either to the shadows of ignorance or to the depravations of error. Moreoyer it has been proved in our exposition of His moral attributes that His veracity and faithfulness are absolutely perfect. Each revelation He makes is therefore *morally true ;* and as the manifestation of infinitely perfect wisdom, altogether *infallible.*

202. (2) *Goodness* is distinguished as absolute and relative. *Absolute goodness* is the perfection of a being, in so far as it cannot be considered in itself without eliciting the approval of a rational and righteous will. *Relative goodness* is the perfection of a being, considered in its aptitude to satisfy the natural tendencies of other beings.

From these definitions it appears easily that God is *supreme goodness* both absolute and relative. He is *supreme absolute goodness* by virtue of His infinitely perfect essence, which contains without any defect everything worthy of approval and love. He is *supreme relative goodness*, for, as we shall see in Book III., no creature can reach the goal of its existence unless it be preserved and directed by Him, who alone is the First Cause of its goodness ; and, as we see in Ethics, no rational being can find the happiness for which it has been made, save through union with Him by perfect knowledge and love. Nay, just as *being*, when taken as a necessary attribute, cannot be predicated except of God, so *goodness* is predicable with absolute necessity of God

w

alone. In this sense our Saviour said, "None is good but God alone." [17]

St. Thomas gives a fuller explanation of this truth in the following words : " God alone is good by His essence. For the goodness of everything is based upon its perfection. Now there is a three-fold perfection of a thing to be distinguished. The first is that which constitutes its existence. To this a second perfection is added, in that the thing existing receives some accidental qualities necessary for its perfect operation. Its third perfection con-sists in attaining something outside itself as the end of its existence. . . . But of these three perfections none belongs to any creature in virtue of its essence. God alone possesses them in this way. Indeed of Him alone can it be said that His essence is His existence ; He alone cannot receive accidental quali-ties, but possesses as identical with His essence what is predicated of others accidentally — for instance, power, wisdom, &c. He also has no end to reach, but is Himself the end of all things. It is consequently evident that God alone is essentially perfect in every respect, which is tantamount to saying that He alone is good in virtue of His essence." [18]

---

[17] St. Luke xviii. 19.

[18] " Solus Deus est bonus per suam essentiam. Unumquodque enim dicitur bonum secundum quod est perfectum. Perfectio autem alicujus rei triplex est. Prima quidem, secundum quod in suo esse constituitur ; secunda vero, prout ei aliqua accidentia superadduntur ad suam perfectam operationem necessaria ; tertia vero perfectio alicujus est per hoc quod aliquid aliud attingit sicut finem. . . . Hæc autem triplex perfectio nulli creato competit

In the following article the Angelic Doctor explains thus the relation of God's goodness to that of creatures: "Everything is said to be good in virtue of the Divine goodness, inasmuch as this is the prototype, the first efficient cause and last end of whatever is good. Nevertheless everything is good in itself, in so far as it is a sort of copy of the Divine Being, from the resemblance to which it is formally denominated good. Thus under one aspect there is *one* goodness of all, under another aspect there are, if we may say so, *many* goodnesses."[10]

Note.—Goodness in a more limited sense signifies reasonable benevolence. That this must be predicated of God in regard to His rational creatures we have proved when treating of the moral attributes.[20]

203. (3) *Beauty* is the inseparable companion of perfect goodness. By the beautiful we mean that which, when intellectually perceived, excites by its

secundum suam essentiam, sed soli Deo, cujus solius essentia est suum esse, et cui non adveniunt aliqua accidentia ; sed quæ de aliis dicuntur accidentaliter, sibi conveniunt essentialiter, ut esse potentem, sapientem, et alia hujusmodi ; ipse etiam ad nihil aliud ordinatur sicut ad finem, sed ipse est ultimus finis omnium rerum. Unde manifestum est quod solus Deus habet omnimodam perfectionem secundum suam essentiam ; et ideo ipse solus est bonus per suam essentiam." (St. Thomas, *Sum. Theol.* i. q. 6. a. 3.

[19] " Unumquodque dicitur bonum bonitate divina, sicut primo principio exemplari, effectivo et finali totius bonitatis. Nihilominus tamen unumquodque dicitur bonum similitudine divinæ bonitatis sibi inhærente, quæ est formaliter sua bonitas, denominans ipsum. Et sic est bonitas una omnium, et etiam multæ bonitates." (*Ibid.* a. 4. c. fin.)

[20] Cf. Bk. II. c. v. sect. 2, § 186.

mere contemplation feelings of satisfaction and delight in the well-disposed will. This idea is happily expressed in the old saying, *Pulcrum est splendor veri*—" Beauty is the lustre of truth."

The description given applies equally to a beautiful edifice, a beautiful statue, a beautiful sermon, a beautiful saying, beautiful music, and to a beautiful idea, a beautiful way of acting, a beautiful character, a beautiful soul.[21]   As our intellect in this life can have no direct intuition but of sensible things, it is impossible for mortal men to contemplate beauty intuitively unless it appears under sensible forms.   Yet its essence is in no way sensible, but purely intellectual.   The most essential note of beauty in corporeal things is proportion of parts to a whole and to one another.   Now proportion *as such* is evidently an object not of sense-perception, but of intellectual apprehension, whether it exists in the region of colour or of sound or of ideas, in the harmony of the animal body, limb with limb, or in the fitness of moral action to the rational nature of the doer.   It follows from this that a brute beast, although it may have an attraction for bright colour, has no true taste for beauty; and that the ability of a man to judge of its presence or absence increases with the power of his intellect to strike a comparison between phenomenal appearance and ideal type.   *Pulchra dicuntur quæ visa placent,*[22] says St. Thomas.   " Things beautiful are

---

[21] Cf. Gœthe's *Aus den Bekenntnissen einer schönen Seele.*

[22] St. Thomas, *Sum. Theol.* 1a. q. 5. art. 4. ad 1.   From the context it appears clearly that it is not the intention of the Angelic

those of which the mental intuition causes delight."
The more comprehensive the mental intuition of
the beautiful, the greater is the spiritual delight
produced by it. Things of which we can have no
direct intuition are to be judged beautiful if it can
be shown that *on the supposition of immediate contemplation* spiritual satisfaction would naturally
arise. This being so, God must be *infinitely
beautiful.* In the section on Divine Life [23] we
draw the conclusion that the comprehensive knowledge which God has of this His perfection necessarily involves in Him a state of infinite happiness.
How much more must this infinite perfection of
the Creator suffice to make finite minds happy
if they are allowed to behold it. As God is
the final end of man, even the knowledge of Him
as He is reflected in the mirror of creatures
would, as is proved in Ethics, become so perfect in
our final state as to cause in us a perfect natural
happiness, supposing us not to have been raised to
a supernatural state, nor ever to have forfeited the
attainment of our last end by sin not pardoned.
Indeed, the millions of infants who die without
baptism every year will rejoice throughout eternity
over the Divine beauty as it is reflected in creation.
Yet their knowledge of God and the happiness
resulting from it cannot be compared with what
Christian faith leads us to live and to long for. By

Doctor to confine the province of the beautiful to *things visible by
the eyes of the body.* He says expressly, "Pulcrum et bonum in
subjecto quidem sunt idem . . . sed ratione differunt."

[23] Bk. II. c. v. sect. 3, § 191.

this faith we are certain that all those who believe in the Word made Flesh with that living faith which works through charity are children of God by adoption. As such they are destined to see God face to face, and to find a torrent of delight in the vision of His eternal and unchangeable beauty. The hope of coming to the enjoyment of this beauty of beauties has guided and strengthened the Apostles and martyrs of all ages in the midst of persecutions and torments. They reckoned with St. Paul "that the sufferings of this time are not worthy to be compared with the glory to come, that shall be revealed in us," [24] when we shall see "the Blessed and only Mighty, the King of kings and Lord of lords, who only hath immortality, and inhabiteth light inaccessible " [25] to the intuition of mortals. The same hope forms even at the end of our materialistic nineteenth century an inexhaustible source of consolation for millions of Christians, who experience in the practice of Christianity the fulfilment of the Divine promise: "He shall know of the doctrine whether it be of God." [26] It is they who truly can rejoice in the thought of their Creator even here on earth, whilst His essence is not seen by them. If all around seems dark, in Him they find light. If everything else be lost, in Him they recover it abundantly. "Wearied with the never-ceasing din of the world, wearied with the monotonous bustle of commerce and of trade, wearied with the hollow pretensions, the duplicity, the jealousies of political

[24] Romans viii. 18.   [25] 1 Tim. vi. 15, 16.
[26] St. John vii. 17.

parties, wearied yet more with the trivialities of social intercourse, and with the solemn littlenesses of individual self-assertion as it jostles its way among the crowd to gain its own wretched hillock—what a joy and consolation to pass by contemplation (if only for an hour) into the bosom of our ever-tranquil God."[27] It was during an hour of this sublimest of all contemplations that St. Augustine exclaimed : " Too late I loved Thee, O Thou, Beauty of ancient days, yet ever new! too late I loved Thee."[28]

[27] Harper, *Sermon on Spiritual Life,* p. 1.

[28] " Sero te amavi, pulchritudo tam antiqua et tam nova, sero te amavi." (St. Aug. *Conf.* x. 27.)

NATURAL THEOLOGY.

BOOK III.
THE ACTION OF GOD UPON THIS WORLD.

PROLEGOMENA.

CONNECTION OF THIS BOOK WITH THE TWO PRECEDING.

204. IN Book I. we showed that the visible universe and the minds of men are indebted for their origin to one personal infinitely perfect God, who created matter and mind by the potency of a sheer exercise of volition. Thus the Christian idea of God is justified before the tribunal of reason under a two-fold aspect; for it became evident that logical reasoning from the deliverance of our senses and consciousness leads to the acknowledgment of what Christian monotheists believe both about the fundamental attributes of God and about His fundamental relation to this world as Creator of all things.

A fuller explanation and defence of the truths implicitly contained in the most fundamental attributes of God (His self-existence, unity, simplicity, infinity), formed the subject-matter of Book II. During the course of it we saw first that the infinite Divine Being is placed above all internal changes by His immutability, above all limits of duration by His eternity, beyond all boundaries of space by His immensity. From these three negative attributes we passed on to the consideration of the intellect and the will of God, those two positive attributes which constitute the Divine life. It appeared clearly that the Creator with an all-comprehensive intellectual grasp comprehends both the infinite depths of His Divinity, and the innumerable multitude of finite beings, possibilities that shall never turn to actualities, and also the whole of past, present, and future existences, including even the future free volitions of rational creatures. Next it was proved that God, knowing that He is infinitely perfect, must love Himself with absolute necessity, whilst He is free to grant or not to grant existence to things distinct from His essence. It was then shown that the exercise of Divine freedom must be one eternal irrevocable choice, and reasons were given for the compatibility of such a choice with the unchangeable state of the Divine Nature. Having after that expounded the holiness of God and the chief moral attributes comprised in it (benevolence, mercy, justice, veracity, and fidelity), we concluded the treatise on the intellectual life of God by demonstrating that He not only lives in the most proper sense of the word, but lives also an infinitely happy life.

From the consideration of the internal perfection

of the Divine will we next proceeded to weigh its relation to possible finite beings, and arrived at the conclusion that under this aspect Divine volition implies infinite power, or omnipotence. The particular attributes of God thus established were in the last chapter of Book II. compared with one another; and it was found that the most fundamental of them all for the purposes of human thought, is the attribute of self-existence; that this attribute therefore deserves the appellation of "Divine Essence;" and that the name most appropriate to the Creator in opposition to His creatures is that revealed by Himself, "Jahveh," or "He who is." The fulness of being implicitly signified by this name led to the final conclusion, that God stands in such a relation to every competent and well-disposed intellect and will as to be, in the most proper sense of the term, supreme truth, supreme goodness, supreme beauty.

The reader sees from this short recapitulation that the whole of Book II. aims at bringing out logically and distinctly the import of the first fundamental truth established in Book I. viz., that "there exists a personal God, one, simple, infinitely perfect Being." It remains now to draw the logical consequences from the second fundamental dogma proved in Book I. viz., that "God is the Creator of the universe."

205. The first question suggested by the great fact of creation is this: How far do existing creatures continue to be dependent on God both as regards the continuance of their being and the exercise of

their activity? It will appear from the answers to be given to this question that under a certain aspect God continually preserves all finite beings and operates immediately in all their operations. These answers call forth at once another query: What is the final goal prefixed by the Creator to the existence and actions of creatures? Is the activity He exerts in their regard such as to deserve the name of Divine providence and government? How shall we reconcile the affirmation of Divine providence and government with the evils of this world, and with what Christians believe about the eternal punishment of the wicked in the life to come? Moreover, it is an historical fact that monotheistic nations of ancient and modern times have believed and are believing still, not only in a Divine government through the means of natural laws, but also in a supernatural interference by special Divine revelations confirmed by prophecies and miracles. What is the judgment of right reason on such a belief?

CHAPTER I.

SECTION I.—*The Divine conservation of creatures.*

Thesis XXXIV.—*Even after it has been created, created being cannot continue to exist without continuous action on the part of God to preserve it in existence. This Divine action is called "conservation."*

206. We may begin by considering how far our created being can be affected in regard to its continuance in existence by other created beings. To preserve a thing is to be in some way or other the cause of its not ceasing to be what it is. In this sense we speak of preserving health, life, good name, innocence, virtue, peace, and so on. Now, as we have proved in Book I., the being of matter *as matter,* and the individual being of each created spirit, human souls included, must be attributed to immediate Divine creation out of nothing. From this it follows that there is something in every creature which lies altogether beyond the domain of created causality, whether to destroy or to continue its existence. For the substance in question is either a purely corporeal thing of a lower or higher order (a piece of inanimate matter, a plant, a dumb animal), or it is a man, or it is a spirit. In the first

case the basis of its individual being is matter, *as matter;* in the second case matter joined to spirit: in the third case spirit alone. Now the production of matter and spirit is production out of nothing, and production out of nothing, as has been previously shown, requires infinite and therefore Divine power. Such an effect manifestly cannot owe its continuance in existence to the action of any creature. The power of every creature and of all creatures together is finite, and finite power is unable to destroy what has its existence in virtue of infinite power. Therefore no creature and no multitudes of creatures can destroy even the smallest piece of matter, or the most degraded of human souls. If they cannot destroy the being of these things, evidently the preservation of such things cannot be ascribed to them.

Hence the preserving influence of creature upon creature is limited to the substantial species of material things, and to the accidental states of substances both material and spiritual. For instance, a sportsman may for a time preserve his dog as a dog by taking care of its health, he may also destroy it by a pistol-shot; but the matter of which the dog is made up cannot be destroyed either by him or by any other creature; it is, so far as created power of destruction goes, absolutely indestructible. An artisan may preserve by practice his acquired skill in his art; yet it does not belong to him to preserve the internal foundation of that skill, his own spiritual soul, and the elementary matter of which his organism is formed.

In their own sphere creatures may preserve a thing either *directly* or *indirectly*. *Direct* preservation is an influence without the continuation of which the thing upon which it is exercised can no longer last. Thus through the action of a source of light upon the organ of vision of sensitive beings, colours are directly preserved as actually visible; for they exist under this aspect only so long as that action lasts. For a blind man the phenomenon of colour exists only potentially, nor can the quality denoted by the term "colour" pass from potential to actual visibility in a room perfectly dark.

A thing is preserved *indirectly*, in that the causes are warded off which would effect its destruction. An example of indirect preservation would be the rescue of a man from drowning.

207. No created being then can preserve in existence either directly or indirectly the underlying entity of any other created being. And now the question arises: Does God preserve all things? And in what sense? The answer given in our thesis is: God preserves all things *directly*.

That He does not preserve all individual things *indirectly* is evident both from experience and reason. In mankind and in the other living beings of this world, a continual corruption and generation of specific existence is witnessed. And reason tells us that human souls and pure spirits are incorruptible substances, consequently not liable to the influence of dissolving causes, and therefore, in so far as their specific being is concerned, not capable of indirect preservation.

But we say that He preserves all things directly, and that without *direct* Divine preservation no created being can continue in existence. As St. Thomas says: "The existence of all creatures depends upon God in such a way that they could not last even for a moment, but would return into nothing, if the influence of Divine power did not keep them in being."[1]

And why so? For the following reasons: Since every created being consists ultimately either of matter or of spirit or is a combination of the two, and neither matter nor spirit can have their origin except in an immediate Divine act, viz., that of creation, it follows that the very basis of the being of each created substance depends for its origin exclusively on the power of God. Such a dependence is manifestly an essential one. It is like the dependence of the daylight on the sun, not like that of the offspring on its parent. But an essential dependence must last so long as the dependent object retains its own proper essence. Thus we arrive at the conclusion that every created essence depends upon the power of God so long as its existence lasts; in other words, that each creature, so long as it exists, is directly preserved by God.

The same inference may be drawn from this consideration: Every creature depends upon the free volition of God for the existence of its inmost

---

[1] "Dependet enim esse cujuslibet creaturæ a Deo, ita quod nec ad momentum subsistere possent, sed in nihilum redigerentur, nisi operatione divinæ virtutis conservarentur in esse." (St. Thomas, *Sum. Theol.* ia. q. 104. art. 1.

being, in that God is free to grant or not to grant existence to finite things. But God can withdraw what depends upon His free-will, a withdrawal not to be conceived as the making of any reality, but only as a *subtraction of preservation.*

Hence God preserves all creatures continually and directly *by not ceasing to act upon them as the cause of their being.*

The last italicized phrase is meant to prevent a wrong conception of Divine preservation. It would be false and childish to conceive it with Bayle as a reiterated creation, postulated by the continual sinking back of creatures into nothingness, from which abyss they must be saved by the continual causation of their being through Divine power. If this opinion were true, there would be properly no preservation at all, but only renewal by Divine creation of interrupted existences. The relation in which Divine preservation stands to creation may be shortly put in this way: Creation is the omnipotent free volition of God conceived as causing the starting into existence of finite beings; preservation is the same omnipotent free volition of God conceived as causing the continuance of the existences already produced. It is therefore right to say: By preservation the creature receives nothing which it has not already got by creation. It would, however, be wrong and false to assert: Creatures are indebted to God immediately indeed for the first beginning of their existence; yet its continuation depends *only* mediately upon the Creator. This statement is to be rejected, for created beings are all under some aspect continually and immediately dependent upon God alone. For the rest it is true that under other aspects, explained above, creatures preserve creatures, but only on the supposition that the basis of their own being, the very root of their "esse," and likewise the basis of the things which they are said to preserve, be kept in existence immediately by Divine power alone.[2]

208. These explanations will throw light upon the following difficulties:

(1) Angels and human souls are incorruptible beings, and consequently cannot lose their existence as individuals of a certain species. But such incorruptible beings do not need preservation. Consequently angels and human souls need no preservation, and the doctrine that God directly preserves all creatures is false.

Answer. In this argument incorruptibility of individual existence is taken for absolute necessity. It is true that human souls and angels cannot be dissolved into component parts, and thus give rise to individual existences of other species. But nevertheless their existence is an effect of free Divine volition, and therefore is contingent, and, absolutely speaking, might cease to be. Faith supported by reason makes us infallibly sure that God will never annihilate either angels or men, and we have also good reason for thinking with St. Thomas that He will not annihilate the elementary matter which forms the basis of all corporeal

---

[2] St. Thomas, *Sum. Theol.* 1a. q. 104. art. 2. "Utrum Deus immediate omnem creaturam conservet."

X.

beings.[3] Yet we have proved above that He could do so by withdrawal of His preservation, *if He willed*. To express this in the technical terms already explained in the chapter on Divine Power: God can annihilate them *potentia absoluta*, not, however, *potentia ordinata*. Hence without His preservation they would be nothing.

(2) The Creator should be able to produce effects superior in stability to those of creatures. But if no effect of God's power can last without being preserved by God, His productions are inferior to those of His creatures: for many productions of creatures, monuments of art for instance, last for centuries without any continuous action of the causes that produced them.

Answer. The apparent strength of this difficulty rests upon its attributing to the causality of creatures what really is due to the power of the Creator. All effects of creatures are modifications or transformations of subjects that owe their existence to Divine creation. After the active influence of a created cause has ceased, its effect continues only on the condition that the subject in which it exists has a natural aptitude for its retention. A chemical compound artificially produced is more or less stable in proportion as it satisfies the affinities of the elements. A machine, the maker of which has violated the

---

[3] Cf. St. Thomas, *Sum. Theol.* 1a. q. 104. art. 4. The holy Doctor teaches in this article that God could annihilate creatures by over-ruling their natural aptitude to persevere in existence. But this would be a sort of miracle, not adapted to the spread of the knowledge and love of God, and therefore not to be expected.

laws imposed upon him by the attractive and resisting forces of its materials, is sure soon to get out of working order. The impress of a seal, which lasts in wax, is lost upon water. In a word, the durability of effects produced by creatures is altogether dependent upon the nature of the created subject in which they are produced. This subject itself has no other subject for its support, and therefore would be nothing, if the free Divine volition that produced it out of nothing, withdrew its omnipotent influence. Consequently the assumption that on the hypothesis of Divine preservation created causes would produce effects superior in stability to those produced by the Creator, is false for two reasons: first, because all stability of effects of creatures is due, not to the efficiency of the creature, but to the subjects produced by the Creator; and secondly, there is no parity between these subjects and the effects of created causes, as the former are productions out of nothing, the latter changes of pre-existing created things.

SECTION 2.—*Simultaneous concurrence of God in the actions of creatures.*

Thesis XXXV.—*God concurs simultaneously in the actions of finite beings.*

209. Hitherto we have treated of the continual direct action of God whereby He sustains creatures in their existence. Now we are to consider His operation regarding their activity. This subject is known in the schools of Catholic Philosophy under the

name of *concursus divinus,* or Divine concurrence. Instead of "concursus" the Angelic Doctor uses constantly other terms. He denotes the Divine co-operation with the actions of finite beings by the general term "operation" (*operatio*); and he specifies it by saying that God moves creatures to action (*Deus movet res ad operandum*), by which he means that this motion to action is exercised inasmuch as God directs, as it were, the active principles and forces of created natures, to their operation (*quasi applicando formas et virtutes rerum ad operationem*), and that, inasmuch as the created activity being thus influenced by Divine motion, all things act in virtue of the Divine power, so much so that He is the cause of all the actions of every agent (*secundum hoc omnia agunt in virtute ipsius Dei; et ita ipse est causa omnium agentium*).[4]

It is difficult to say which of the two modes of expression is better. Whether we use the modern term "concursus" or whether we follow the terminology of St. Thomas, and say that God's influence upon the activity of creatures is a sort of motion or application exercised upon their faculties, that He operates in their operation, and that creatures act in virtue of Divine power : all these technical terms may be easily misunderstood unless accurately explained. Misunderstanding of terms is here the more to be guarded against, because there is something in the dependence of finite activities upon the action of God, which has become a

---

[4] Cf. St. Thomas, *Sum Theol.* 1a. q. 105. art. 3. 4. 5; 1a. 2æ. q. 10. art. 1. and 4.; *De Potentia,* iii. a. 7; *Contra Gent.* iii. 67—70.

subject of controversy among Catholic philosophers, although they agree with one another up to a certain point. That all actions of creatures, simultaneously with their dependence upon created causes, have also a certain dependence upon the action of the Creator, nobody denies. The difference of opinion is about the nature of the dependence.

To the best of our ability we shall first put before the reader the doctrine held by ourselves on this subject, and afterwards the controversy about the necessity of what is called *physical premotion* or *predetermination.*

210. Let us begin by distinguishing various Divine operations or concurrences regarding the activity of creatures.

(*a*) *Natural and supernatural concurrence.*

By the concurrence which is merely *natural* God helps creatures to act and work in harmony with their natural faculties; whilst by *supernatural* concurrence He elevates them to a way of acting to which their nature with its faculties is inadequately proportioned, although it may be raised to the same by a special Divine operation. Thus God concurs naturally with material things, in that they act in agreement with the chemical, mechanical, and biological laws which rule the energies of their nature. He concurs also naturally with the spiritual faculties of man, intellect and will, as often as their operation is proportioned to the psychological laws inherent in the human soul. But He concurs supernaturally with the forces of His creatures, when He makes use of them as ministerial or instrumental causes for the extraordinary Divine operation known by the name of miracle, which we shall consider in chapter iii.   We may remark also by the way—though this is a truth which lies beyond the cognizance of reason and is only guaranteed by revelation—that God exercises a supernatural concurrence in those actions which, according to Christian revelation, are performed under the influence of His actual grace, which consists in supernatural illumination of the intellect, and comfort, encouragement, and strength of the will.   Thus a good preparation for and devout reception of the sacraments of the Church, an effectual prayer, in fine every action by which a reasonable creature *positively* prepares itself for final union with God (and *a fortiori*, every good work meriting reward in Heaven) requires a supernatural concurrence of the Divinity.

(*b*) *Mediate and immediate concurrence.*

By *mediate* concurrence God prepares the creature for a certain action : by *immediate* concurrence He causes it to act really either with necessity or with freedom according to its nature.   In mediate concurrence several stages are discernible, which we may best illustrate with reference to a particular free action, say an alms bestowed by a charitable person on a man in need who has offended him. To this action God has concurred mediately (a) by creating that man, (β) by preserving him, (γ) by helping him to acquire the habit of kindness and generosity, (δ) by directing through supernatural or natural causes his attention to the reasons for which he should practise charity precisely just now.

The last sort of mediate concurrence is called *moral* concurrence, and thus we arrive at a third distinction :

(c) *Moral and physical concurrence.*

Moral concurrence is only possible with regard to free acts. It consists in the suggestion of motives to good actions, and in making such actions appear desirable. Thus by moral concurrence God draws the will, but He does not force it. We may distinguish a natural moral concurrence, exercised through the medium of rational creatures, and a supernatural exercised immediately by God Himself.

By natural moral concurrence God causes those influences of created beings, for instance of parents, teachers, good friends, upon our intellect and will, which incline us naturally to choose what is right and to reject what is wrong. But incomparably more excellent is the supernatural moral concurrence, known to Christians under the name of Divine illuminations and inspirations, by which the Holy Ghost moves our souls to saving actions, in such a way that it depends upon the free-will of man whether he chooses to follow his Heavenly Guide or "to kick against the goad."

In contrast with this moral concurrence, God's immediate influence upon the creature in the moment of its action, and precisely upon its faculties considered as acting, is called *physical* concurrence.

To signify that all capabilities of creatures for action must be reduced to Divine creation and preservation, and that the exercise of these capabilities can never take place but with dependence upon Divine volition, scholastics say that God concurs with His creatures in action as the first cause, whilst the creatures are second causes.

211. To prove the existence of a supernatural concurrence of God belongs to apologetic and dogmatic Theology. We shall show its possibility and harmony with reason in chap. iii. when treating of miracles. As regards natural concurrence, it is enough to prove that every action of every creature depends immediately upon God. From this it will follow that all the influences by which one creature impels another to action must be considered as a *mediate* Divine concurrence; which concurrence will be moral, if the influence exerted proceeds immediately from a rational creature and consists in the suggestion of motives to a good action.

But what of suggestions to evil? Why cannot the harangue of a disloyal demagogue exciting people to rebellion against their lawful sovereign be held as a suggestion made to them under *mediate* moral concurrence on the part of God?

In order to give to questions like this a satisfactory answer, we have to weigh carefully the relation of God to moral evil. We shall do this in chapter ii., and from the explanations given there it will become evident that God neither intends sin, nor approves of sin, nor helps to sin, nor in sustaining the natural activity of creatures, does anything which He should omit in order to prevent sin.

These explanations presupposed, we may answer in short to the question proposed, no man is rightly held responsible for suggestions to evil which in some way arise out of his action as out of their mediate cause unless he either intends to bring about the suggestion by his way of acting, or shows his approval of the suggestion, or does not hinder it, although he *not only could* but also *should* do so. Now, no one of these conditions is realized in God when He concurs with rational creatures in their suggestions to evil. Therefore He cannot be said *mediately* to suggest it.

212. As appears from what we have said, our task of proving the existence of Divine concurrence philosophically, reduces itself to the demonstration of an immediate or physical influence of the Creator upon the action of His creature. When we speak of an immediate influence we do not mean to say that the action of the creature depends *under all aspects* immediately upon God. This assertion would be a virtual denial of created activity, and particularly of that activity known under the name of free volition.

In order that the reader may understand under what aspect we argue the action of a creature to depend mediately upon God, and under what aspect we say it depends immediately upon God and the acting creature together, we must recall some truths regarding action already touched upon in Book II., when we were occupied in showing the harmony of Divine freedom with Divine immutability, and again when we treated of the life of God.

What we do assert is that, although under one aspect the action of a creature is truly its own action depending on its own activity, under another aspect it is at the same time dependent upon God, and this not only mediately but immediately. In other words, the creature in action depends upon a causal exercise of the omnipotent Divine Will, not only for the existence and preservation of its nature and faculties, but also for the actual exercise of those faculties; so much so that it can use none of them unless the Creator in the very moment when the faculty is used, supports it with the efficacy of His Divine power. To this power the creature owes not only its faculties as applicable for action, but also as applied to act.

If the former of these two different ways of dependence existed without the latter, Divine concurrence would only be mediate. It then could be likened to what a watchmaker does for his watches. His concurrence with the continual motion of the watch is manifestly only mediate. Whether he wakes or sleeps, whether he thinks of the watch or not, the watch goes for as long as the laws of mechanics and dynamics will allow. But neither can the watch go, nor the watchmaker work in its construction, nor any creature do anything whatsoever, unless in the very moment in which the action takes place God wills that the faculty from which it flows be really exercised.

213. This it is what we mean by immediate Divine concurrence. But no sooner is the position stated than we feel obliged to guard it against misunderstanding. We said just now that God by the power of His will, is a true cause of every action at the very moment when it proceeds from

the faculty of His creature. Above we said, and every Christian believes, that God cannot approve of sin. How are these two statements compatible? The answer involves a fuller explanation of our position.

In every action that proceeds from a morally free faculty two characteristics are to be distinguished. The first is the use of liberty or the act of choosing. This act considered *precisely as such* is not due to the exercise of created freedom, but it is that very exercise itself, and follows necessarily from the free nature of the creature, so long as God wills that that nature shall have its proper play and field of action. The free creature is not free to exercise its freedom or not to exercise it, it is only free to exercise it with regard to any particular object proposed as eligible, either accepting or not caring to accept that object. It is then clear that the free act of the creature, in that it is an exercise of freedom, can depend immediately both upon God and the creature, and can nevertheless depend immediately upon the creature alone, in that it is rather acceptance than neglect of a particular object. God willing the exercise of freedom at the moment when it is exercised, implicitly wills that there be a choice made by the creature. This choice is not a change, but an immanent act of the will, consisting in what we may call the *fixing* or *clamping* of one or other of two alternatives, namely, the refusal or the acceptance of this object, this thought, this desire, this deed, this word, here and now eligible to me. By the fact that God grants the *actual use* of freedom, He grants the action of choice without determining its issue. So St. Thomas teaches expressly when he says: "The act, as determined to be this or that, is from no other agent than from the will itself."[5]

These explanations will enable the reader to understand how far the free volition of a rational creature is due immediately both to God and to the creature, how far it is immediately due to the creature alone, how far that which is the creature's own doing is approved of by God, and how far it is disapproved of by His will without being prevented by His power.

Inasmuch as free volition is the use of a faculty natural to rational creatures, or, as scholastics are wont to say, an *actus physicus*, it is the immediate effect both of God willing the use of the free-will, and of the creature having this use actually under God, as a natural result of its faculty of freedom. Inasmuch, however, as the use of freedom with regard to a certain object, say an alluring imagination, is acceptance and not refusal or *vice versa*, it is a self-determination immediately due to the creature alone. If the acceptance or refusal the free creature makes is in harmony with the moral law laid down by the Creator, it is approved of by Him. If it is against that law, He disapproves of it, and cannot be said to will it, unless by this phrase be signified that He wills not to impede it. In other words, at the moment of the free choice

[5] "Quod determinate exeat in hunc actum vel in illum, non est ab alio agente sed ab ipsa voluntate." (*Sent.* II. d. 39. q. 1. a. 1.)

He wills positively that His creature shall have the actual use of freedom; and willing this, He leaves it to the creature to determine whether this use shall be such or such with regard to the object in question, whether eventually it shall be virtuous or sinful. The creature determines this, not by producing a reality independently of God—this would be absurd—but simply by immanent volition or nolition, neither of which means production, in the sense of the effecting of a new physical actuality. Both volition and nolition are only productions in the sense of causing a definite relation of will to a certain object apt to be chosen, and at a moment in which the will has sufficient actuality for choosing. The will itself alone causes immediately this its relation to the object; in other words, it alone is the proximate cause of its free self-determination, but only in virtue of an actuality, upon the bringing about of which God as Prime Cause has immediate influence. (Cf. pp. 266 and 302.)

Thus it remains true that there is no actual being in the creature independent of God, at the same time the free action of the creature, *considered precisely as self-determination to one alternative out of two or more*, depends immediately upon the creature alone as a consequence of *moral freedom*.

Having cleared away the danger of misunderstanding as regards the immediate concurrence of God to all operations of creatures, we may now proceed to prove that there is such concurrence.

214. In the preceding section on Divine preservation it was shown that no created being can last

even for a moment without being kept in existence by the continuation of the same omnipotent Divine volition that caused it to be. As Father Faber has beautifully said : " The home of the creature is the hand of the Creator." From it there is no escape, so long as the creature exists. The pen may drop from the hand of the writer, it does not lose thereby its existence, though it be no longer applied to the work of writing; but the creature is so absolutely under the sway of Divine omnipotence, as to have no being at all apart therefrom. Now the omnipotence which preserves the creature is not a blind force. No, God knows from eternity the nature of every creature that He preserves, from the tiniest piece of matter up to the loftiest spirit. Decreeing its existence and its preservation, He foresees what will naturally follow, if He chooses to preserve the creature in a state harmonizing with its nature. He sees that such a state is impossible without actual operation on the part of the creature. Moreover, He comprehends perfectly the relation between nature and action, and thus He foresees that under certain conditions of existence a certain natural action of the creature will either be inseparably connected with its existence or not. In the former case [6] He knows that decreeing its existence implies

---

[6] We put this case only hypothetically. We do not state that there is really any individual action of a finite being, not only continually and connaturally, but inseparably connected with its existence, though perhaps the self-consciousness of an angel may be such an action. See St. Thomas, *Sum. Theol.* 1a. q. 56. art. 1. in corp. etc. ad 3.

decreeing its action; in the latter case He sees that it depends upon Him to prevent, if He will, the natural outpouring of the activity of the creature, at the same time that He preserves the creature in being.   In either case He cannot decree the existence of a creature for a certain moment, together with the existence of the natural conditions prerequired for action, and the existence of its unchecked natural activity, without decreeing thereby the actual use of the faculties of the creature, or in other words the action itself *considered precisely as actual exercise of created activity.*

Let us now call to mind what we have proved in Book II., that the decrees of God stand unchangeable, and that His Will is by itself infinite power.   In virtue then of the same omnipotent volition by which God from eternity has decreed the existence of the unchecked activity of the creature, He causes that activity at the moment when the creature operates, not as a Divine operation, but as an operation natural to a finite faculty.   Therefore we say that He causes it simultaneously with the creature as the primary cause, whilst the creature is the secondary cause of the same.   Seeing and willing beforehand any given natural operation of any creature, He forms what we call technically *the decree of simultaneous concurrence* with the action.   When the creature comes to exercise this activity, God sees what this exercise means, and wills at the same time that it shall take place.   This is His simultaneous concurrence with the creature to its action, in so far precisely as that action is an outcome of the natural being which the creature possesses at the time.

Evidently, therefore, there is no action of any creature independent of the Divine Will, or that would take place at all, if that Supreme Will did not intend the action efficaciously and simultaneously, inasmuch as it is an exercise of a natural faculty.

The efficacious intention of the Divine Will which influences the created agent is not directed merely to the existence of the agent with its faculties and habits, but to its existence precisely *as acting in harmony with its natural exigency of action.* In other words, the action of the creature is not only mediately dependent upon Divine volition, but immediately, because not only in its source, but in its own reality, it is foreseen and decreed by God from eternity; and as it has been decreed, so it is willed and produced in time by God as the first cause and by the creature as the second cause. Thus one of the schoolmen, Durandus, who will only admit a mediate concurrence of God to the actions of creatures, does not express the full truth. On the other hand, the Divine concurrence is mediate in this sense, that between God (who efficaciously wills the action of the creature, not as His action, but as the action of a finite being) and the actual action of a created faculty, there exists really the creature with its faculty as proximate cause of the same action which is attributed to God as its First Cause. He is its First Cause, in that the creature owes the actual exercise of its faculty to the fact that God, at the very moment when the faculty acts, intends (what indeed He has intended from eternity) that it shall not only have a potential or habitual fitness for actual application, but shall really proceed to that actual application. St. Thomas expresses this truth in the words: *Omnia agunt in virtute ipsius Dei, et ita ipse est causa omnium actionum agentium*—"Every being that acts is in the exercise of its action dependent upon an influence proceeding from God Himself, and thus He is the cause of all actions of active beings."

215. Against the doctrine of immediate Divine concurrence thus explained and proved, two difficulties occur.

(1) If the action of the creature is also God's action, it would seem that nothing remains for the creature to do. For God does what He does sufficiently well, and consequently we may reason thus: If God concurs in the operation of the creature, this operation is sufficiently explained by His causality alone. But what is sufficiently explained by one causality, is not to be attributed to another. Therefore what is called the action of the creature is properly not attributable to it, but to God, which is equivalent to saying that the creature does not act at all.

Answer. God could, of course, produce without the intervention of any created agent the same physical *effects* which He enables them to produce by His concurrence with their activity. He could

---

[7] St. Thomas, *Sum. Theol.* 1a. q. 105. art. 5. in corp.; *De Potentia,* q. 3. art. 7.

Y

for instance thus make a steam-engine, but in that case the steam-engine would not have been the work of man, whereas this latter is what, on the supposition of creation, God wills, and what is in itself a worthy object of Divine volition. If, however, He chooses to have created agents, He must "concur" with them in their activity in such a way as not to suppress the application of it, but rather to grant this application by the nature of His concurrence.

(2) The statement that there exists no action of any creature, unless supported by an efficacious Divine volition which has for its term that very action, implies that even sinful actions are efficaciously willed by God, which is absurd, as being in evident contradiction with the Divine holiness.

Answer. All that the said statement implies is that God wills to grant the actual use of freedom with regard to the objects by which creatures are tempted to sin; not that He efficaciously draws them into sin or helps to sin *as sin.*

Section 3.—*Controverted question about physical premotion and predetermination.*

Thesis XXXVI.—*The theory of physical predetermination in the sense in which it is understood in the Catholic schools is not supported by any cogent reasons, and it makes the explanation and defence of moral freedom unnecessarily difficult.*

216. Whilst all Catholic philosophers and theologians assert unanimously that every action of

creatures depends simultaneously upon God, they differ in their explanation of the nature of that simultaneous dependence. The doctrine enunciated in the thesis is that of Molina. The opposite doctrine is generally called Thomism, on the plea that it is that of St. Thomas, although we are by no means prepared to admit that the Saint is rightly interpreted by those who impute to him this sense. It is necessary to give an outline of this famous controversy, because it appertains to a question concerning which some conclusions must be reached in any treatise on Natural Theology which aims at being complete. We must be understood, however, in advocating our own conclusions, to speak with all becoming deference of the views of our opponents, many of whom bear names worthy of the highest honour among Catholic philosophers.

What, then, is meant by physical predetermination? It does not signify Divine " premotion " in general—that is to say, any sort of Divine moral or physical help towards action which precedes the action, but it denotes quite a particular sort of Divine premotion. As we shall explain below, Divine premotion in general cannot be denied by any Catholic. Not only does God premove His creatures morally, He premoves them also physically. At least He exercises such an influence upon them as may rightly go by this name. But physical predetermination, as upheld by its advocates, is a transitory impulse to action produced immediately by God in the faculty of a creature as often as the latter is to act, an impulse so perfectly adapted to the nature of the agent that a certain particular action will infallibly result. And so far is this said to be the case that God, as the adherents of this doctrine explain, knows the future action of a creature by knowing the premotion that He has decreed for it. Nevertheless, while maintaining thus much, they are far from denying the moral freedom of rational beings.

According to them the physical predetermination, which draws the free-will of a man to a particular choice, causes this choice *infallibly*, but not *necessarily*. Our self-determination, they say, is both the certain result of Divine predetermination and the outcome of the use of moral freedom granted by that very predetermination. God predetermining the creature does not lead it to a necessary, but to a free self-determination, and at the same time He leads it infallibly to that choice to which His predetermination, taken together with the disposition of the creature that receives it, naturally tends. Nevertheless God does not predetermine any one to a sin. True, His predetermination causes the free choice *which* is sinful, but He does not cause it *as* sinful. Its sinfulness is caused by the bad disposition of the created will in which the Divine predetermination is received.[8]

If we object to this that it is exceedingly difficult to understand how a creature thus predetermined can possibly have the actual use of its freedom, our opponents do not deny that there is some mystery

---

[8] See Goudin in *Philosophia*, Pars IV. q. 4 (Edit. Parisiensis, 1851), pp. 224—283, especially pp. 228—239 and pp. 264—267.

in this. But they refer us to the incomprehensibility of Divine causation at once most sweet and most efficacious. Its sweetness manifests itself in this, that the predetermining Divine premotion causes the creature to act, not anyhow, but only in such a manner as is in keeping with its nature. Therefore in an irrational creature God causes a necessary action, but in the rational will of angels and men He causes free actions, as often as the use of freedom is due to their nature.

217. But why insist upon this predetermination? Why refuse the doctrine stated in the thesis? Chiefly, they reply, for these reasons:

(1) Without physical predetermination the supreme dominion of God over His creatures and the infallibility of His Providence cannot be sufficiently explained. The Molinists, who teach only a simultaneous concurrence, and do not admit that God premoves free creatures otherwise than morally, by showing them certain actions in a pleasing or displeasing light, make the Creator a simple co-operator with His creatures—nay, in a certain sense they subordinate His action to the action of the creature; for, if God does not predetermine the action of the free creature, then the free creature must predetermine the Divine concurrence, as the latter in itself does not tend to this or to that free volition. How, then, can it remain true that God is the first free cause? [9]

(2) As Catholic Philosophy has for its guiding

---

[9] Goudin, *Ibid.* pp. 263, 264, § 11, " Probatur ultimo præmotio ex inconvenientibus."

star Catholic Theology, a philosophical opinion
which agrees less well with the teachings of the
Fathers of the Church and with common Catholic
doctrine should not be favoured, although the
Church has not condemned it. But the teaching
of the Molinists on Divine concurrence does not
well agree with the doctrine of St. Augustine, who
teaches expressly : *Deus de voluntatibus hominum,
quod vult cum vult facit* [10]—" God makes of the wills
of men what He wills, when He wills it."   And
does not the Church represent to us the special
benefit of efficacious grace as a physical predetermination when she directs her priests to pray : *Ut
Deus nostras etiam rebelles compellat propitius ad se
voluntates ; ut convertat nos,* &c.—" That God may
compel our wills, even when they are rebellious, to
Himself; that He may convert us," &c.[11]

218. We hope the summary given here of the
view of our opponents is a fair one.   Let us, then,
now give our answer, which will be done best by
following the tenor of our thesis.

First of all, we admit that God in more than
one sense premoves all His creatures to action,
inasmuch as premotion designates a direction to a
certain kind of activity, and the actuation of created
faculties in harmony with the eternal decrees of
Providence.   Is not the very fact of creation and

---

[10] *De Correptione et Gratia,* c. xiv.   Cf. Prov. xxi.: *Sicut divisiones
aquarum, ita cor regis in manu Domini est, quocumque voluerit, inclinabit
illud*—" As the divisions of waters, so the heart of the King is in the
hand of the Lord ; whithersoever He will He shall turn it."

[11] Cf. Goudin, *Ibid.* pp. 245, 246.

preservation a sort of Divine premotion? No creature can perform any other species of action than that for which it has faculties from the Creator; and on the supposition of its preservation, it needs must act in harmony with the natural tendency of its faculties so far as natural actions are concerned. If we turn to those which are supernatural, the creature can perform none of them save in agreement with the supernatural powers added to its nature by the Creator. All this is true premotion, and no Molinist denies aught of it.

Nay, as appears from our exposition in sect. 2, Molinists do not shrink from saying with St. Thomas —*Deus est causa nobis non solum voluntatis sed etiam volendi*—"God causes in us not only our faculty of will, but even our actual volition." 'And again: *Deus est causa omnis actionis*—"God is the cause of every action." [12]

But all these phrases are easily explained without physical predetermination. God's concurrence at the moment of our free volition consists in our opinion precisely in this, that His power grants us not only the faculty of choosing, but the actual exercise of free choice. By His causality our will is impelled to the desire of good in general, whenever our intellect represents any particular good either real or apparent; but He causes this desire in such a way that we ourselves alone determine whether we will accept or reject this or that particular thing which seems good to us.

The issue of our choice is from eternity known

[12] *Contra Gent.* l. 3. c. 89.

to Him, simply because it is one of the objective future truths, all of which must be present to the intuition of His eternal infinitely perfect intellect. This knowledge, inasmuch as it represents the action of the creature conditioned by the decree of simultaneous concurrence under any given circumstances, we have called in Book II. *scientia media.*[13] The simultaneous concurrence of God with acts of free-will coincides with the causation of the actual longing for good in general, which longing is included in every volition of a particular good, as the *genus* in the individual, or as "animal" is included in "Peter."

It is not therefore true that in the Molinist system God does not cause the creature's action, especially not the actual volition of free creatures. All that can be said is that, according to Molinists, God does not cause free action under such an aspect as to make it imperative on the creature by its very nature.

219. We return to the objections of the adherents of physical predetermination.

Their first objection was that with the negation of a predetermining premotion the guidance of created activity, essentially belonging to the supreme Lord of all things, is denied to Him. From the explanations already given it appears that this objection lacks weight. It was started in the Thomist schools on the occasion of Molina's celebrated

---

[13] We here beg the reader to remember that in the *positive* explanation of the *scientia media* we do not stand by Molina, but *against* him with Suarez. (Cf. pp. 282, seq.)

but perhaps not very dignified comparison of the simultaneous concurrence of God with creatures, to two men towing a boat or carrying a burden. Molina's aim was to show that creatures, especially rational creatures, exercising their natural activity, are in their own order really principal causes of those effects to which their faculties are proportioned.

Let us show this in a concrete instance. God concurs with the action of the writer, He concurs also with the action of the pen. Is not the writer then a principal cause in the order of secondary causes, and the pen an instrument? True, compared with God the First Cause, the writer himself may be likened to an instrument, in so far as in the exercise of his activity he depends altogether upon the supporting power of His Creator. Yet He certainly cannot be said to receive from God an impulse for action perfectly like that given by a writer to his pen. To say that would be to deny human freedom. It is idle, therefore, to appeal with Goudin[14] and others to this illustration of Molina, as a proof that Molinists conceive the Divine concurrence as a sort of help collateral and co-ordinate with the operation of the creature. Nor can it be shown that our doctrine is opposed to St. Thomas on the ground that he rejected the same illustration which Molina used. His rejection was based upon the well-grounded anticipation that it might easily be misunderstood. Molina made use of it because he thought that his meaning would be

[14] *Philosophia,* Pars. IV. p. 232.

sufficiently gathered from the context. But if you will have it to mean that God causes one part of the action and the creature another part, just as two men towing a boat cause each a part only of the total motion, the illustration does not hold. And thus St. Thomas took it. If, however, you apply it to free creatures, to indicate that the action of a creature really depends upon two causes, neither of which is physically predetermined, the illustration cannot be considered as a mark of a false conception of Divine concurrence.

That in this sense it was not rejected by the Angelic Doctor, is to us quite evident.

220. And now as to the objection that in our system the creature must predetermine the concurrence of God, because that concurrence is in itself indifferent. This difficulty would have force, if we affirmed the simultaneous concurrence of God without asserting at the same time the *scientia media*. By this knowledge God foresees from eternity which choice any rational creature under given definite circumstances would make on the hypothesis that He on His part decreed simultaneously to concur with it in the actual exercise of its freedom.

In the light then of this knowledge God freely decrees from eternity to grant the use of freedom requisite for the creature to act and make its choice. He comprehends also from eternity the alternatives that are open to the choice of the created free being. Moreover, by virtue of the *scientia media*, He foresees the choice, in so far as it depends proximately upon the creature alone, or in

other words, is an actual preference of one alternative to the other, based upon the actuality
necessary for choosing, which actuality is granted
by the free decree of the Creator.

Nor can it be said that Molinism mars Christian
humility and leads men to 'neglect to pray for
efficacious graces for the performance of saving
and meritorious actions. Molinists teach that
every salutary and, *a fortiori*, every meritorious
action we perform is due to a *premoving*, though
not *predetermining* grace of the Almighty, which
by the *scientia media* He foresaw that we would use.
He could have granted another grace perfectly
sufficient for the performance of the good work,
but one which He knew we would freely despise.
Why did He give us the one rather than the other?
Because He loved us with a special love.

A Molinist then has the strongest motives to ask
for those graces of which God foresees he will make
a good use. Such a prayer would be equivalent to
that of Holy Church: *Converte nos Deus salutaris
noster*—" Convert us, God our Saviour." *Nostras
etiam rebelles compelle ad te voluntates*—" Compel to
Thee our rebellious wills."

It would seem, therefore, that there is nothing in
the supreme dominion of God and the Catholic
doctrine of efficacious grace to make us shrink from
Molinism.

Let us see now whether the harmony between
human freedom and Divine concurrence be indeed
as apparent on the theory of physical predetermination as upon that of *scientia media* and simul-

taneous concurrence. Let us take a concrete instance, and imagine a human being making the first free choice in his life, and that a choice deliberately sinful. How this could come about in the system we defend is clear enough. In the moment of choice the free creature owes to God the actual use of freedom. But the determination to the one alternative rather than to the other, included in that use of freedom, is, according to Molinists, not predetermined but only foreseen in the case of a sinful choice. In the case of a good choice, it may have been *absolutely intended*, but was not physically *predetermined*. How does the same choice come about in the system of the Thomists? Whether it be a good or a bad one, it is physically predetermined. And yet they say, and must say, that God does not predetermine a man to sin *as sin*. Whence then, we ask, does the first sin a man commits take its rise? We ask *about the first*, in order to preclude at once the evasion, that a man by his sin might have deserved to receive a predetermination to a choice that would infallibly be sinful, although it would always be sinful through the man's own fault. Such a solution of the difficulty we are proposing is in itself very obscure, and certainly not applicable to the *first* sin. If it be true that the sinful choice must infallibly follow from the combination of the physical predetermination with the disposition of the will that receives it, at the moment when it receives it, the reality of the use of freedom under such a predetermination is indeed an insoluble mystery.

CHAPTER II.

SECTION I.—*The existence of Divine Providence.*

Thesis XXXVII.—*All things created are under the sway of Divine Providence, and none of them can frustrate the final end absolutely intended by the Creator, or move towards it in a way and under circumstances not foreseen by His intellect, or not freely either approved or at least tolerated by His most holy will. The final end of creatures consists in the first place in a certain degree of manifestation of the Divine perfections in the created likenesses of God, and in the second place in the perfect union of rational creatures with their Creator by knowledge and love. This is technically expressed by saying that the end of creation is God's external glory both objective and formal and the happiness of rational creatures.*

221. Providence as well as prudence (which is its doublet), considered in its etymological meaning, is equivalent to *foresight*. This etymological signification of the word coincides pretty well with the real import of what we call *prudence* in a man and *providence* in God. We say that a man is prudent

when the whole tenor of his life justifies the supposition that in his undertakings he has a definite object in view, and uses constantly the means fit for the attainment of his purpose. In a similar sense we attribute providence to God; for this predicate is given to Him in order to imply that He has settled from eternity the final goal toward which the whole of His creation and each particular creature is to be directed, that He has ordained the means by which the end shall be reached, and that He rules in the course of ages all events so perfectly as that nothing shall occur to bar His final and absolute intention.

It was this idea of Providence that suggested to the deep Christian philosopher, Boëthius, the following definition of it, which was adopted by St. Thomas: " Providence is the all-regulating and stable plan of God, the supreme Ruler of the universe."[1]

To be more explicit, we may give the definition another form and say: " Providence is God the supreme Lord of the universe Himself, inasmuch as He directs all things to an end fixed by Him, in harmony with His eternal plan.

The verification of this definition supposes the existence of two Divine operations with regard to creatures:

(1) The assignment of an end to all things and of ways by which they shall reach it.

---

[1] " Providentia est ipsa divina ratio in summo omnium principe constituta, quæ cuncta disponit." (St. Thomas, *Sum. Theol.* 1a. q. 22. art. 1.)

(2) Actual direction of all things to that end.

222. Can it be proved that Providence thus explained really exists? Or shall we say with the artisan-philosopher Chubb and other more recent deists, that the existence of a Creator cannot be denied, but that His influence upon this world does not extend beyond laying the foundation of it, which being laid all things go on as best they can without their author watching their course or interfering in any way? Against this deistic position we enunciate our thesis in its several parts.

First we say that God has prefixed a final end to everything created, and that He allows nothing to frustrate that end or move towards it otherwise than as He foresees and either approves or at least tolerates.

We call attention to the phrase, *approves or at least tolerates.* Why do we not say simply: Whatever happens is God's will? Because this expression might be taken to mean that even the sins committed by rational creatures are willed by God, at least as means to an end. This of course would be inconsistent with God's holiness. Although He can tolerate sin, and can turn the misery following it into an occasion of good, He never can approve of or wish for sin in order to reach His end. We express this in scholastic terms shortly by saying that God wills sin, not *positively* but *permissively.* The term *permissively* does not imply that God gives permission to sin, but means only that for good reasons He does not hinder those sins which rational creatures commit through the abuse of their free-will. Having thus made clear the meaning of our statement, we may proceed to prove its truth.

It has been demonstrated in Books I. and II. that the one self-existing personal God has created all things, and that He is infinitely wise and powerful. Moreover, we have shown in chapter i. of this Book that the being of each creature depends continually upon Him for its existence, and that no action of a creature can come about except under His concurrence. Now it is evident that an infinitely wise and good Being cannot act without intending a good end, nor in His actions lose sight of that end. It is also evident that all effects of Divine action are decreed from eternity. It follows that the origin, the duration, the various phases of existence and action of each particular creature were from eternity willed by God, either positively or permissively, with a view to a certain end. Moreover, it follows that the influence which He continually exercises upon the activity of creatures is in harmony with His eternal plan, and involves the continual intention of the end.

As we have seen in Book II., God is really identical with an intellect of Infinite Wisdom and a will of Infinite Goodness. By His Infinite Wisdom He understands from eternity the end to be reached by creation, and the various ways in which by His omnipotence He might reach it. His will of infinite goodness embraces the end He has in view and fixes by irrevocable decree the ways in which it shall be reached. Abiding in Himself by His absolutely perfect essence, He watches and directs

in the course of time the exercise of every faculty
of His creatures. He watches and directs it without
any toil or labour, paying equal attention to the
whole and to the minutest details. As by one
eternal glance of His infinite understanding He
comprehends the dimensions of space, and calculates
the distances and orbits of the heavenly bodies,
and by one omnipotent volition keeps the whole
machinery of the universe in motion, with a continual regard to the final goal it is to reach; so by
the same eternal all-penetrating intuition does He
read the most secret thoughts of every mind,
observe the most minute oscillations of every
organic cell, and count the most insignificant vibra-
tions of every atom of matter, ruling by His omnipotent will all things so that there is no thought of
any mind, no oscillation of any cell, no vibration
of any atom, which is not in some way or other duly
subordinated to the end He intends.

223. And this end—wherein does it consist?
Evidently it must be an external manifestation of
His internal perfection; not a manifestation in the
pantheistic sense, as though God evolved Himself,
as it were, into the visible and invisible universe,
but a manifestation by the production of finite
created likenesses of the infinite Divine essence.
That the end of the world created can be nothing
else is evident from a truth demonstrated in Book II.
We showed there that God loves Himself with
absolute necessity, and cannot love anything else
but with reference to His own infinite goodness.
Now the external manifestation of the Divine per-

z

fection through created likenesses is called in scholastic language, God's *external glory*, just as His internal perfection as known to Himself alone is called His *internal glory*. Moreover, scholastics distinguish between *external objective* and *external formal glory*. By the external objective glory of God they mean created things in so far as they are adapted by their very existence and activity to bear witness to the Divine perfection, on the supposition that somewhere in creation there are intelligent beings, who can intellectually perceive them and form a judgment on their nature. The external formal glory of God is the acknowledgment of His perfection produced in the minds of intellectual creatures by the contemplation of His works.

Supposing these definitions, it is so evident that the Creator of the world intends His external objective and formal glory, that without such an intention we cannot even conceive creation to be possible. For it is repugnant to reason that a finite being should exist, the nature of which is not a copy, however imperfect, of the essence of the One infinite Being; consequently God, producing creatures, intends the production of likenesses of His own essence, as so many mirrors in which His infinite goodness is reflected under some aspect or other. If He did not intend this, He would be acting without any knowledge or intention at all— a supposition absolutely alien to His wisdom. But if He intends it, His intention is directed to what we have defined as His *external objective* glory. Moreover, as He cannot love anything but with

reference to His own goodness, so He must will
that the activities of created intellects and wills
shall be related to that goodness according to their
natures. But they cannot be related to it rightly
save by the acknowledgment that God is what He
is, the supreme Truth, Goodness, and Beauty. To
this acknowledgment all rational creatures must
finally arrive. If they are not impeded in the right
use of their reason, they will arrive at it in the
course of this life, unless through their own fault
they prefer darkness to light. If it be impossible
for them to know God before they leave this life,
as in the case of the innumerable multitudes of
children who die before the use of reason, at their
entrance into the next life the Creator will manifest
Himself to their immortal souls, draw them to His
love, and thereby make them happy. Not indeed
with the supernatural beatitude of which we learn
from revelation, but with an enduring natural
happiness.

Those who wilfully shut their mind against the
knowledge of their Creator, at all events will be
undeceived in the moment when they depart from
this life. As so many other delusions vanish when
death puts an end to our earthly existence, so before
all others that delusion of delusions will disappear,
which makes man believe that there is no personal
God who rules the world.

The Monotheist and the Agnostic will then agree
perfectly in the recognition of that God, whose
eternal power and divinity St. Paul[2] declares to

[2] Rom. i. 20.

be clearly visible in His works. They will both recognize their God, but with very different feelings.

The one will *then be forced* to acknowledge Him as infinitely good, albeit he still refuses to love Him; the other, if indeed he perseveres till the end of his days in acknowledging his Creator both in theory and practice according to the lights received, will know and love Him, and thus reach what is called in our thesis, the *secondary end* of creation, the beatitude for which rational creatures are destined. This secondary end God does not intend absolutely, but conditionally. He says as it were to every rational creature with reference to eternal salvation or final misery: "I have set before you life and death, blessing and cursing. Choose therefore life."[3] If man, by either expressly denying or practically ignoring his dependence upon God, obstinately refuses to choose life, it is not so much his Creator that condemns him, as his own malice, which changes him from a vessel of Divine mercy into a victim of Divine justice. God has implanted in the heart of man a nature longing for perfect happiness. In vain does man strive to quench his thirst for happiness with the perishable goods of this world. He possesses them only for a short while, and whilst he is enjoying them, the better part of his being does not cease to crave instinctively for the fulness of truth and goodness and beauty, which is to be found nowhere but in God alone. Now if the nature of man is thus naturally driven towards God as the source of its beatitude, it follows evi-

[3] Deut. xxx 19.

dently that it is the intention of our Maker to cause our happiness by perfect knowledge and love of Himself, at least on the condition that we co-operate with His benevolent designs.

No human being, however wretched he may be, is excluded by God from final happiness, unless through his own fault he makes himself unworthy of it, by persevering in a state of rebellion up to his last breath. St. Paul's words are in harmony with our rational inference when he says that " God will have all men to be saved."[4] How could it be otherwise?

224. Here, no doubt, many a reader is tempted to say: " All well and good; but I am at a loss to see how you can affirm that even the uncivilized savage is under the influence of the Divine light, which you say, guides every human being to his last end who does not deliberately turn away from it? To this grave difficulty which in theology meets with a deal of attention, we may be content to give a compendious answer in a philosophical treatise. It is clearly God's arrangement that men should depend largely upon one another for their instruction and progress in knowledge of all kinds, religious knowledge included. The necessary consequence of this is that through the neglect and malice of some who should be the natural teachers and leaders of their fellow-men, the latter should suffer. But God can rectify the evil.

225. But what about the secondary end of the irrational creation? Shall we say that the elements,

<hr>

[4] 1 Tim. ii. 4.

plants, and dumb animals are destined also to glorify God formally by knowledge and love, and thus to become happy through Him? Evidently this would be absurd. Even the highest among irrational creatures, the dumb animals, are unable to form a rational judgment on anything, to have a rational desire of anything, to reflect upon happiness, to wish for happiness, or to grieve for its absence. Their knowledge is but a reaction of their sensitive organism upon impressions produced in them by material things. Their cravings are blind emotions, resulting from the combination of the innate instinct proper to their species, with impressions made upon them. It is impossible that such beings should know and love God, or be happy in Him. Shall we then say that their end is not to glorify God *formally*, but only *objectively*, to be realizations of Divine thoughts, to be, as it were, books written by infinite wisdom? This is true as far as it goes, and there are those who think that it was in no sense necessary for God to go further and place a crown on His creation by the creation of rational creatures. But at all events, the objective praise which they render Him would have far less meaning, if there were no beings who could read the Divine ideas expressed in their existence. Those beings are the rational souls of men; and in a far higher degree, the pure spirits called angels. It is to them and through them that the heavens tell the glory of God, and the firmament announces the works of His hands. Yet we cannot say that the material world below men is properly meant for the use of angels. These do not need to be roused by sensible impressions to the evolution of their intellects. Being altogether independent of matter, they are endowed with innate ideas, and therefore able to know and love God, without going first through a process of intellectual development aided by material impressions. Only those rational beings who are compounds of matter and spirit, stand in need of such helps. Man, therefore, must be the favoured creature, for whose utility the Divine Majesty has created the visible universe that surrounds us. And indeed everywhere we find irrational creatures supplying the wants of human nature. They serve mankind partly by providing nourishment, clothing, shelter, and other bodily conveniences; partly by stirring up their intellects and wills to the pursuit of arts and sciences, and by leading them through the knowledge of creatures to that of the Creator; and last but not least, by affording opportunities for the practice of moral virtues, patience especially, and resignation to the inscrutable ways of their Creator.

226. From the doctrine of Providence thus proved and explained, two important corollaries are to be drawn. The first is this: God does not intend the final well-being of any individual living creature of this world except man. And man himself is to be perfectly happy, not here on earth, but hereafter.

It is therefore quite intelligible, that God should allow millions of irrational creatures to be sacrificed for the sake of man, to serve his eternal welfare remotely or proximately. No less reconcilable is it

with Divine Providence, that under certain conditions mortal men should be wasted by contagious
diseases, emaciated by famine, or fall in the flower
of their age on the battlefield.   In a word: *God
cares more for one immortal soul that does not resist
Him, than for the whole of the material universe.*

God must rule His creatures with a wise regard
for their natural dignity, according as that is greater
or less.   Now the human soul stands by its nature
in an infinitely nearer relation to God than the most
perfect of dumb animals.   It is an image of the
Creator, whilst every other living creature of this
world exhibits only some trace of His Majesty.   It
owes its origin immediately to His creative power;
whilst a dumb animal is a living erection made by
secondary causes on the groundwork laid by God
in the creation of matter and life.   The rational soul
alone is able and destined to know and love God, and
thus to be personally happy, whilst everything else is
made to reveal the Creator to His rational creatures,
and to promote their eternal welfare during a short
period of time, till that day shall come of which
St. Peter says, that on it "the heavens shall pass
away with great violence, and the elements shall
be melted with heat, and the earth and the works
in it shall be burnt up."[5]

The other corollary we are to derive from the
great truth of Divine Providence may be thus formulated: Every man, however low his social position, ought to be treated with reverence by his
fellow-man, as a personal being destined for an

[5] 2 St. Peter iii. 10.

eternal exaltation and happiness infinitely greater
than all the aims of temporal ambition. On the
other hand, dumb animals must be left in their
own sphere, and be treated as *things*, not cared for
as *persons*, not accepted as *subjects of right* against
whom injustice can be committed, but as *living
instruments* which man may utilize in every reasonable
way.

SECTION 2.—*The relation of Providence to existing evil.*

Thesis XXXVIII.—*Neither from the evils which
exist in this world, nor from those which, according to
Divine revelation, await the wicked in the life to come,
can any lawful inference derogatory to Divine Providence
be drawn.*

227. One of the most harassing questions which
have ever wearied the brains of philosophers, and
stimulated the zeal of Christian apologists, is as to
the possibility of such an enormous amount of evil
in a world created by an infinitely good God, and
continually under the sway of His Providence.

Absolutely speaking, this difficulty against the
moral attributes of the Creator is sufficiently solved
by an appeal to the arguments by which we have
proved to demonstration the existence of one
personal, infinitely perfect, and infinitely wise God.
These arguments are built on evident premisses,
according to the rules of sound Logic. The opponent of the doctrine proved has first to show a want
of internal soundness in our arguments before he
can hope to destroy them by difficulties. No

puzzling doubt, however great, can overthrow evident conclusions.   A man charged with a crime,
who has manifestly proved his *alibi*, cannot possibly
be the perpetrator, although from accidental circumstances grave suspicions may have arisen against
him.   In a similar way, when once it has been
evidently proved that God exists, and is infinitely
good; the evils of this world cannot be attributed
to the absence of a wise and benevolent Providence,
even if the existence of those evils remain to a large
extent a riddle to us.   A man who waited to render
homage to his Creator till he had solved all the
problems, to the solution of which his curiosity
might urge him, would act far more absurdly than
a child who refused to honour and obey his parents
till they had justified to his mind all the details of
their housekeeping.   The distance between a child's
mental capacity and that of his parents is, after all,
finite: but God's mind is infinitely above ours.

228.   Yet this answer, though substantially adequate, it is clearly desirable to supplement by a
detailed account of the relation in which evil stands
to the infinitely good will of God.   Such an account
we must now endeavour to render, and before all
things it is necessary to fix accurately the sense of
the term *evil*.   Some modern philosophers take evil
to be any absence of good in a thing.   They distinguish, consequently, three sorts of evils, metaphysical, physical, and moral.   *Metaphysical evil* is
understood by them to be the absence of a certain
perfection in a being, the nature of which is incompatible with such a perfection.   Thus, for instance,

the absence of feeling in a stone, the absence of reason in a dumb animal, and the absence of learning in an infant, are in this view metaphysical evils. By *physical evil* they mean a defect which mars the natural integrity of a being, or interferes with a proper development of its activity. Thus, under the category of physical evil come, bodily diseases of whatever kind, mental imbecility, liability to great fits of passion preceding the use of free-will, want, destruction of property by drought or inunda-tions, violent death, &c. Under the term of *moral evil* they comprise the deviation of the free-will from the moral law, and the actions proceeding from a will thus gone astray, as lying, theft, murder. In order that such volitions and actions may be considered as moral evils in the strict sense of the word, their source must be a will deliberately malicious. Otherwise, we have only what moralists call *material* sin, not *formal*.

In this explanation of evils nothing seems to be objectionable but that the term *evil* is taken in a wider sense than its usual application allows. Men commonly do not call every imperfection an evil, especially where the imperfection is the mere absence of a perfection not due to a thing. Every-thing is good, inasmuch as its state of existence harmonizes perfectly with its nature. A nature of a lower order is in itself less good than a nature of a higher order. Yet the essence of that lower nature does not involve what is properly called *evil*. The word *evil* signifies not the mere absence of a perfection, but its absence in a being to which under a certain aspect it is due.   Therefore, only physical and moral evils are evils in the strict sense of the word.

229. What are called metaphysical evils cannot possibly militate against the infinite goodness of the Creator.   To abolish them would mean to annihilate all creatures. A created being, either infinitely perfect, or at least so perfect that none more perfect could be created, is a contradiction in terms. The hypothesis of an infinitely perfect creature would involve the existence of two infinite beings, disproved in the First Book. The hypothesis of a creature so perfect that none more perfect could be, would amount to an implicit denial of the infinite power of the Creator.   We have already shown in Book I. that an absolutely perfect world is impossible.   The world of an infinitely good God can only be relatively perfect, that is to say, perfectly adapted to its end as intended by the Creator.   In Section 1 of this Book, we have seen that God intends by creation the manifestation of His goodness, or His external glory, and the beatitude of rational creatures.   Neither the one nor the other can be intended in an infinite degree. In other words, God can neither intend that any particular creature, or any multitude of creatures, should adequately represent His unbounded perfection; nor can He intend that any purely finite creature should enjoy a happiness of infinite intensity.   He must, therefore, intend both the primary and the secondary end of creation to be realized within certain limits.   Now, every finite degree of

external glory of God falls infinitely short of an adequate expression of the infinite Divine goodness. Comparing, therefore, finite degrees of external manifestation with the adequate expression of the Divinity, we may say that the difference between, 1, 100, and 1,000,000 degrees vanishes. Which of these degrees shall God intend in creation? Surely, whichever He pleases. The selection depends entirely on His free-will. He does not need any creature. He may, therefore, choose among the indefinite multitude of possible beings without violating any of His perfections; yet so that He shall always attain His own glory, both *objective* and *formal;* subordinate the course of things perfectly to the end He has in view, and conduct to final happiness those rational creatures who obey the voice of their conscience. With these restrictions, we affirm that no amount of imperfection in created natures can be adduced as an exception against the statement of the monotheist: "An infinitely good and wise God rules this world."

230. Supposing, then, that God creates a world filled with creatures of a nature under many aspects very imperfect—an hypothesis doubtless verified in this world of ours, the *possibility* of *moral* evil, and the *natural* necessity of *physical* evil, is sufficiently explained. Man has a free-will. By his very nature he is such that he can commit sin. Again, both man and the rest of the living creatures of this world, in consequence of their imperfect nature, must be liable to many physical sufferings, unless God is continually to work miracles for their

deliverance. Does, then, the infinite goodness of God require that by supernatural interference He should prevent all physical and moral evils? The answer is evidently to be given in the negative.

231. First, as regards physical evils, God cannot, indeed, intend them for their own sake. He cannot delight in the misery and sufferings of His creatures. But there is no reason whatever to prove that He may not allow these evils, with the intention to compensate them by some good occasioned thereby. Nay, He may even intend them as means to an end. It is not necessary that He should lay open to our view the particular final cause of every disease and every misfortune; it is enough for us to know that He is infinitely good, infinitely wise and just. Knowing thus much, we are certain of two truths which must satisfy every reasonable thinker. The first is, that an infinitely good, and wise, and just God must draw some good out of every evil He allows, and cannot allow any without a reason worthy of His infinite wisdom. The second may be formulated thus. A human mind, though able to get a true knowledge of God amply sufficient to guide the man on his way to his last end, is manifestly unfit to comprehend the eternal counsels of the Almighty. Add to this, that in many cases experience and history show to the faithful Christian distinctly, how in the hand of Providence physical evils become instruments of great boons in the moral order. Poverty and sickness teach man most forcibly his nothingness, and open his mind to the consolations of religion. The blood of the martyrs

became the fertile seed of Christianity, whilst the ignominious death of Christ our Saviour enhanced the glory of His Resurrection, brought out the Divine origin of His Church, and opened to fallen mankind the road that leads to the Heavenly City, where "God shall wipe away all tears from their eyes ; and death shall be no more, nor mourning, nor crying, nor sorrow shall be any more."[6]

None can understand this fully, unless he believes that God became Man, that as Man He died upon the Cross, and afterwards ascended glorious into Heaven. The belief in these truths makes it easily conceivable that through many tribulations we must enter into the Kingdom of God. An acquaintance with the life and doctrines of Christ and His Apostles goes far to reconcile the believer in Christianity with the hard lot of the poor, and the promiscuous distribution of temporal goods, and of merely natural mental gifts among just and unjust. A Christian knows that there is another life, in which both the unbridled sensuality and supercilious cruelty of Dives and the patient resignation and heroic suffering of Lazarus will be duly rewarded. And reflecting how vastly the natural endowments of Lucifer surpass the most splendid human genius, he no longer wonders at beholding at times among men the spectacle of great abilities thrown away in a bad cause.

232. But this reflection involves another difficulty far greater than that drawn from mere physical evils. God foresaw from eternity the fall of Lucifer and

[6] Apoc. xxi. 4.

the evil angels. He foresaw all the sins of man.
Why did He not hinder them?

Let us first see in what relation God stands to
moral evil. Moral evil in the strict sense of the
word consists in a free turning away of the created
will from the law laid down by God. God necessarily loves His own goodness and everything else in
relation to it. He can, therefore, never approve of
a created free being deliberately ignoring its true
position to Him. But sin manifestly involves a
deliberate refusal of the creature to stand to God
in that attitude of subject to ruler, which is the
proper posture of a creature before its Creator. No
sin, therefore, can be pleasing to God. He manifests
His disapproval of it to every man who commits sin,
and that in the very moment when he is about to
commit it. For sin *in the strict sense of the word* is
not committed without disobedience to the voice of
conscience, which re-echoes the will of the Supreme
Lawgiver. But it is one thing to disapprove of sin,
and quite another thing not to impede it. God does
not impede sin; although, absolutely speaking, this
was possible for Him. Yet we must not forget that
He is infinitely free as well as infinitely powerful. He
can, therefore, tolerate sin, if this toleration is not
opposed to His Divine perfections. But it is not
opposed to any one of them; as will easily appear
on comparing it with those perfections which at first
sight it would seem to violate, namely, His wisdom,
His holiness, His justice, and His mercy.

233. First, then, it may be argued as an objection,
that God does not attain the end He intends by

tolerating sin; for the sinner does not glorify God as he ought to do, and forfeits his own happiness, if he dies in the state of grievous sin. We reply that the end which God intends is His own glory, and that on such terms as to leave it to the choice of the free creature to become throughout eternity a living monument of His beatifying love or of His rigorous justice. As regards the happiness of the free creature, He intends that happiness only on condition that the creature prepares for the same before the time of probation expires with the close of this earthly life.

234. But is the toleration of sin compatible with the sanctity of God? No sin can be committed, unless God concurs to the sinful action. But in doing so He seems to approve of sin; for there is nothing which could necessitate Him to lend the sinner His aid. In answer to this difficulty, let us repeat briefly the solution already given in the chapter on Divine concurrence. (pp. 364 seq. and 370.) We there showed that God does not concur in the sin itself, nor does He encourage the sinner to abuse his free-will. The concurrence of God, which the sinner abuses, consists in this, that God grants him the use of the moral freedom that belongs to his nature. To do so He has reasons worthy of His infinite wisdom, although incomprehensible to human minds.

235. But scarcely is this answer given, when another difficulty arises: God puts one man in circumstances in which it is very easy to avoid sin, and He places another in positions which make sin,

AA

apparently, unavoidable. Is such an unequal treatment of two creatures of the same human nature
not against Divine justice? Is it not acceptance of
persons? Compare the case of a well trained child
of good Christian parents with that of a youth who
grows up in the surroundings of vice and impiety.

We answer in the first place that God's justice
does not oblige Him to treat creatures of the same
nature exactly in the same way. The justice of
God is not commutative, but distributive. It is not
manifested by paying to creatures what they have
any right to ask of Him, but in granting them what
He cannot refuse to their nature and their merits
without denying His own goodness, wisdom, and
benevolence. If then He grants thus much to all
men, the objection against His justice ceases,
although He may make the grant to one in a
sufficient, to another in an abundant degree.
Certainly nobody can prove that poor, ignorant,
and badly educated people fall into or are punished
by God for really grievous sins, the avoidance of
which was not made morally possible for them,
either naturally or supernaturally by special internal
graces. Their acts often do not involve that malice
which prompts better-endowed minds to similar
excesses. Ignorance frequently excuses them from
grievous guilt, when they do things objectively very
serious. From reason and revelation we must conclude that no man is ever necessitated to violate the
law of God culpably, and that every sin imputable
to man is caused only by abuse of freedom against
the voice of conscience. Add to this, that through-

out the Old and New Testament God calls Himself
with a sort of preference the protector of the poor;
and indicates that their human frailties will be
judged with great mercy. For what else is the
meaning of these passages of Scripture: "He
that despiseth the poor reproacheth his Maker;"[7]
"He that hath mercy on the poor lendeth to
the Lord;"[8] "He" (the Messiah) "shall judge the
poor of the people and He shall save the children
of the poor;" "He shall spare the poor and needy
and He shall save the souls of the poor;"[9] "He"
(the Messiah) "shall judge the poor with justice;"[10]
"To him that is little, mercy shall be granted;
but the mighty shall be mightily tormented," &c.;[11]
"The prayer out of the mouth of the poor shall
reach the ears of God;"[12] "The Lord will not
accept any person against a poor man;"[13] and
the poverty of the Word Incarnate, His perpetual
companion during life, what else does it signify
than that the poor are dear to God? If they are
dear to Him, it is impossible that any one of them
should perish finally unless by his own grievous
fault. What we have said of poor and uninstructed
men may be applied to all those who without their
own fault are in great danger of sin. Experience
proves that they are often protected in quite an
astonishing way, if they use those precautions which
Providence has placed within their reach.

236. But how is it consonant with the mercy of

---

[7] Prov. xvii. 5.   [8] Prov. xix. 17.   [9] Psalm lxxi. 4, 13.
[10] Isaias xi. 4.   [11] Wisdom vi. 7.   [12] Ecclus. xxi. 6.
[13] Ecclus. xxxv. 16.

God, to grant the sinner moral freedom, when He foresees that the wretched man will abuse it and ruin himself? A father surely should not hand his son a loaded pistol, at a time when the latter shows himself overcome by disgust of life and ready to get rid of it at the first convenient opportunity. Really, however, there is an infinite disparity between the two cases. The father is bound by human and Divine law to follow another line of action. He is the head of a family and not the ruler of the universe. It is not with him to draw out the fundamental laws of his domestic government. Through the voice of his conscience he is informed of the will of his Maker. And his conscience tells him that he does grievous wrong by thus occasioning the death of his son without any sufficient reason. No motive can be made out for putting the temptation in his way but wanton cruelty and desire of the suicide of his charge. God, on the contrary, in granting moral freedom does not intend that the sinner shall abuse it. By warning him through the voice of conscience He manifests clearly that He wishes him to turn away from the temptation. His foreseeing that the free creature will go wrong could only obscure His mercy, if it were not easily understood that He has quite sufficient reason for allowing the use of freedom, although this use becomes mischievous through the fault of the creature.

We may insist upon the natural harmony between a free creature and the use of freedom ; we may call attention to the truth that God can and will

elicit good from evil, that He is free to grant or
not to grant those special privileges of grace by
which He preserves saints at times, that sufficient
grace to avoid formal sin is offered to every one.
Considerations like these suffice to show that the
argument raised against the mercy of God from the
existence of moral evil is unsound, although they
do not unveil the mystery of Divine wisdom that
shrouds from our view the reasons for which, in
particular cases, moral evils are not prevented. We
are only allowed to see some of the Divine artifices
by which our incomprehensible Creator raises upon
the spiritual ruin caused by sin, the most splendid
edifices of virtue and true greatness, or causes the
malice of the wicked to be one of the many rungs
in the ladder by which His faithful servants ascend
to the height of Divine charity and intimate union
with God.   Thus the fallen Peter becomes the
immoveable Rock of the Church, the strength of his
brethren, the model of pastors, the undaunted hero
whom nothing can separate from his crucified
Master.   On the other hand, the rage of unbelievers
causes St. Stephen to practise heroic charity, makes
St. Lawrence exult upon the gridiron, and peoples
Heaven with an innumerable multitude of martyrs.

237. "Yet," continues our objector, "according
to Christian belief, eternal punishment is the lot of
him who dies in grievous sin.   Why should this be ?
Why should those who refuse grace up to death
lose for ever all chance of salvation ? "

Before answering, let us formulate one principle.
It is this : What Infinite Wisdom deems just must

a priori be approved by a finite understanding. But we have proved the First Cause of all things to be infinitely perfect and wise, and may we not reasonably expect that among the arrangements of Infinite Wisdom there will be many beyond the grasp of our limited faculties? However, let us see what human reason makes of the arguments of our opponent.

First, then, it is alleged that according to justice there must be proportion between the magnitude of a crime and the punishment inflicted for it, and that this does not seem to be the case if a grievous sin committed in the twinkling of an eye is to be expiated by never-ending torments.

This reasoning rests manifestly on the wrong supposition that the magnitude of crime is to be measured by the time required for its perpetration. If this were the case, the boy who plays truant for half a day would be a far greater criminal than the ruffian who in half an hour commits a dozen murders. Common sense does not take this view of the matter. Whilst committing the boy to the cane, it delivers the murderer to the gallows. Every one agrees that by the crimes committed within the space of thirty minutes, the murderer has forfeited twelve times over all the benefits which he might have enjoyed in human society on earth for forty or fifty years. It is evident then that time cannot be the standard by which punishment is to be determined. Not the duration of a bad deed, but its internal wickedness, must be the measure of the expiation due to it. But its wickedness increases in proportion as the obligation is sacred which is deliberately violated. Now it is evident that no obligation of man towards man can stand comparison for a moment with the obligation of man to obey God. The right of God to the obedience of His reasonable creature is absolute and infinite. No right can be more strict; and every other right is based upon it. A wilful violation, therefore, of this right implies a malice which opposes itself to the foundation of all orders. It is, in comparison with social disorders, considered as violations of merely human rights, an infinite moral disorder. Hence it is justly punished with an infinite penalty. But a finite creature cannot suffer a penalty infinite in intensity. The duration, therefore, of the penalty must be infinite. This must be insisted upon all the more emphatically, because the soul of a man who dies in mortal sin leaves this world in a state of opposition to its Creator. The distortion of the human understanding and will, caused by a deliberate refusal to acknowledge God as Supreme Master, cannot be repaired when the time of preparation for man's last end has passed. Death puts a term to that time. Consequently, the free-will of man remains for ever in the same relation to God in which it is in the moment of the separation of soul and body. The will of one, therefore, who dies impenitent, after having committed grievous sin, remains for ever averted from God, refusing to embrace lovingly the only Being in which the created spirit can find his beatitude. Happiness is incompatible with such a state. On the contrary, it must be a state of the deepest dissatisfaction and misery; for it is impossible that a rational and spiritual nature should ever find rest and peace unless it be united with God, the source of all goodness, and beauty, and truth. The misery of the dying, impenitent sinner lasts then as long as the perversity of his will. His will is incorrigible; hence his misery must be irremediable.

Accordingly, there is perfect harmony between Divine justice and the most essential feature of eternal punishment as proposed by Catholic doctrine. Catholic theologians agree that Hell would cease to be Hell, if the damned could only enjoy the Beatific Vision of God. Whatever may be the nature of the *fire of Hell* and its effects upon the damned, it is certain that the pain which it causes is nothing in comparison with the distress and despair produced by the consciousness of having for ever forfeited access to the only true source of peace and happiness. It is, however, a connatural consequence of this greatest of all penalties, that the damned should suffer positively through the intervention of creatures. He who has refused to make use of creatures as instruments in the service of his Creator, is justly punished by experiencing pain through their influence. Hence our reason sees how congruous it is that, according to the law of God, rebellion against Him should be punished in the next world through the instrumentality of a real, material being, bearing some similarity to earthly fire. The " fire " of the sun has remotely a share in all the benefits God grants us through His creatures for our salvation. A contempt of those benefits is appropriately avenged by a substance similar to that by the aid of which the benefits were conferred, that is, *by fire*.

In what way this will be done is irrelevant to our discussion here. Readers may consult St. Thomas.[14]

238. Let us now turn to the objection against Divine mercy based upon the same doctrine of eternal punishment. "Whatever may be the demands of justice!" exclaims the unbeliever, "infinite mercy requires the final extinction of all punishment, all the more so because eternal punishment is useless, and consequently its infliction real cruelty!"

Let us judge of the relation between mercy and punishment, not according to blind sentiment, but in the light of reason. First as regards the infinity of Divine mercy. To place limitations to the Divine mercy as it is in itself, one must show that that mercy somehow falls short of the standard required by Infinite Wisdom. But how shall the infidel show this? Not certainly by pointing out that the effects of God's mercy are limited. In fact it seems intrinsically repugnant that creatures should act according to their nature, and yet evil be removed from them without any limit. To answer, however, more positively we may solve the difficulty thus. As Divine Mercy is infinitely perfect because it is in perfect harmony with Infinite Wisdom, so Divine Justice is infinitely perfect for the same reason. Consequently, *a priori*, there is no ground why, in the

[14] St. Thomas, *Sum. Theol.* 3a; Suppl. q. 70. a. 3. § "Et ideo dicendum;" and *Ibid.* q. 97. art. 5.

relation of God towards His reasonable creatures, either one or other of these two attributes should be manifested exclusively. It would appear more proper that both should shine forth in their effects. Of course, God owes it to His own goodness that the joint glorification of these two attributes should be in harmony with the final happiness of all reasonable creatures, on the supposition that none of them refuse to fulfil the conditions laid down for the attainment of that happiness. But if *some* submit to their Creator, and *others rebel* against Him, it behoves the dignity of God to make a final irrevocable distinction between loyal subjects and obstinate rebels. This distinction may be made in such a way that the everlasting punishment of the wicked shall itself be a manifestation both of justice and of mercy,—of justice in point of duration, and of mercy in point of intensity. According to St. Thomas, this is what is actually done. He says: "In the damnation of the reprobate, mercy manifests itself, not by putting a stop to the penalty inflicted, but by alleviating it somewhat, so as to exact less than what is really due."[15]

239. From this discussion on Providence, in respect of the permission of evil and the infliction of eternal punishment, it is, we hope, evident that the Christian philosopher, after having proved on philosophical grounds the existence and attributes of God, may face boldly any difficulty by which adver-

---

[15] "In damnatione reproborum apparet misericordia non quidem totaliter relaxans sed aliqualiter allevians dum punit citra condignum." (St. Thomas, *Sum. Theol.* 1a. q. 21. art. 4. ad 1.)

saries try to undermine his conclusions. To do more than dispel the fallacies with which unbelief opposes the evidences of reason and the testimonies of Christianity in favour of an infinitely wise and good Providence, is a task neither necessary nor possible. It is not necessary; because after the truth of Divine Providence has been established, man knows enough for taking a proper view of life. Under such a Providence as Natural Theology discloses to our reason, and Christian revelation proposes to our faith, life is certainly worth living, in obedience to the voice of conscience and in opposition to the impulse of blind passion. All the duties imposed upon us by the voice of conscience can be fulfilled without investigation of the secret counsels and hidden ways of the Supreme Being. No need to lose time in such investigations. When once we clearly understand that we are essentially servants of an infinitely good Master, it behoves us to pay Him adoration, confidence, and love, and to be anxious rather about a complete knowledge of the duty of the creature to its Creator than about the ways by which the Creator guides His creature.

CHAPTER III.

SECTION I.—*Miracles conceivable and possible.*

Thesis XXXIX.—*Miracles, as believed in by Christian monotheists, involve nothing self-contradictory or absolutely impossible, nor are they in any way opposed to the existence of physical law. Consequently, they are intrinsically and extrinsically possible, and by no means effects unworthy of a wise Governor of the Universe.*

240. In the present section we are only concerned with the possibility of miracles; in the next we shall discuss whether they come within the range of human knowledge. Our thesis says, first that miracles are not self-contradictory, or that the proper notion of a miracle does not involve any union of mutually inconsistent ideas.

To prove this it will be necessary to inquire what is meant by "a miracle." In a wider sense, we call "a miracle" anything astonishing. Thus, we may speak of "miracles of beauty," "of learning," "of virtue." And we may call any effect of an unknown cause "a miracle." But the Christian, theological sense of the word *miracle* is far more restricted, and very definite. In this sense no event is called a miracle, unless it be due to quite a special interference of God. Yet not even every such event is a miracle. Something must be added, as will appear from the two following definitions of *miracle*, the first of which is given by St. Thomas, the second adopted by modern theologians.

241. According to St. Thomas, " miracles are effects wrought by the power of God alone in things which have a natural tendency to a contrary effect, or to a contrary way of producing it."[1]

In explanation of this definition we have to make the following remarks :

(*a*) St. Thomas requires for the existence of a miracle that the effect in question should be attributable exclusively to Divine power. It appears from the context of his doctrine that he means to say : The principal cause of a miracle is God alone ; a creature can only be instrumental in its operation, either by disposing the matter in which, by virtue of the Divine volition alone, the miracle is produced, or by obtaining miracles from God through prayers or good works, or by commanding in the name of God that a miracle shall take place. Such a command supposes a special, Divine inspiration, through which the person who works the miracle is made sure that his command will be efficacious.[2]

To some readers the objection may occur : You say, God alone is the principal cause of a miracle.

---

[1] " Illa quæ sola virtute divina fiunt in illis rebus, in quibus est naturalis ordo ad contrarium effectum vel ad contrarium modum faciendi, dicuntur proprie miracula " (*De Potentia*, q. 6. *De Miraculis*, art. 2. in corp.).

[2] Cf. St. Thomas, *ibid*. a. 4.

But God is the principal cause of every positive effect. Therefore, according to your explanation, every positive effect is a miracle? The answer to this objection is that God is the principal cause of a miracle, not merely in the sense of *prime cause*, but inasmuch as *principal cause* denotes a cause endowed with natural faculties proportioned to a certain effect, and is thus opposed to *instrumental cause*, which by itself alone has no perfect natural aptitude for the effect in which it is said to be instrumental, but is raised to that aptitude by a special impulse and direction proceeding from the principal cause. Thus, in the action of painting, God is the *prime cause;* the artist is the *principal cause;* and his brush and pallet are the *instrumental causes* of the picture. The action of painting is, therefore, a human action depending upon ordinary Divine concurrence; but it is not a Divine action. Though God be the *prime cause,* human faculties are proportioned to such an action, and therefore the painter is the *principal cause* of it. But a miracle is an *effect which, considered in the concrete with all its circumstances,* is manifestly proportioned to the Divine power alone. Elias prayed, and the wet wood caught fire miraculously, not because the natural conditions prerequired for this effect were present, but because God willed it so on account of the prayer of the Prophet. The man born blind, who washed himself in the pool of Siloe by the command of our Lord, was cured, not because the washing was proportioned to the cure, but because the Incarnate Son of God willed it so on condition of this act of obedience. The man born blind was to a certain extent the principal cause of his going to the pool and washing himself there; but the Son of God was not only the *prime*, but also the sole *principal* and *proper* cause of the miracle.[3] (*b*) By the additional words, "in things which have a natural tendency to a contrary effect, or to a contrary way of producing it," St. Thomas implies that the effect of a miracle is either something which in the ordinary course of nature never happens, or something which in the ordinary course of nature does not happen in this way. Of the first kind is the raising of a dead man to life again, of the second kind the cure of a very serious disease by a simple command.

242. After having given his definition, the Angelic Doctor, by way of further explanation, indicates two series of facts, which at first sight would seem to be miracles, but are not miracles in the sense in which Catholic theologians use the term.

The first series is formed by the hidden effects of nature—(*ea quæ natura facit nobis tamen vel alicui occulta*). There are natural effects, the natural cause of which is unknown. That cause may be either some hidden force or forces of nature acting by themselves, or it may be forces of nature applied by the natural faculties of man in an artificial way, or it may be forces of nature utilized by pure spirits, supposing they act only with their natural faculties. All these effects are wonderful and marvellous, but not miracles.

[3] Cf. 3 Kings xviii. 30—39; St. John ix.

The second series is made up of actions which are Divine, but occur regularly in the *ordinary* natural or supernatural course of things—(*ea quæ Deus facit nec aliter nata sunt fieri nisi a Deo*). Such actions are: (1) The creation of each individual human soul, which takes place through purely Divine power as often as the substratum of a human body has been duly prepared by natural causes. As we have shown in Book I., no human soul can come into existence otherwise than through immediate Divine creation. But this creation follows a certain rule, laid down by God from eternity to be followed regularly; and moreover it follows a rule which must be observed, if God wills mankind to continue to exist in agreement with the exigencies of their nature. The creation of a human soul, then, though a purely Divine action, is neither a miracle nor a supernatural action in the strict sense of the word. It is not a miracle, because it is in harmony with the ordinary course of things: it is not a supernatural action, because it is necessary for the completion of human nature. Also the first creation of pure spirits and of matter, though most marvellous, does not come under the category of miracles, because by that creation the very foundation of created nature was laid. Christians believe also in other actions, transcending not only the faculties of creatures, but even the exigencies grounded on their nature and their faculties; and therefore strictly supernatural actions, yet not miracles. Such actions are the *infusion* or *increase* of *sanctifying grace* through the sacraments of the

Church, and through acts of perfect contrition. Such are also all *illuminations* and *inspirations* of the Holy Ghost, by which men are prepared and helped to the performance of saving and meritorious works. These actions are not miracles, because they follow the ordinary course of constant super-natural influence of God upon rational creatures, in accordance with the general direction of His Providence in the present order of things towards a supernatural beatitude.

The conversion of St. Paul no doubt was preceded and accompanied by miracles in the strict sense of the word. The conversion itself may be rightly called a miracle of grace; but it was not a miracle in the ordinary sense, because it was not a supernatural and extraordinary change produced by God in Saul as in a living, corporeal being; but the change was made in his spiritual faculties. Miracles, as understood by St. Thomas and Catholic theologians, are extraordinary Divine operations in nature, that is to say, in the sphere of sensible corporeal things.

243. To express this clearly, modern theologians define a miracle to be a *sensible, unusual, Divine, and supernatural work.*[4] (a) A miracle is defined "a sensible work," because the definition does not extend beyond those extraordinary supernatural

---

[4] "Opus sensibile, divinitus factum, insolitum, supernaturale." (Cf. T. Pesch, *Instit. Phil. Nat.* p. 711.) Whilst agreeing in the substance, different modern representatives of Catholic Theology and Philosophy vary in the form of the definition. To our mind the form adopted l.c. recommends itself for great precision.

BB

facts which imply changes perceptible through the senses.

(*b*) A miracle is defined " an unusual work," because it is opposed to the ordinary course of nature, or to the ordinary way in which corporeal things under similar circumstances act and react on one another. The mere frequency of a miracle in comparatively few spots of the globe does not take away its character of being "an unusual work." To use the words of St. Thomas: " If daily some blind man were made to see, this would nevertheless be a miracle, because opposed to the ordinary course of nature."[5]

(*c*) A miracle is called " a Divine work," because it is due to a special positive agency of God. The co-operation of even the holiest and most wonderful of the saints in the miracles which they are said to work, does not extend beyond acting as impetrators, or as instrumental and ministerial causes, as explained above.

(*d*) A miracle is called not only a Divine, but also a supernatural work, because it is not one of those Divine works which complete the natural existence of corporeal things, man included. To these works belong the first creation of the world and the continual creation of individual souls.

Note.—In the language of Scripture miracles are often called *signs, prodigies, virtues.* The word *sign* refers to the intention God has in working miracles. He wills thereby to *speak to* man in a sensible way. The name *prodigy* points to the *wonder* excited in

[5] *Sent.* ii. dist. 18. q. 1. art. 3. ad 2.

human minds by the sight of miracles; whilst the
word *virtues* implies that they are manifestations of
power, supreme and Divine.

244. Against the definition of miracles just explained, a difficulty may be raised from a division
of miracles very common in Catholic schools, and
mentioned repeatedly by St. Thomas. Miracles are
divided into miracles *above nature, beside nature, and
against nature* — (*miracula supra naturam, præter
naturam, contra naturam*). *Above nature* are those
miracles which are worked in material subjects, in
which in the ordinary course of nature similar effects
never occur. Thus, it never happens naturally,
that a dead and decomposing body rises to' life
again. Therefore, the resurrection of Lazarus was
a miracle *above* nature.[6]

Beside nature are those miracles that occur in
material subjects, in which through the forces of
nature, either left to themselves or artificially
applied, similar effects do occur. Here an effect
is known to be miraculous by its occurring at a
prophesied time, or simply upon the word of a
thaumaturgus, and that in cases in which similar
effects could not have been obtained through natural
forces otherwise than gradually and with no certainty
about the success. Thus, the fact that in Egypt,
upon the word of Moses, all the first-born of men
and beasts died in one night, whilst the Israelites
were spared, was a miracle beside nature. Such a
miracle also was the sudden withering of the hand
of Jeroboam, when he stretched it out against the

___

[6] Cf. St. John xi. 43, 44.

420   *THE ACTION OF GOD UPON THIS WORLD.*

Prophet of God; and the blindness of the sorcerer Elymas, caused upon the prediction of St. Paul.[7]

Against nature are the miracles which happen in material subjects that naturally tend to a contrary effect, and are not prevented from producing their effect by any natural cause. Thus, the preservation of the three companions of Daniel was a miracle against nature; also the going back of the shadow upon the sun-dial of Achaz.[8]

This is the division of miracles which is substantially to be found in St. Thomas.[9] The term "nature," which is taken as the standard of this division, means the whole of corporeal substances and their forces acting under ordinary Divine concurrence, either by themselves alone, or under some artificial direction of rational creatures. We must note that the miracles which are said to be *against nature,* are in no way against the essence or against the final end of natural substances, but only against the course of action these substances would take, if God had not from eternity decreed for special reasons to interfere with it.

But how to combine the division with the definition? The definition says, that every miracle is *supernatural,* or *above nature.* In the division, on the contrary, only one class of miracles is marked as being *above nature.* The solution is to be found in the fact that in the definition the miraculous effect

---

[7] Cf. Exodus xi. xii.; 3 Kings xiii.; Acts xiii. 8—12.

[8] Cf. Daniel iii. 21—24; 4 Kings xx.

[9] St. Thomas, *Sent.* ii. dist. 18. q. 1. art. 3. solutio; *De Potentia,* q. 6. art. 2. ad 3m.

is considered as it exists in the concrete, with all its circumstances, knowable to a diligent observer. When thus viewed, every real miracle must be pronounced to be supernatural, or a Divine effect. But a miraculous effect, though manifestly Divine when viewed adequately, may be taken into consideration inadequately and the question asked: How does this effect stand to the efficiency of mere natural forces, abstraction being made from all particular circumstances? This consideration leads to the result that some miracles are *above nature*, others *beside nature*, others *against nature*. Therefore, the definition is not opposed to the division; because in the definition the miraculous effect is viewed as happening under all the peculiar circumstances under which it does happen: whilst the division of miracles is made by comparing the effect with the forces of nature, abstracting from concrete circumstances. And thus far of the definition and division of miracles.

245. That miracles are conceivable and not intrinsically absurd, is easily shown. They are by hypothesis extraordinary effects of Divine power in corporeal things, beyond the powers of creatures. There is certainly nothing in this concept approaching to self-contradiction. The power of creatures is finite. It is, therefore, conceivable that God should work in created things in a way impossible to creatures; and that not in the ordinary way, which the continuation of created existences and activities implies, but in a manner quite extraordinary. Again, as we have seen, God is infinitely powerful and free.

If He is infinitely powerful, He certainly can produce effects in corporeal things, which no created activity left to itself could produce under the circumstances. And if He is infinitely free, He cannot be said to have been necessitated from eternity so to order the course of created activities as to leave no room for His own immediate interference further than was altogether necessary for the continuance of the world. Miracles are consequently conceivable as works of God's absolute power.

246. It remains to be considered whether they can be combined with the eternal decrees of God. God, it may be urged, cannot contradict Himself. Now, universal experience leads to the conclusion that the material substances of the universe follow natural laws, or certain uniform ways of action, so that under the same circumstances the same effects occur. These natural laws must have been decreed by God from eternity. If so, what room remains for extraordinary interference? Some such train of reasoning seems to have been in Dr. Carpenter's mind, when he penned the following lines: " In regard to the Physical Universe then, it might be better to substitute for the phrase, 'Government by Laws,' 'Government according to Laws': meaning thereby the direct exertion of the Divine Will or operation of the First Cause, in the forces of Nature, according to certain constant uniformities which are simply unchangeable, because—having been originally the expression of Infinite Wisdom—any change would be for the worse." [10]

[10] *Mental Physiology*, p. 706.

There is much truth in these words, but not the whole truth. God's decrees are indeed irrevocable, and the course of nature is at least generally uniform. Were it otherwise, mankind would be held in a state of perpetual suspense by the unavoidable and insoluble question: What will happen next? There would be no stimulus to labour where no fruit could be counted on; and human life, if possible at all, would be in a condition of abject misery.

But the one concession, that God governs the world according to natural laws, does not involve the other, that in every particular case the general law is applied. There are exceptions made in human legislation, where it is foreseen that a general enactment would bear too hard upon a particular case. So the Creator may foresee from eternity that in this case and that an exception to the general course of nature will serve His purpose better than the maintenance of the uniformity; and He may decree that exception accordingly from all eternity. Let us suppose, at least for argument's sake, that it is God's eternal design to raise some of His rational creatures to a union with Himself in knowledge and love, far more intimate than any that their nature could lay claim to. This being so, God could no doubt decree to communicate His benevolent designs to particular chosen legates, and to commission them with the promulgation of those designs to mankind. In order now to give these His legates an incontestable authority, He could decree to make known to them what they could not possibly know by natural means, namely, the future free actions of men with all their particular circumstances. Such a decree itself would be a decree to interfere with the psychological law of the natural dependence of the human mind upon ideas gathered from experience or elaborated by reason. It would be a suspension of a psychological law for a higher end and in a particular case only. There is nothing repugnant in all this. If, then, God can thus inter fere with a psychological law on behalf of a Prophet whom He sends, why should He be unable to give His Prophet still more authority, by decreeing that in particular cases a prayer, a command, a touch, or even a mere volition of that Prophet should be followed by an extraordinary effect in a corporeal thing? There is again nothing unworthy of God in this supposition. No decrees are repealed, but from eternity the rule and the exception from the rule are settled with one act of Divine volition in the light of infinite knowledge and with an intention *not to help nature to that for which as a work of God it is competent by its natural forces, but to raise it to a higher level out of pure generous love.*

247. Once we understand that *God is infinite intellect and will, and acts by mere volition according to eternal decrees,* we can have no difficulty in solving modern arguments against the possibility of miracles. Almost all are variations of those of Spinoza.[11] This author starts from the supposition that God must from eternity will everything He knows, a supposition disproved by us in Book II., where we treated

[11] *Tract. Theol. Polit. c. 6.*

of the free-will of God. (Cf. pp. 295, seq.) We showed there that God wills nothing with absolute necessity but His own existence. Arguing in particular against those miracles which the scholastics called against nature, Spinoza says [12] that such miracles would involve either the absence of general laws of nature, or the supposition that God could act against the laws of His own nature. This difficulty is done away with by what we have shown in Book I., that the self-evolving God of Spinozism exists only in the imagination of pantheists. The phrase, ";' against nature," means, as we have seen, no more than this, that the natural tendency to action proper to a corporeal being in a particular case remains potential, instead of becoming actual, as it would have become had not God decreed to make this case an exception to the general rule.

"But," continues Spinoza, "if miracles are, strictly speaking, all above nature, then you must admit a break in the necessary and immutable course of nature; which is absurd. It would follow also that the principles of reason are violable; for after all they are but laws of nature. In that case we are unable to trust them, unable to prove the existence of God; and thus miracles, far from being a help to the knowledge of God, prove a total impediment to that knowledge."

This argument confounds in the first place the course of nature as decreed by the Divine mind from eternity with the course of nature as it commonly occurs in human experience. Under

[13] Loc. cit.

the former respect it is absolutely immutable, not under the latter; and this suffices for the possibility of miracles, as has been shown in the proof of our thesis. If in a particular case the common rule is not followed, if, for instance, water changes miraculously into wine, it does not follow that equally well in another particular case two and two might become five, and thus a principle of reason be violated. If Spinoza had studied St. Thomas, he would have found the solution of his difficulty.[13] St. Thomas says, that if we speak of an action against *principles of nature* (or more accurately, against the natural tendency of physical forces), we imply thereby that such an action surpasses created agencies, from which it does not follow that the Almighty Creator cannot effect it, supposing it to be in keeping with His justice and wisdom. But the *principles of reason* are not tendencies of physical forces, but enunciations of

---

[13] *De Potentia*, q. 6. art. i. obj. 11. As this passage is one of the many in which Aquinas anticipated modern difficulties, we will give it in full. The obj. 11 runs thus: "Sicuti ratio humana a Deo est, ita et natura. Sed contra principia rationis Deus facere non potest, sicut quod genus de specie non prædicetur, vel quod latus quadrati sit commensurabile diametro. Ergo nec contra principia naturæ Deus facere potest." His answer is: "Ad undecimum dicendum, quod logicus et mathematicus considerant tantum res secundum principia formalia; unde nihil est impossibile in logicis et mathematicis, nisi quod est contra rei formalem rationem. Et hujusmodi impossibile in se contradictionem claudit, et sic est per se impossibile. Talia autem impossibilia Deus facere non potest. Naturalis (*i.e.* the physicist and biologist) autem applicat ad determinatam materiam; unde reputat impossibile etiam id quod est huic impossibile. Nihil autem prohibet Deum posse facere quæ sunt inferioribus agentibus impossibilia."

inviolable truths, which cannot be set aside by any rational being without the ruin of all certainty, much less be over-ruled by God, Who is the First Truth and the Source of all truth.

Spinoza's difficulty regarding the perturbation of order by miracles has been repeated by Voltaire, Strauss, and others, and seems to be a chief stumbling-block for many, because they forget the distinction between order as conceived by God and order as manifested in the uniformity of nature. Order under the first aspect reigns everywhere; order under the second aspect is the normal thing, but there are exceptions for wise reasons. Such exceptions are no more perturbations of the laws of nature than in human society privileges modifying the tenor of a general, civil, or criminal law, granted by the lawgiver at the same time he establishes the law, and granted with wise limitations, can be called abrogations of the law itself.

SECTION 2.—*Miracles can be known as such.*

Thesis XL.—*By careful inquiry the extraordinary Divine operations called miracles can be sufficiently distinguished from the wonders of nature and art, and from the operations of created spirits.*

248. Affirming in our thesis that miracles are knowable, we do not maintain that every particular miracle is sufficiently open to all inquirers. All we hold is, that those in whose favour God works miracles, and to whom He wishes thereby to manifest Himself in an extraordinary way, cannot

fail to discover Him as the Author of those effects.
Our argument is simply this. God never works
miracles but for an end worthy of Himself. He
works them in order to draw men nearer to Himself by extraordinary manifestations of His Divine
attributes, of His power, wisdom, benevolence,
mercy, justice. His miracles are intended to be
a solid comfort to men of good-will, and an earnest
and terrifying warning to those who revolt against
the voice of their conscience. They are, as it were,
a Divine speech, expressed, not by Divine words,
but by Divine deeds. Now, is it possible that God
should thus address men without offering them
sufficient means to ascertain that He has spoken?
To suppose this would involve the denial either of
God's power or of God's wisdom. The supposition
in fact amounts to this, either that God cannot
make Himself known as the Author of these special
works, or that He does not care to do so. Take
the first alternative, and you deny God's power;
take the second, and you deny His wisdom. In
both cases you think of the Creator in a way
altogether incompatible with His perfection. Men
are able to stamp their works with such indisputable
signs of their individuality as that nobody, on
sufficient inquiry, can see any reason for suspend-
ing his judgment as to their origin. And should the
Creator be powerless to manifest Himself by equally
clear evidences? Men of common sense do not
annoy their fellow-men with ambiguous communi-
cations, the proper meaning and origin of which
nobody can discover; and shall the infinitely wise

God speak the language of signs and wonders in such a way that no amount of reasonable inquiry can throw light upon the real speaker? ' Such suppositions cannot be entertained for a moment. But to acknowledge them as absurd is equivalent to the statement that miracles are really knowable *if duly inquired into*.

249. This last-mentioned condition must be added. Otherwise we may take for miraculous what are really no more than hidden effects of nature, artificial tricks of men, or operations of created spirits, surpassing men in their acuteness of intellect and in their power of applying the forces of nature to ends of their own. The first and second of these cases is possible, and has happened often enough. The third case is of course put down as impossible by materialists, extreme evolutionists, and agnostics. If there are any other thinkers, not in this class, who still do not believe in rational beings higher than man, and yet infinitely distant from the Creator, then, we must say, their stand-point is not conformable to reason and history, and is besides opposed to a fundamental truth of Christianity. Reason *a priori* finds it far more probable that between the one infinite spirit and human souls not purely spiritual, there should exist created pure spirits, than that they should not exist. History testifies that the belief in such spirits among civilized nations is as old as mankind. The history of magnetism and spiritualism countenances this supposition, that some purely spiritual creatures do at times make their influence sensibly felt in this

world. Such is the judgment of many Catholic theologians, who have studied the history of spiritualism with great attention.[14]

250. It appears then that created rational beings higher than man, or at least other than human, influence this visible world. Shall we then call their influence miraculous? According to the definition of a miracle we cannot do so, unless they act not by mere natural power but as instruments of God. Now St. Thomas, speaking from the stand-point of Christian Revelation, and consequently taking for granted that there are good spirits (*holy angels*) and evil spirits (*demons* or *devils*), lays it down. as an evident corollary of revealed doctrine that God, whilst using good angels as moral instruments for miraculous effects, never grants to evil spirits greater power than they have by nature, but

[14] Not long ago the *Spectator* wrote as follows: " He [the writer] would assert that no one who has studied what are now called euphemistically the phenomena of hypnotism, and the various states of distinct personal consciousness which the French physicians elicit in their hypnotic patients, should doubt that the old doctrine of one spirit over-riding another in the same organism is as good an explanation of the facts as any other which can be suggested; indeed, a great deal better, in his opinion—he speaks only of himself —than Mr. Myers' theory of different strata of consciousness. . . . Though the writer speaks only for himself in saying what he does, the present generation has, in his opinion, ample and absolute evidence, if it will only bear patiently with fools and knaves and impostors of all kinds in seeking it, that alien intelligences not acting through any human body—and sometimes intelligences of a very mean order—do produce definite physical effects on this world, and do sometimes induce aberrations of mind in men and women which rise to a point of virtual insanity." (*Spectator*, Feb. 9, 1889, " Professor Huxley and Agnosticism," p. 195.)

on the contrary, often restrains their natural energy.[15]

Whatever such spirits do, is done, as the Angelic Doctor says, "by skilfully utilizing through motion the potential energies latent in nature"—*adhibendo corporalia semina per motum localem.*[16] This they do with an incredible velocity, and an insight into possible combination of natural forces of which man can form no idea.

251. Thus for a due inquiry into miracles, we need a double series of criteria; the first to guard us against taking for miracles mere natural effects, caused by physical forces left to themselves or artificially applied by men; whilst the second helps us to distinguish miracles from the effects of evil spirits. As the good angels never go about to deceive men by their artifices, we do not want a series of criteria to mark off their natural operations from true miracles.

Before the application of these criteria, the historical truth of *the fact itself* must first be tested. Inquiry must be made as to "Who reports the fact?" "Could such a witness know the truth,

---

[15] Cf. *Sum. Theol.* I. q. 110. art. 3. et art. 4. and *De Potentia*, q. 6. art. 3. art. 4. art. 5. In the last place he says distinctly: "Sicut Angeli boni per gratiam aliquid possunt ultra naturalem virtutem, ita Angeli mali minus possunt ex divina providentia eos reprimente, quam possint secundum naturalem virtutem. . . . Cum operatio miraculosa sit quoddam divinum testimonium indicativum divinæ virtutis et veritatis; si dæmonibus quorum est tota voluntas ad malum, aliqua potestas daretur faciendi miracula, Deus falsitatis eorum testis existeret; quod divinam bonitatem non decet."

[16] St. Thomas, *Sum. Theol.* 1a. q. 110. art. 4. ad 3.

or is it likely that he was deceived?" "Is the veracity of the witness above suspicion?" If the answer to these three questions is favourable, we are morally certain of the existence of the fact, as reported by one or more immediate or mediate witnesses, according to the ordinary rules of testimony.[17] When this certainty has been reached, the criteria of the miraculous character of the fact come into application.

252. (1) Criteria by which we may judge whether a well attested fact *apparently* miraculous, is or is not to be assigned to hidden physical causes, either left to themselves or applied by men.

(*a*) An effect, which of its very nature is out of proportion to the efficacy of physical forces however combined by human ingenuity, must be due to a cause transcending physical nature and the will of man. Such an effect would be the raising to life again of a human body dead and buried and in a state of decomposition.

(*b*) If an effect be within the competence of physical and human causes under certain conditions, but not under the conditions present in this particular well attested instance, such an effect must be attributed to an agency above that of nature and man. The sudden cure of leprosy or blindness by a mere form of words would be such an effect.

(*c*) As often as a well attested effect is produced after physical means have been applied, which according to the judgment of experts are not quite

[17] See the *First Principles* of this series, c. vii.

out of proportion to the production of the effect, yet not likely to produce it, we are not sufficiently warranted to put the effect down to a superhuman cause. Of this sort are cures of certain nervous diseases by such influences upon the imagination as naturally cause considerable shocks to the system, and might thus have remedied the disorder.

253. (2) Criteria by which miracles are distinguished from wonders worked by evil spirits.

Note.—For the application of these criteria it is supposed that those of the first series have been applied, and that there is no longer any doubt about the superhuman character of the effect.

(*a*) A well attested effect of such a nature that it could not have been produced by any physical forces however well arranged must be Divine. By certain material unseen influences, guided by created spirits, diseases may be cured; and even hidden things may be revealed. But it seems inconceivable that any such influence should bring back the soul of a dead man to a body already in a state of decay.

(*b*) However marvellous and well attested an effect may be, yet if by its very nature it tends to discredit beliefs, which can be proved to rest upon a Divine foundation, and to have been confirmed by real prophecies and true miracles, it is certainly not Divine, but attributable only to fallen spirits opposed to God. Such were the effects produced through the instrumentality of Simon Magus,[18] of Elymas,[19] of Apollonius of Tyana,[20] and of various so-called

[18] Acts viii. 9.   [19] Acts xiii. 8.
[20] Lactantius, *Instit. Div.* v. c. 3.

CC

idols.[21]   We have been warned beforehand that
"many false prophets shall arise and shall seduce
many,"[22] and that a time shall come "when that
wicked one shall be revealed . . . whose coming is
according to the working of Satan in all power and
signs and lying wonders."[23]

(*c*) Superhuman effects which contain anything
manifestly unworthy of the Creator, cannot in
reason be put down to Divine influence.   Therefore
St. Thomas, attributing certain magic arts of the
middle ages to superhuman influences, brings this
argument among others to show that evil spirits
are concerned in them.   "To favour things which
are contrary to virtue is not the work of a good
spirit, but these arts favour such things; for they
result in adultery, theft, murder, and other evil
deeds. . . . Therefore," &c.[24]

(*d*) If neither the nature of a superhuman effect,
nor the human person who is instrumental in producing it, nor the object for the attainment of which
it is produced, nor the circumstances under which
it occurs, show anything to excite reasonable suspicion of demoniac influence, the effect must be
considered as a Divine work.   *A fortiori* must it be

---

[21] See St. Augustine, *De Civit. Dei*, Bk. XXII. cc 9, 10.   Cf. also
Euseb. *Eccles. Hist.* iv. c. 3, a passage quoted from the Christian
apologist, Quadratus.   Cf. the excellent work, *System der göttlichen
Thaten des Christenthums*, by Professor Dr. F. X. Dieringer.

[22] St. Matt. xxiv. 11.   [23] 2 Thess. ii. 8, 9.

[24] "Præstare enim patrocinium aliquibus quæ sunt contraria
virtuti non est alicujus intellectus bene dispositi.   Hoc autem fit ex
hujusmodi artibus; fiunt enim plerumque adulteria, furta, homicidia,
et alia hujusmodi maleficia procurantur. . . . Non est ergo," etc.
(St. Thomas, *Contra Gent.* iii. c. 106.)

considered such, if with increasing inquiry, made with a humble and sincere desire to know the truth, evidences from all sides concur to prove that God alone can be the author of the wonder in question.[25]

Objections against the knowableness of miracles, as distinguished from the possibility of them, may be reduced to the two following, the first of which is Hume's celebrated argument as restated by Mill, the second has frequently been brought forward by various unbelievers.

254. (1) Mill, repeating Hume's argument,[26] reasons thus: "The evidence of miracles consists of testimony. The ground of our reliance on testimony is our experience, that certain conditions being supposed, testimony is generally veracious. But the same experience tells us that even under the best conditions testimony is frequently either intentionally or unintentionally false. When therefore the fact to which testimony is produced is one, the happening of which would be more at variance with experience than the falsehood of testimony, we ought not to believe it. And this rule all prudent persons observe in the conduct of life. Those who do not are sure to suffer for their credulity.

" Now a miracle (the argument goes on) is in the highest possible degree contradictory to experience;

[25] "Non pertinet ad providentiam Dei, non permittere falsa signa quæ ad probationem et profectum electorum prosunt; sed pertinet ad providentiam Dei, dare auxilium ac modum quo possint dijudicari et cognosci, quia non est divinæ bonitatis et sapientiæ ut permittat hominem tentari ultra id quod potest." (Cf. Suarez, *De Mysteriis vitæ Christi*, d. 31, sect. 2.)

[26] *Essays on Religion*, pp. 219, seq.

for if it were not contradictory to experience, it would not be a miracle. The very reason for its being regarded as a miracle is, that it is a breach of the law of nature, that is, of an otherwise invariable and inviolable uniformity in the succession of natural events. There is therefore the very strongest reason for disbelieving it that experience can give for disbelieving anything. But the mendacity or error of witnesses, even though numerous and of fair character, is quite within the bounds of common experience. That supposition, therefore, ought to be preferred."

Answer. This sort of reasoning manifestly begs the question. It is said that it is an *invariable* experience that miracles never occur; therefore they never occur. But that is just the question, whether the experience against miracles is *really* invariable? According to most trustworthy sources of historical knowledge there never has been such an invariable experience. Nor is this unbroken uniformity demonstrable *a priori* by any argument available to show that *God cannot work miracles.* We have proved that He can. Therefore the assertion of invariable uniformity is not borne out either by testimony or theory.

Nor can the interruption of the uniformity of the course of nature in comparatively few cases, and those settled from eternity by infinite Wisdom, reasonably be called a breach of law. As well call every limitation included in the tenor of a law a breach of the same.

Then it is said that witnesses are never free

from the suspicion of mendacity. *Foolish* and *unreasonable* suspicion, granted. But can we *reasonably* suspect all witnesses, however numerous and however fair their character may be, even when they attest their experiences on oath, as is done in the processes of beatifications and canonizations in the Catholic Church?

255. The second objection may be thus stated in its general form: "Even the best attested facts alleged as miraculous may be due to some hidden physical causes of which we do not know; for who can know all the forces of nature?"

Answer. Of course we cannot be certain that the event is miraculous, before reasonable inquiry has been made, what has been done in the case, and what has not been done. But such an inquiry may surely show that no physical forces, competent to that effect, have been applied, though they may exist in nature. For instance, a man who suffers from a disease, say a malignant tumour, pronounced fatal by several good physicians, is cured on a sudden and perfectly by addressing a short prayer to God through the intercession of a Saint. It is absolutely certain that his cure is a Divine effect. If he will not be satisfied about this, he might as well doubt whether his thirst to-day is quenched by the liquid that he drinks to-day.

Thus not only the natural Providence of God, in which every monotheist believes, but also His supernatural Providence, the great consolation and strength of the Christian during life and at the hour of death, stands perfectly in conformity with reason.

APPENDIX I.

WHEN treating of physical predetermination,[1] we remarked that we were by no means prepared to admit that St. Thomas is rightly interpreted by those who find it laid down in his works, and we now submit our reasons for taking him to sanction the Molinists rather than the so-called Thomist teaching. Our object in doing so is to satisfy those of our readers who are specially interested in the views of the great Doctor. In order to prove our point we have only to refer to his doctrine on the way in which God moves the human will, on the nature of moral freedom, on the origin of free volitions and on the Divine foresight of these volitions.

A. And first, as regards the Divine motion by which human wills are influenced, the Angelic Doctor discusses this subject under the heading, "Utrum voluntas moveatur a Deo solo sicut ab exteriori principio."[2]

---

[1] *Natural Theology*, p. 371.

[2] St.Thomas, *Sum. Theol.* 1a. 2æ. q. 9. a. 6. ad 3m. " Deus movet voluntatem hominis, sicut universalis motor, ad universale objectum voluntatis, quod est bonum ; et sine hac universali motione homo non potest aliquid velle ; sed homo per rationem determinat se ad volendum hoc vel illud, quod est vere bonum vel apparens bonum. Sed tamen interdum specialiter Deus movet aliquos ad aliquid determinate volendum, quod est bonum, sicut in his quos movet per gratiam."

There he teaches that the human will is moved
from without, and that the external principle by
which it is moved, is no other than God, and this
for two reasons: first, because He is the Creator of
the rational soul; and secondly, because He is the
universal good.

Against this doctrine he puts the following
objection: "God does not cause anything but what
is good, according to Gen. i. 31, 'God saw all the
things that He had made, and they were very good.'
Therefore, if the human will were moved only by
God, it never would be moved to anything bad; and
yet, as St. Augustine says, 'it is the will that sins
and it is the will that acts rightly.'"

In answer to this difficulty St. Thomas says:
"God moves the will of man as universal mover to
the universal object of the will, which is good taken
in general; and without this universal motion man
cannot will anything; but man determines himself
under application of his reason to the volition of
this or that thing, which is really or apparently
good. Nevertheless, sometimes God moves some
to a determinate particular volition of something
good. This is the case with those whom He moves
by His grace." Comparing these clear words of
Aquinas with the expositions of those who defend
physical predetermination, we are struck by a considerable difference.

On the one hand St. Thomas teaches that God
commonly does not cause the acts of the human will
except in so far as they involve a craving for something good. The determination, which particular

good shall be chosen to satisfy that craving, is,
according to him, not due to God but to man, who
by a free consent to a particular practical judgment
of his reason, moves his will, now to this, now to
that object.

Those on the contrary who maintain physical
predetermination, tell us that the motions of the
human will towards precisely those particular goods
which we choose, are predetermined by God, and
therefore come about infallibly. Again, St. Thomas
teaches indeed that God *sometimes* premoves men to
some particular good, but the holy Doctor does not
specify how this is done. He leaves it therefore
open to us to explain that motion, as we have
explained it, in solving the Thomistic difficulty
drawn from the nature of efficacious grace. (Cf.
p. 379.)

B. If we now turn to the idea of freedom as
explained by St. Thomas, we find him again opposed
to the predeterminists.

Contra Gentes, iii. c. 112.— St. Thomas is explaining the different relations of rational and
irrational creatures to Divine Providence. God,
he says, governs rational creatures for their own
sake, the irrational for the sake of the rational.
His first reason for this doctrine is the existence
of freedom of will in the rational, and the absence
of it in the irrational world. In what then consists
that freedom? These are his own words: "Free
is that being which can rule its own action; for
free is he who is the cause of himself; whereas
that which by a sort of necessity is driven to action,

is in a state incompatible with freedom."[3] As regards this passage, we know very well that the adherents of physical predetermination say explicitly that the predetermined creature really rules its own action under God, and that the predetermining motion of God by no means necessitates the creature to a certain action, but only draws it to the same infallibly. Let all this pass, however difficult it may be to understand. But we beg leave to ask one question: In what sense does St. Thomas say that the free being is the cause of himself? We all know that he does not mean to imply that man, on account of his freedom of will, must have in himself the principle of his existence. Nor can his saying be explained in this sense, that the free rational creature causes its own action independently of God; for he teaches expressly that God operates in all operations of His creatures. Is it then his meaning that the free creature causes its action in dependence upon God? No, because thus understood, he would say nothing of the free creature that would be at all peculiar to a free creature as such. All creatures depend upon the Creator in their actions. There remains, then, only this interpretation, that the free creature, whilst dependent upon God for action, depends proximately upon itself alone as regards its determination to this or that action. This interpretation thoroughly agrees with another saying of the Angelic Doctor: "It is

---

[3] "Quod dominium sui actus habet, liberum est in agendo; liber enim est qui sui causa est; quod autem quadam necessitate ab alio agitur ad operandum, servituti subjectum est."

peculiar to the rational nature that it tends to an end in such a way as to move and lead itself thereunto, whilst an irrational creature must tend to it as moved and led by another."[4] Who this other is, St. Thomas says clearly immediately before, in the words: " The whole of irrational nature stands to God in the relation of an instrument to its principal cause."[5] The inference to be drawn from this is, manifestly, that rational creatures, *acting as rational creatures, that is to say, using their freedom of will,* are not set in action by God as instruments by their principal causes. On the contrary, he represents them as principal causes of their own self-determination, on the supposition that they actually enjoy the use of freedom.

C. If we now ask the Angelic Doctor to explain himself more fully, and name the agency that carries the free-will to one alternative rather than another, he answers quite frankly that it is none other than the free-will itself. The passage to which we refer is *Sent.* ii. d. 39, q. i. art. i. in corp. St. Thomas teaches there that the human will, through man's own fault, may fall into sin. He adds that in the will we must distinguish between the faculty and the act. " The will as a faculty," he says, " is not from ourselves, but from God, and therefore cannot be sin in us, but the act of that faculty may be sin, because it is

---

[4] " Proprium est naturæ rationalis, ut tendat in finem, quasi se agens vel ducens ad finem, naturæ vero irrationalis, quasi ab alio acta vel ducta." (*Sum. Theol.* 1a. 2æ. q. 1. a. 2. in corp.)

[5] " Tota irrationalis natura comparatur ad Deum sicut instrumentum ad agens principale." (*Ibid.*)

from us."[6]   He wishes, however, to make us understand that the act of which he here speaks is not the actual use of freedom *as such* (this no doubt is also from God), but the actual use of freedom inasmuch as it means *the actual preference of one alternative before another, when the creature is actually free to choose either.*   To leave not a shadow of doubt regarding this his real meaning, he adds expressly, " That the will embraces this or that determinate particular action, is not owing to any agency other than the will itself."[7]

It would seem that this passage of St. Thomas is not only implicitly but explicitly opposed to physical predetermination.   For the predeterminists maintain that each particular determination of the free-will is predetermined by God, and that the knowledge God has of the infallible future existence of the free acts of men is involved in the knowledge of the decree by which He has settled the exercise of His predetermining influence upon human wills.

D. In the latter part of this statement we find another contradiction between so-called Thomism and St. Thomas.   Aquinas teaches that the reason why God knows future free actions is this, that they *in themselves* are present to Divine intuition, *not only in their causes.*   " Further, events considered in their individual future existence, can only be known by God, to whom they are present even then, when in

---

[6] " Voluntas potentiæ, cum a nobis non sit, sed a Deo, in nobis non potest esse peccatum, sed actus ejus qui a nobis est."

[7] " Quod determinate exeat in hunc actum vel in illum, non est ab alio determinante, sed ab ipsa voluntate."

the course of things they are still future, inasmuch
as His eternal intuition extends itself by one act
over the whole course of time."[8] Of course this
must in the first place be true of those future events
which do not follow necessarily from their causes;
consequently, of free actions. These actions are
in the most proper sense of the word *contingent*
effects, and therefore it is certain that, according
to St. Thomas, future free actions of creatures are
known by God directly, not in the decrees by
which they are caused.

Nay, he goes so far as to exclude the possibility
of the latter knowledge, when he says: "A contingent event may be considered inasmuch as it has
pre-existence in its cause ; and thus it is considered
as something both future and not determined as yet
to one definite issue (because a cause which acts
not necessarily may turn to this or to that of two
alternatives opposite to each other) ; and under this
aspect a contingent event cannot be known for
certain by any knowledge whatsoever."[9]

Then the Angelic Doctor goes on to say that
God knows nevertheless future contingent events,
because not only their causes, but their future par-

---

[8] " In se ipsis quidem futura cognosci non possunt nisi a Deo,
cui etiam sunt præsentia, dum in cursu rerum sunt futura, in
quantum ejus æternus intuitus simul fertur supra totum temporis
cursum." (St. Thomas, *Sum. Theol.* 1a. q. 86. art. 4. in corp.)

[9] "Potest considerari contingens ut est in sua causa; et sic
consideratur ut futurum, et ut contingens nondum determinatum
ad unum (quia causa contingens se habet ad opposita) ; et sic contingens non subditur per certitudinem alicui cognitioni." (St. Thomas,
Sum. Theol. 1a. q. 14 art. 13. in corp.)

ticular existences are open to His eternal intuition. The reader will remember that this doctrine coincides with the teaching of the Suarezian Molinists given by us in Book II., who advocate the *scientia media*, which is nothing else than an immediate intuition of the conditionally future existence of free actions. St. Thomas certainly does not seem to hold that the future free actions of rational creatures are known by God in His predetermining decrees, as in the real and infallibly operating causes of those actions.

E. Among all the passages which Thomists love to quote from St. Thomas in favour of predetermining premotion, there is none which really proves physical predetermination to be his doctrine, although there are many which prove premotion in general, and even in particular, inasmuch as it can be conceived without physical predetermining influence. We are the last persons to deny that this sort of premotion, which we have explained and approved (p. 374, § 218), was before the mind of St. Thomas, when he compared the operation of God in created agencies to the motion by which an artist applies his instrument to cut something.[10] The truths really contained in this simile may be stated thus:

1. As the natural aptitude of an instrument for cutting is without effect unless it is applied by the artist to some material, so the natural faculties existing in creatures to produce changes in other creatures are of no avail, unless God by His Providence brings them mediately or immediately into

---

[10] St. Thomas, *Sum. Theol.* 1a. q. 105. art. 5. in corp. et ad 3; *De Potentia*, q. 3. art. 7. in corp. § "Sciendum namque," et ad 7.

relation with matter to act upon. What is, for instance, the best orator without an audience, the best master without pupils?

2. As the artist can freely drop the instrument, and thus put a stop to its cutting, so God by His absolute power could, save for His free decree to act otherwise, efface any creature from the order of existing things, and thus abolish its activity. He can also make creatures cease to act without subtracting their preservation, simply by not willing that they shall be in a state fit for certain actions. Thus, for instance, He destroyed the influence of Elymas by striking him on a sudden with blindness.[11]

3. As the action of the instrument is directed by the artist's intellect and will to the end that he intends, so every action of creatures is turned by Divine Providence into a means to the last end of all creation, the external manifestation of God's perfections.

We should have good hope of harmony between Molinists and Thomists, if Molinists would bring their true doctrine regarding premotion more explicitly to the front, and if Thomists would distinguish carefully between premotion to free action in general, and premotion to this or that particular free election; and again between the Divine knowledge of a particular future free action, as possible to the will under a certain condition, and the Divine knowledge of the same action, as infallibly to come about under that condition. It is true, in order that a free volition under a given condition may be

[11] Acts xiii. 11.

really and adequately possible to us, God must have decreed from eternity to concur with us by granting us the actual use of freedom. But the decree to grant this actual use is not a decree to influence the free-will in such a way that *by the physical nature of the said influence* our free choice in one direction is predetermined. On the contrary, according to reason and to St. Thomas's teaching, it is a decree, physically thus to influence the free-will (naturally or supernaturally) that *in virtue of its actual physical state it must exercise its freedom,* that is to say, must accept, or omit to accept, any object proposed by the understanding as eligible.

APPENDIX II.

THE pantheistic system of Spinoza, embodied in his Ethics, is worked out with so much simulation of mathematical exactness, that to some authors, particularly to the German philosopher, Frederick H. Jacobi, it appeared to be *theoretically* irrefutable. We have already argued the absurdity of the two fundamental dogmas of Spinoza's monism.[1] Moreover, we have set forth the ambiguity of two of his most important definitions, and pointed out the paralogism introduced by their use in the very first step of his reasoning.[2] This, however, we could not do without referring to the connection between the first six propositions of the Ethics. In order now to enable our reader to see this connection, and to judge for himself as to the safety of the road cut by Spinoza to his famous Proposition VI., " One substance cannot be produced by another substance," we will examine thoroughly into the first six propositions of his Ethics.

Let us begin by singling out of the eight definitions and seven axioms with which the Ethics open, those which form the groundwork of the propositions we are concerned about. They are Definitions

---

[1] *Natural Theology*, Th. X. pp. 112, seq.
[2] Loc. cit. Bk. I. c. v. sect. 6, pp. 200, seq.

DD

III., IV., V., and Axioms I., IV., V. Our comment on these fundamental principles will show that all of them are more or less ambiguous, and may therefore be applied in a true or in a false sense.

As regards Definitions III. and V. in particular, we shall sum up here what we have said on them at greater length in Bk. I. c. v. sect. 6.

Definition III. " By substance I mean that which is in itself and is conceived by itself." (*Per substantiam intelligo id quod in se est, et per se concipitur.*)

Comment. This definition may signify either (1) A substance is a natural whole, a complete individual being, in opposition to parts, properties, or modifications of such a being ; or (2) a substance is a self-existing being.

In the first sense the definition is true, in the second arbitrary and false. (§ 79.)

Definition IV. " By attribute I understand that which the understanding apprehends in substance as constituting its essence." (*Per attributum intelligo id quod intellectus de substantia percipit tanquam ejus essentiam constituens.*)

Comment. The definition does not cover all attributes, but only the attributes of God, the one self-existing Being. Of course the Divine attributes are identical with the simple Divine essence. Each of them may therefore be said to constitute that essence, although self-existence is said to do so with most propriety.[3] Of the attributes of creatures we cannot say this. Some of them *complete one another*

---

[3] Cf. Bk. II. c. vii.

to constitute an essence (*e.g.*, animality and rationality in man) ; others are conceived as *flowing from* the essence of a being (*e.g.*, understanding and freewill) ; others again are *accidental modifications added* to substance (*e.g.*, learning in man).

We have then to choose between two alternatives. Either we must pronounce Spinoza's definition of "substance" to be taken in the second, false sense explained above, or we must reject his definition of attribute as altogether inadequate.

Definition V. "By mode I mean the affections of a substance, or that which is in something else, by which also it is apprehended." (*Per modum intelligo substantiæ affectiones, sive id quod in alio est, per quod etiam concipitur.*)

Comment. This definition allows of three interpretations : (1) A mode is that which gives to anything its specific character (*e.g.*, the principle of life to a dog). (2) A mode is a property accompanying a being, so to speak, by its acts (*e.g.*, understanding, moral freedom). (3) A mode is an accidental modification (*e.g.*, skill).

Only in its second or third interpretation does Spinoza's definition of "mode" harmonize *sufficiently* with common parlance ; *perfectly* in the third alone.

And now as to the three axioms :

Axiom I. is thus worded : "All that is, is either in itself or in something else." (*Omnia, quæ sunt, vel in se, vel in alio sunt.*)

Comment. According to the different meanings that may be attached to the phrase, "in itself," this axiom signifies either, (1) everything is either a

subject or a determination of a subject, which
determination may be substantial or accidental
(a substantial or accidental form) ; or (2) everything is either self-existent or inherent in self-existence.

In the first sense the axiom is true, in the
second intrinsically contradictory, because in self-
existence there can be no inherent determinations
really distinct from it. (Th. VIII. and Th. XXII.)

Axiom IV. " Knowledge of an effect depends
on knowledge of a cause, and involves the same."
(*Effectus cognitio a cognitione causæ dependet, et eandem
involvit.*)

Comment. This means either (1) an effect *as an
effect* cannot be known without the conception of a
cause ; or (2) a thing which is an effect cannot be
known, unless it be conceived together with its
cause.

In the first sense the axiom expresses a self-
evident truism ; in the second it is manifestly false.
A child knows his home, his parents and relations,
his toys, &c., before he in any way reflects upon the
causes of these things. And accurate self-introspection will convince any one that his first conception of things is an apprehension of their existence
and of some of their attributes (extension, colour,
&c.), involving no notion of cause.

Axiom V. " Things that have nothing in common
one with another cannot be understood through one
another, or the conception of one does not involve
the conception of the other." (*Quæ nihil commune
cum se invicem habent, etiam per se invicem intelligi*

non possunt, sive conceptus unius alterius conceptum non involvit.)

Comment. This axiom may be explained in two ways : (1) Things really diverse cannot be explained by means of one another, unless under some aspect they are conceivable by a common idea. (2) Things really diverse can under no aspect be conceived by a common idea, because they have really nothing in common.

The first sense is true, the second false, involving, as it does, the absurd position of nominalism, that there are no universal ideas based upon the objective similarity of diverse essences.

Now let us see how Spinoza proves his first six propositions by the help of the ambiguous principles just explained. We give a translation both of his propositions and of his demonstrations, *omitting nothing;* and add our respective comments to each.

Proposition I. " Substance is prior in nature to its affections." (*Substantia prior est natura suis affectibus.*)

Demonstration. " This is comprised in Definitions III. and IV."

Comment. We have already fully commented on this first step of Spinoza's reasonings. (Bk. I. c. v. sect. 6.) Therefore it will suffice to remark here shortly that Proposition I. is true, if you take Definition III. in the first, and Definition V. in the second or third sense explained above. In other words, if you suppose that *substance* signifies any natural whole, and *mode* either a natural property or an accidental modification of such a whole, Proposition I. cannot be denied. If you, however, take Definition III. in the second and false sense to mean a self-existing being, and Definition V. in any of the three meanings compatible with its ambiguity, Spinoza's Proposition I. means that "a self-existent being is prior in nature either to its specific determination or to its natural properties, or to its accidental modifications," an assertion which involves the absurdity that self-existence is a changeable subject. (Cf. Th. XXII.) In Spinoza's system there is no room for Proposition I. but in its second false sense, as will appear from the following:

Proposition II. "Two substances having different attributes have nothing in common with one another." (*Duæ substantiæ diversa attributa habentes, nihil inter se commune habent.*)

Demonstration. "This too appears from Definition III.; for each must be comprised in itself and conceived by itself; or, the conception of the one does not involve the conception of the other."

Comment. If to signify any being complete in itself as a natural whole Definition III. is taken in its first (true) meaning, Proposition II. is false, because diverse natural wholes, of however different attributes, may nevertheless, under one or other aspect, resemble one another, and on account of this similarity have the same attribute in common, inasmuch as its import is realized in each of them. Thus, for instance, a man and his dog have the same attribute, "animality," in common. Of either of them I say, with perfect truth, "This substance is an animal." And I say also rightly, "The substance which is really identical with the animal *dog* is other than that which is really identical with the animal *man.*" If, however, Spinoza's Definition III. is taken in its second (false) meaning, so as to make *substance* identical with *self-existence*, there is no *raison d'être* for Proposition II. ; because self-existence can only be one substance. (Th. VII.)

Proposition III. " Of things that have nothing in common, one cannot be the cause of another." (*Quæ res nihil commune inter se habent, earum una alterius causa esse non potest.*)

Demonstration. " If the things have nothing in common, neither can they (by Axiom V.) be understood one from the other, and so (by Axiom IV.) they cannot be causes of one another : *q.e.d.*"

Comment. If the phrase, " to have something in common," is applied in a sense quite usual, so as to mean, " to have the same predicate," Proposition III. is based on a false supposition, because there are no things which would not have at least the predicate " being " in common.

If, however, the phrase, " to have nothing in common," shall mean " to exist as diverse realities," Proposition III. is false, and the proof given by Spinoza does not really support it, unless each of the two ambiguous Axioms V. and IV. be taken in its second false meaning, pointed out above. Indeed, Spinoza's conclusion would only follow if it be supposed that Axiom V., " Things that have nothing in common one with another cannot be understood through one another," is true if you take it to mean, " Diverse things under no aspect can be conceived by a common idea ; " and that the truth enunciated by Axiom IV., " Knowledge of an effect depends on knowledge of a cause, and involves the same," is no other but this manifest falsehood, " The idea of an effect, however the latter may be viewed, involves necessarily the idea of its cause."

Proposition IV. " Two or more different things are distinguished from each other either by diversity of the attributes of substances, or by diversity in the affections of these same substances." (*Duæ aut plures res distinctæ vel inter se distinguuntur ex diversitate attributorum substantiarum, vel ex diversitate earundem affectionum.*)

Demonstration. " All that is, is either in itself or in something else (by Axiom I.), that is to say, there is nothing out of or beyond the understanding except substances and their affections (by Definitions III. and V.). There is consequently nothing out of the understanding by which individual things can be distinguished from each other except substances, or—and this comes to the same thing— their attributes and affections (by Definition IV.)"

Comment. Different things are in the first place distinguished from one another by their different substantial being, and secondarily by their attributes and affections. In commenting upon Definition IV. we have given reasons to show that there is a difference between the substantial being of created things, or what we may call their physical essence, and the attributes of that essence. Moreover, while the essential attribute remains the same, the affections of an individual thing may vary indefinitely.

The same man of whom I have to predicate constantly moral responsibility may attach his heart now to money, now to pleasure, now to virtue, &c.

It appears then that Proposition IV. is altogether false, and based upon a false application of the inadequate Definition IV. In order to be in harmony with truth, Proposition IV. must be thus worded: "Two or more different things are distinguished from each other by their different undivided substantial being; from this primary difference there follows a difference in their attributes, and in their affections, or accidental modifications, if they are capable of any such." The restriction, "if they," &c., is added with reference to the Divine substance, which is immutable.

Proposition V. "In the order of existence there cannot be two or more substances of the same nature or attribute." (*In rerum natura non possunt dari duæ aut plures substantiæ ejusdem naturæ sive attributi.*)

Demonstration. "Did several distinct substances exist, they would be distinguished from each other either by diversity of attributes or by diversity of affections [modes] (as appears by the proposition immediately preceding); if by diversity of attributes only, it were then conceded that there is but one substance of the same attribute; if by diversity of affections, then inasmuch as substance is prior in nature to its affections (by Proposition I.), if we set aside its affections, and consider the substance in itself, which is to consider it truly (by Definitions III. and V.), the substance in that case could not be conceived as distinct from anything else; so that, as stated in the preceding proposition, there cannot be several substances, but one substance only."

Comment. First of all, Spinoza appeals in vain to his Proposition IV. as a firm basis of that under consideration; for we have shown above that Proposition IV. is false, and based upon false reasoning.

In development of his proof of the present proposition, Spinoza adds another piece of false information by telling us that, setting aside affections of substances, and considering them "in themselves, or truly," there is no longer any distinction of substances. This false statement he bases upon Definition III. and Definition V. Yet it does not follow from these definitions, unless we take Definition III. in its second, false sense, so as to define *substance* to be *self-existence*.

We see then that Proposition V., which has been sometimes termed the *Argumentum Achilleum* of Spinoza, deserves that name in that it is really *vulnerable*, like Achilles, if only you strike at the vulnerable spot.

The truth underlying Proposition V. amounts to this, that two different substances cannot have the same *physical* attribute in common. But nobody wishes to signify this, when he says that two substantial beings, say Peter and Paul, have the attribute "rationality" in common. The meaning is that, as regards the import of this attribute, they resemble each other perfectly, and that there is consequently in their different *physical* substantiality a real foundation for a *logical* identity of attribute.

Proposition VI. " One substance cannot be produced by another substance." (*Una substantia non potest produci ab alia substantia.*)

Demonstration. " In the preceding proposition we have seen that there cannot in the order of existence be two substances of the same attribute, or that have anything in common (by Proposition II.) ; and so (by Proposition III.) one cannot be the cause of, or be produced by another : *q.e.d.*"

To the demonstration Spinoza adds by way of corollary, " Substance cannot be produced by anything else." And in order to make this corollary, which on the hypothesis that Proposition VI. was really proved, is evident enough, still more plausible, he supports it by the *reductio ad absurdum* in this manner : " If substance could be produced by something else, the knowledge of substance would have to depend on a knowledge of its cause (by Axiom IV.), in which case it would not be substance (by Definition III.)."

Comment. As appears clearly from the demonstration of Proposition VI., it rests entirely on Proposition V., Proposition II., and Proposition III., all of them ambiguous, and only applicable to support Proposition VI., if they are taken in a sense manifestly false, and sophistically supposed by Spinoza as really proved.

For the demonstration of this Proposition VI. to hold, we must assume that (*a*) there cannot be several substances of the same *logical* attribute, grounded on their *physical* similarity (false sense of Proposition V.); (*b*) two substances having *physically* different attributes, have nothing *logically* in common, based upon real physical similarity (false sense of Proposition II.); (*c*) things that have nothing *physically* in common (or that are, considered in their physical existence, not *one* thing, but *many* things), cannot be cause and effect (false sense of Proposition III.).

Only, I say, by assuming all these false interpretations of ambiguously worded propositions, can any connection be made out between the premises and the conclusion of the demonstration by which Spinoza proves Proposition VI. Consequently this proposition, which is the whole foundation of his pantheistic monism, must be pronounced to be *a miserable sophism*.

The same verdict must be given on the accessory proof contained in the corollary. A simple appeal to Axiom IV. and Definition III., so Spinoza thinks, is enough to show that "substance cannot be produced by anything else." Indeed, if you interpret Axiom IV. to mean that an effect *under no aspect* is conceivable without the conception implying the conception of its cause; and if you take Definition III. to imply that "substance" is synonymous with "self-existence," the conclusion in due course runs that no effect can be a substance, and that consequently there is only One substance effecting changes in itself. But such a process of reasoning, taken for what it is really worth, evinces no more than that from two absurd premises there follows as usual an equally absurd conclusion.

APPENDIX III.

IMMEDIATE CONSCIOUSNESS OF GOD IN THE PATRISTIC WRITINGS.

SEVERAL distinguished scholars of our own century have been of opinion that in the writings of the early defenders of the Christian faith, particularly in those of St. Justin, Clement of Alexandria, Tertullian, and St. Augustine, passages were found which showed that their authors, in opposition to scholasticism, believed in an immediate natural knowledge of God. Thorough information on this subject is given by Kleutgen, *Philosophie Scholastique* (translated from the German), nn. 427—489. He shows that the meaning of the sayings alleged in no way disagrees with the common teaching of the schoolmen.

The passages to which our opponents appeal, may aptly be divided into two classes, inasmuch as in some of them the knowledge of God is spoken of *as belonging to human nature*, whilst in others man is said *to know truth in God*, the First, Unchangeable Truth.

Careful examination shows, however, that the first class of passages do not imply any belief in an innate idea of God, or any direct intuition of Him in His relation to finite beings. They are only designed to express strongly that human reason, *connaturally developed and applied*, cannot fail to arrive at the knowledge of the Creator.

As regards the other statements, which affirm that we know truth in God, their real import is that the natural light of our reason, by which we perceive truth, is in its existence and activity a sort of faint copy of God, the self-existing Infinite Truth, and caused by Him. We say in common parlance that we see things of this world in the light of the sun. By this phrase we imply indeed a dependence of our actual vision of things round about us upon the influence of the sun. Yet we do not imply *a gazing at the sun as the reason why we are able to see things.* In a similar way, St. Augustine says in answer to the question, *Where* we see the truth of our affirmations ? that we see it neither in ourselves nor in other men, but in God, the Unchangeable Truth.[1] By this assertion he impresses upon us the dependence of our ability for discerning truth upon Divine creation and concurrence ; but he can in no way be said to advocate an immediate consciousness of God, as is well shown by Kleutgen, loc. cit. n. 472, seq.

[1] *Confess.* Lib. XII. c. 25.

APPENDIX IV.

ST. THOMAS AND THE IDEA OF INDETERMINATE

BEING.

A DISTINGUISHED student of Rosmini's philosophy called some years ago our attention to these words of St. Thomas: "Anima semper intelligit se et Deum indeterminate."[1] He found in them a support of Rosmini's hypothesis that we are born with a dim perception of God *as being*. (Cf. p. 14.) Assuredly an interpretation like this would upset the whole of St. Thomas's psychology as contained in his commentaries on Aristotle's *De Anima*, and in *Sum. Theol.* i. qq. 75—89.

But what does St. Thomas mean by those words? Considering.the whole context in which they occur, and comparing it with the doctrine of Aquinas on the *Intellectus agens*, especially with the remarkable assertion, "*Intellectus agens est agens tantum et nulla modo patiens*,"[2] and with the more explicit teaching laid down in ii. *Sent.* dist. 17. q. 2. a. 1. § "*Et ideo remotis omnibus prædictis erroribus*," we have arrived at the following interpretation, which the reader may kindly consider and examine: In virtue of its spiritual nature and of the spontaneous activity of the *intellectus agens*

---

[1] In i. *Sent.* dist. 3. q. 4. a. 5.

[2] *Sum. Theol.* 1a. 2a. q. 50. a. 5. ad 2.

flowing from it, the soul possesses habitually all needful capacity for being awakened to self-consciousness and for ascending by degrees to the knowledge of its Creator. So far forth we may say, then, that the soul always knows its own existence and God *indeterminately;* that is to say, such is the natural sympathy between the organic faculty called *imagination,* and the spiritual faculty called *intellectus agens,* that immediately upon due determination of the imaginative faculty, the soul will arrive in the first place at the intellectual perception of material things; concomitantly, in the second place, at self-consciousness, inasmuch as it knows its own knowing; and finally, in virtue of its natural tendency to investigate the causes of things perceived, by degrees it will arrive at the knowledge of the First Cause, or God.[3]

[3] Cf. St. Thomas, Qq. Disp. *De Veritate,* q. x. a. 8. et *Sum. Theol.* q. 88. a. 1. et a. 3.

APPENDIX V.

THE LOGICAL CONNECTION BETWEEN THE UNITY AND INFINITY OF GOD.

MANY authors of Latin text-books of Philosophy agree with us in proving the Unity of God from His Self-existence. Yet for the most part they treat of the Infinity of God before having proved His Unity, and then in proving the Unity they avail themselves not only of our argument drawn from Self-existence, but appeal also to the premised doctrine on the Infinity. We prefer the order followed by St. Thomas in the *Summa Contra Gentiles*, and by Suarez in his *Disputationes Metaphysicæ*. In both of these works the Unity is treated of before the Infinity.[1]

To our mind this order alone is in strict harmony with Logic *on the supposition that we reason upon merely natural grounds.* Of course, even before proving that there can be but One undivided self-existent essence, we are able to show that all contingent reality must be based upon the order of being denoted by the term self-existence, abstracting altogether from the question, whether in that order there is only one being possible or several separately existing beings. Yet this alone does not suffice for

---

[1] Cf. St. Thomas, *Contra Gent.* i. c. 42. et c. 43.; Suarez, *Metaph.* disp. 29. sect. 2. et disp. 30. sect. 2.

EE

the proof that there is an Infinite Being. The existence of such a being implies the existence of One undivided essence of so high a perfection that there is no perfection, either real or conceivable, but has in that One essence, in that One undivided being, some kind of equivalent. How can we make sure that such an essence exists, unless we prove first that Self-existence is by its very nature not only One *metaphysical*, but also One *physical* essence? As long as you leave it in the dark, whether or not there is an intrinsic contradiction in the supposition of many self-existences, you cannot possibly be certain that there is a being comprising in its own essence the source of all reality conceivable. Indeed, on the hypothesis of the internal possibility of several self-existent beings, none of them would be the source of all reality, because none would possess the actual perfection of the rest, formally or eminently; consequently none of them would be really infinite. We must therefore first lay open the intrinsic absurdity contained in the assertion of several self-existent beings, before we can prove the Infinity of God by evident natural reasons.

APPENDIX VI.

In Bk. I. Th. XV. we laid down the tenet that Creation is not only good, but even very good, nay, in a certain sense, best, inasmuch as in all its departments there is a perfect adaptation of means to such ends as are absolutely intended by the Creator.

Let us in this place test briefly the reasons which have led three distinguished monotheistic philosophers, Leibnitz, Malebranche, and Rosmini, to maintain that our world is not only the best of worlds, in the sense just explained, but the very best world possible.

(A) Leibnitz argues thus : " If among all possible worlds there were not one which is best, God would not have created any of them. . . . There is an infinity of possible worlds, and of these God must have chosen the best, because He does nothing but in agreement with His supreme Reason."[1]

Answer. We agree with the assumption that there is an infinity of possible worlds, that is to say, an indefinite number of possible systems of

---

[1] " S'il n'y avait pas le meilleur (optimum) parmi tous les mondes possibles, Dieu n'en avait produit aucun . . . il y a une infinité de mondes possibles, dont il faut que Dieu ait choisi le meilleur, puisqu'il ne fait rien sans agir suivant la suprême Raison." (Opp. Edit. Erdmann, p. 506.)

finite things, or, as we are accustomed to say, of possible universes. But from this it in no way follows that God must have chosen the very best of them for creation. In fact, as no universe is rightly called possible, unless it can be produced by Omnipotence under the guidance of Infinite Wisdom, it follows from the assumption of an infinity of possible worlds that there are in the Divine Mind worlds without number, *each of them good enough for creation.* Consequently there is neither any possible world which, when created, would not be *relatively* the best, nor is there any which ought to be called *the very best of all.* If there were any world really possible which would not be *relatively* best, infinite Wisdom would fall short of its absolute aims. On the other hand, if there were any world *absolutely* best, Infinite Power, *i.e.,* power not exhaustible, would be exhausted by its creation.

(B) Malebranche's reason for exaggerated optimism is equally weak. He thought that any world not the very best possible was incompatible with the end of creation, inasmuch as this end is the external glory of God, or, what comes to the same thing, the manifestation of His goodness, and the making that goodness to be acknowledged by rational creatures in the highest degree possible. Besides, it seemed to him that infinitely perfect Wisdom necessarily produces a work so perfect as that none can be more perfect.[2]

---

[2] Cf. *Recherche de la Vérité*, Lib. IV. c. i.; *Traité de la Nature et de la Grâce*, 2, 51.

Answer. Although God owes it to His own perfection to aim at the manifestation of His goodness
in His works, and thus seek what is commonly
called His external glory, yet we should be wrong
in asserting that He must seek that glory in the
highest degree possible. To say so is to put
bounds to God's supreme freedom, and to ignore
His omnipotence, which cannot be limited to any
degree of created perfection. Malebranche seems
to have overlooked the fact that an adequate manifestation of God's power and wisdom is intrinsically
impossible; whilst for an inadequate showing forth
of both of them there suffices the creation and
perfect adaptation to ends of any system into which
rational creatures enter.

(C) Rosmini considered this world to be the
only one in harmony with the goodness of God,
inasmuch as in it the greatest good was produced
by the smallest means.[3]

Answer. This assertion seems to extol the wisdom
of God, while really it depreciates it. Must not
Infinite Wisdom be capable of arranging systems
of creatures for the manifestation of God's goodness in endless many ways? Of course we do not
mean to say that there is an actually infinite number
of possible worlds, but we contend that *the multitude
of possible worlds transcends any given number.* Out
of such an *endless* multitude, which cannot be

---

[3] "Alla dimanda: perchè (Iddio) volle creare questo mondo,
anzichè un altro, dee respondersi: perchè questo mondo era degno
della somma bontà come quello che col minimo mezzo produceva il
mazzimo bene, e perciò fu il solo possibile." (Teodicea, n. 651.)

gathered together *in the form of a number*, God chooses freely a particular universe. Yet this choice is not exercised by successive comparison of the terms at choice. Such a comparison, as Rosmini says rightly, would be impossible. Rather, the Divine choice is made upon a comprehensive view of the Divine Essence, involving a clear insight into all possibilities of finite essences and their combinations, inasmuch as the Divine Essence is the prototype of an endless multitude of contingent beings.[4]

The moderate optimism advocated by us against Leibnitz, Malebranche, and Rosmini, is in perfect harmony with the doctrine of St. Thomas, as the reader may see for himself by reading *Sum. Theol.* q. 25. a. 5. and a. 6. Very clear is also the following

[4] "Medium illud quo Deus cognoscit, scilicet essentia sua, est infinitorum similitudo quæ ipsum imitari possunt." (St. Thomas, Qq. Disp. *De Veritate,* q. 2. a. 9.) Cf. the deep explanation given by St. Thomas throughout the whole of *Sum. Theol.* 1a. q. 14. a. 12.: "Utrum Deus possit cognoscere infinita." Upon many disputes about this subject great light is thrown by the following saying of St. Augustine: *Quamvis infinitorum numerus nullus sit numerus, non est tamen incomprehensibilis ei cujus scientiæ non est numerus*—"Although an infinite multitude cannot be gathered in any number, yet it is not beyond the comprehension of Him whose knowledge is not limited to things that can be summed up in numbers." (*De Civitate Dei,* Lib. XII. c. 18.) Mark, however, the difference between "infinite" or "indefinite multitude," and "actually infinite multitude of actually existing things." The former is incomprehensible to us, but really comprehended by God; the latter is intrinsically contradictory, as may be seen, pp. 55 and 98, seq., where we deny the possibility of an actually infinite multitude of things and events, either having existed successively, or now existing simultaneously. But whilst such a multitude is impossible, multitudes ever increasing and never complete are not only possible but actual in the minds of rational creatures, as St. Thomas, loc cit. rightly remarks.

statement of his: "God necessarily wills His own goodness, and therefore naturally intends its manifestation by the production of creatures. Yet the things actually created do not stand in such a correspondence to His goodness, as though without them the Divine goodness could not be manifested. For as it is manifested by the things that are and by the present order of the world, so it might be manifested by other creatures and by another arrangement of creatures. From this it follows that, without contradicting His goodness, justice, and wisdom, God could create other things than those created."[5] No less pronounced is this remark of the Angel of the School: "Over and above the things created, God can create things of quite different qualities, new species, new genera of creatures, in fine, other worlds; and no Creation can exhaust the power of the Creator."[6]

[5] "Finis naturalis divinæ voluntatis est ejus bonitas, quam non velle non potest. Sed fini huic non commensurantur creaturæ ita, quod sine his divina bonitas manifestari non possit; quod Deus intendit ex creaturis. Sicut enim manifestatur divina bonitas per has res quæ nunc sunt et per hunc rerum ordinem; ita potest manifestari per alias creaturas et alio modo ordinatas. Et ideo divina voluntas, absque præjudicio bonitatis, justitiæ et sapientiæ, potest se extendere in alia quam quæ fecit." (Qq. Disp. *De Potentia*, q. 1. a. 5.)

[6] "Super omnia quæ Deus fecit, adhuc possit alia dissimilia facere, et novas species et nova genera et alios mundos; nec unquam id quod factum est, facientis virtutem adæquare potest." (Qq. Disp. *De Veritate*, q. xx. a. 4. § "In utraque.")

INDEX.

E E*

ENGLISH MANUALS

OF

CATHOLIC PHILOSOPHY.

(STONYHURST SERIES.)

EDITED BY

RICHARD F. CLARKE, S.J.

EXTRACT FROM A LETTER OF
HIS HOLINESS THE POPE TO THE BISHOP OF SALFORD
ON THE STONYHURST PHILOSOPHY.

"You will easily understand, Venerable Brother, the pleasure
We felt in what you lately reported to Us about the College of
Stonyhurst in your diocese, namely, that by the efforts of the
superiors of this College, an excellent course of the exact sciences
has been successfully set on foot, by establishing professorships,
and by publishing in the vernacular for their students text-books
of Philosophy, following the principles of St. Thomas Aquinas.
On this work We earnestly congratulate the superiors and teachers
of the College, and by letter We wish affectionately to express Our
good-will towards them."

---

1. **Logic.** By RICHARD F. CLARKE, S.J., formerly
Fellow and Tutor of St. John's College, Oxford; Classical
Examiner in the Royal University of Ireland. Price 5s.

2. **First Principles of Knowledge.** By JOHN
RICKABY, S.J., Professor of Logic and General Metaphysics at St. Mary's Hall, Stonyhurst. 2nd Ed. Price 5s.

3. **Moral Philosophy. (Ethics and Natural Law.)**
By JOSEPH RICKABY, S.J., M.A. Lond.; Professor of
Ethics at St. Mary's Hall, Stonyhurst. 2nd Ed. Price 5s.

4. **Natural Theology.** By BERNARD BOEDDER, S.J.,
Professor of Natural Theology at St. Mary's Hall,
Stonyhurst. Price 6s. 6d.

5. **Psychology.** By MICHAEL MAHER, S.J., M.A. Lond.;
Professor of Mental Philosophy at Stonyhurst College.
Price 6s. 6d.

6. **General Metaphysics.** By JOHN RICKABY, S.J.
Price 5s

In the Press.

A Manual of Political Economy. By C. S. DEVAS,
Esq., M.A., Examiner in Political Economy in the Royal
University of Ireland. Price 6s. 6d.

Some Opinions of the Press on the first three Vols.

LOGIC.

"We must congratulate the editor of the series of Catholic Manuals of Philosophy on affording such a valuable contribution to English Catholic literature. The easy style throughout, the clearness of exposition, and the well-chosen examples, make the book at once attractive to the general reader, and of inestimable use to the special student. But the highest excellence of the work, and the one which characterises the series conceived and edited by the author, is sympathy with the intellectual atmosphere in which we live, with its difficulties, with its strength, and with its weakness."—*The Tablet*, April 13, 1889.

"An excellent text-book of Aristotelian logic, interesting, vivid, sometimes almost racy in its illustrations, while from first to last it never, so far as we have noticed, diverges from Aristotelian orthodoxy."—*Guardian*.

"Though Father Clarke mainly concerns himself with Formal Logic, he occasionally, for the sake of edification, makes excursions into wider fields. Adopting the standpoint of 'moderate realism,' he directs his chief attack against the limitation of the Principle of Contradiction, the nominalist statement of the Principle of Identity, and the theory of conception set forth by Mill. The arguments usually employed in these time-honoured controversies are marshalled with much vigour. . . . The uncontroversial portions of the book are extremely clear, and the descriptions of the various forms of syllogism as little dry as their subject-matter permits."— *Saturday Review*, April 20, 1889.

"Father Clarke has most successfully accomplished his high purpose, and makes the study of a comparatively dry subject most interesting and attractive. The book cannot fail to be of supreme advantage to all engaged in the teaching or acquiring of sound philosophical principles."—*Freeman's Journal*, March 15, 1889.

"To converts from Protestantism educated in the English Universities, and bewildered by the discrepancies created by the perversions to which they were in early life accustomed, the existence of such a text-book will be particularly useful. The task has been executed with remarkable ability. It is not possible to make the study of logic as easy as reading a novel, but the author has the power of rendering the work of the serious learner comparatively easy, and no conscientious reader of fair intelligence need shrink from the mastery of this difficult branch with such aid as this book affords."—*Cork Examiner*, March 8, 1889.

"In its general outline it follows the order of the Formal Logic which is still required in the Oxford schools, and is familiar to most people who are in any way interested in philosophy. The author has had a wider aim in view than merely providing a manual for Catholics; he would appeal also to perplexed Protestants, and to women who have shared the advantages of higher education."— *Church Quarterly*, April, 1889.

FIRST PRINCIPLES OF KNOWLEDGE.

"The volume before us is a solid fundamental exposition of what is known by modern logicians as 'Applied Logic,' or a treatise on the 'Philosophy of Certitude.' It defends the objective reality of human thought against the false systems of idealism."—*Ave Maria Magazine*, April, 1889.

"It is a hopeful sign of the times that a Catholic professor should freely enter the lists of debate in opposition to acknowledged masters of recent philosophy. The Jesuit Father is no respecter of persons."—*Journal of Education*, April 1, 1889.

"These Manuals are worthy of the widest circulation. They will clear away many popular delusions, much confusion of thought and language. They will help to strengthen many minds to strive fearlessly and perseveringly in the search of truth."—*Bombay Catholic Examiner*, April 19, 1889.

"It is a valuable treatise in every sense of the word. We have read it with the greatest pleasure. The style carries on the reader, and the several points are introduced with a truth and accuracy in pleasing contrast to the lumbering sophistries of many who call themselves philosophers and are not."—*Catholic Times*, April 5, 1889.

"The burden of Mr. Rickaby's utterance is that Idealism is wrong and Realism is right; that Idealism is a mere blind, concealing a general scepticism as to the possibility of truth at all, whereas Realism alone will explain the facts of knowledge, and strengthen a man's conviction of the validity of his rational processes.—*Church Quarterly*.

MORAL PHILOSOPHY.

"Father Rickaby's *Moral Philosophy, or Ethics and Natural Law* (Longmans) is the first of a series of 'Manuals of Catholic Philosophy.' The author is a member of the Society of Jesus, and his work embodies the substance of a course of lectures delivered for eight years in succession to the scholastics of that Society, at St. Mary's, Stonyhurst. The arrangement is methodical, and the style clear and condensed. Many of the sections are supplied with lists of passages for reading, selected from such authors as Plato, Aristotle, St. Thomas Aquinas, Paley, and Mr. Ruskin. The work is a new and important departure, and deserves to be read by others than those for whom it is primarily intended."—*Scottish Review*.

"The style of the book is bright and easy, and the English (as we need not say) extremely good. . . . The manual will be welcome on all sides as a sound, original, and fairly complete English treatise on the groundwork of morality."—*Dublin Review*.

"The work, to the ordinary reader, is interesting enough to absorb the attention; to the student of Ethics it has a double value—simplicity of style, as well as full knowledge of the subject and its various branches. We are glad that the price of the book puts it within reach of the great mass of the people."—*Catholic Times*, October, 1888.

"As regards the style of the book, it is, as a rule, clear, terse, and simple; and there are many passages marked alike by sound sense and by elevation of tone."—*Journal of Education*.

" Father Rickaby, with his Aristotelian and scholastic training, is always definite and clear, distrustful of sentiment, with an answer ready for every assailant."—*Mind*, No. 54.

" Father Rickaby's style of exposition will be found singularly clear and fresh, and his power of elucidating the bearing of an abstruse thought by some historical illustrations singularly happy. It should be specified also as one of the features in the book, that it keeps close on the track of Aristotle, and is careful to expound his pregnant but perplexing epigrams."—*The Month*.

" The authority of the moral law is asserted admirably as a binding Imperative, and not as a mere utterance of the autonomous reason. And there are many true and valuable statements in most parts of the book."—*Church Quarterly*, April, 1889.

" It is one of a series of ' Manuals of Catholic Philosophy ' in course of issue, and embodies the substance of lectures delivered by the author during eight successive years to the students of the Jesuit Society at Stonyhurst. The book is marked with several of the merits usually found in the educational writings of the Jesuits : orderly method, lucid arrangement, clear, definite, and incisive wording, competent familiarity with the literature of the subject, both ancient and modern."—*Church Times*, May 3, 1889.

" These three volumes form a part of a series of works intended to present in an easily accessible form the philosophy which the Roman Church delights to honour. They are written by three different members of the Society of Jesus, and though remarkably similar in tone present some few differences of detail. The third—that on Ethics—is rendered additionally interesting by a list of authorities appended to each section. The style of the three is popular and easily intelligible; the principles are fully illustrated by concrete examples."—*Church Quarterly*.

" In the two volumes named below (*First Principles of Knowledge* and *Logic*), we have set forth in clear and vigorous English the doctrine of knowledge and the principles of reasoning taught by the learned and subtle Aquinas in the thirteenth century, but adapted to the needs of students and controversialists of the nineteenth century by teachers who, like St. Thomas himself, are able to discuss doubts without doubting, to hold converse with sceptics of every school, and still to hold to the faith. . . . To those who would like to know exactly the form that philosophy takes when she enters the service of ' The Church ' the volumes may be commended."—*Inquirer*, Sept. 21, 1889.

Benziger Brothers, New York, Cincinnati, and Chicago.